THE
FLORIDA
KEYS

THE FLORIDA KEYS

A History & Guide

1992—93 Edition

Joy Williams

Illustrations by Robert Carawan

Random House • New York

Library of Congress Cataloging-in-Publication Data

Williams, Joy.
The Florida Keys: a history & guide/by Joy Williams:
illustrations by Robert Carawan.—1992–93 ed.
p. cm.
Includes index
ISBN 0-679-73736-7 (pbk.)
1. Florida Keys (Fla.)—Description and travel—Guidebooks.
2. Florida Keys (Fla.)—History. I. Title.
F317.M7W54 1991
917.59′410463—dc20   91-52658

For Caitlin, the one and only

CONTENTS

Introduction   ix

The Upper Keys   1
  Key Largo   7
  Diving   11
  John Pennecamp Coral Reef State Park   14
  Where to Stay   19
  Where to Eat   21

  Tavernier   23
  Plantation Key   25
  The Back Country   28
  Windley Key   33
  Upper Matecumbe Key   37
  Islamorada   39
  Where to Eat   40
  Where to Stay   41

  Lignumvitae and Indian Keys   42
  Lower Matecumbe Key   48
  Long Key   52

The Middle Keys   57
  Key Vaca   67
  Marathon   69
  Where to Stay   72
  Where to Eat   73

  Fishing   74
  The Seven-Mile Bridge   80
  Bahia Honda Key   83

The Lower Keys   87
  Big Pine Key   92
  No Name Key   97
  The Torch Keys   98
  Ramrod Key   103

Cudjoe Key 105
Sugarloaf Key 108
Stock Island and Approaches to Key West 113

Key West 117
The Streets 121
Changes and Confusions 123
Mystery and History 125
Collapse and Resurrection, Collapse and
  Restoration 129
Tourist Town 134
A Walk Up Duval Street 154
Beaches and Salt Ponds 167
Galleries and Antiques 169
Newspapers 170
Writers 173
Forts, Towers, and Museums 182
Old Town 190
The Graveyard 197
Where to Stay 200
Where to Eat 210
Bars 217
Fishing, Diving, and the Waters Beyond 222
Fort Jefferson and the Dry Tortugas 224

Index 229

INTRODUCTION

The Florida Keys do not run due south. They drift southwest, Route 1 running more east–west than north–south. The Gulf side is actually Florida Bay, the upper reaches of which belong to the Everglades. The bay side is called the "back country" or "outback." The Atlantic side is actually the Straits of Florida, where wide Hawk Channel runs out from shore to the reef, which stretches the length of the Keys. Beyond the reef is the Gulf Stream—"out front"—that great oceanic river whose demarcation is clearly seen, the water being a profound and fabulous blue. Beyond the Gulf Stream lies, then, the ocean.

The Keys run from Biscayne Bay to the Dry Tortugas, a distance of some 180 miles. No road runs to the keys north of Key Largo—Sands, Elliott, and Old Rhodes—and the Tortugas are 70 watery, wild miles from Key West. The distance accessible by car is some 106 miles—from Key Largo to Key West. That road, originally built in the 1930's, replaced Henry Flagler's Florida East Coast Extension railroad line, an amazing piece of engineering which had linked the Keys since 1912 and which was destroyed by a hurricane in 1935. The Mile Markers which are referred to in this guide—green signs with white numerals, posted on the right-hand shoulder—were first placed along the Keys by the railroad.

On a map, the Keys look fairly improbable—and Route 1, the line that drops down their sprinkled length, improbable too. The possibilities are vast, but the road itself is simple, which explains why some travelers begin at Key Largo, hang onto the steering wheel, and don't stop until Key West, heeding the billboards' urging, Go All The Way, with all its attendant, randy implications of reckless fulfillment. Other travelers arrive in the Keys, love them, stick close to Islamorada, and wouldn't dream of going all the way, considering Key West weird, if not bizarre, as though that singular and raffish place was at the bottom of an ever-darkening well.

But of course the Keys don't really go from light to dark. The Keys sparkle downward, warm and bright, full of light and air and a bit of intrigue. The Keys are relaxed, a little reckless. The Keys are water and sky, horizon, daybreak, spectacular sunsets, the cup of night. The least interesting thing about them is the road, but the road, as is its nature, allows entrance. The road is the beginning.

There are some automobile guides, such as the old Sanborn Guides to Mexico, that are wonderfully jittery backseat companions, not pointing out cathedrals and markets (because the route in question is manifestly lacking in cathedrals and markets), but taking great pains to point out everything else. A child selling an iguana is *here;* half a kilometer down the road you will pass a most peculiarly shaped boulder; a bit beyond that there was once a Pemex station, though unfortunately, a Pemex station is no longer there, only a tire dump; two kilometers away the road curves. . . . And so on.

The Keys once lent themselves to this sort of innocent treatment, and in a way they still do. There is the road, and there are the dutiful descending markers accompanying your every mile, suggesting that a trip is little more than coloring your own experience between provided lines. At MM #— there is an egret; at MM #— there's a pretty view between two violet jacaranda trees; at MM #—, if you can wait that long, is a bar where the bartender wears live snakes wrapped around her neck and wrists—her "pretties," she calls them. . . . And so on.

Time passes, of course. The snake lady is run over one night as she is crossing the road. Someone builds his dream house in front of the pretty view, cutting down the jacaranda trees in the process. But the Keys, though no longer the empty, silent stretches they once were, still markedly lack (you might as well be told) historical and cultural monuments. And the osprey still builds his nest larger each year at MM #—. And the tarpon still roll and flash each spring under the bridge at MM #—. And certainly at MM #— the disreputable bar remains. The best way to enjoy the Keys is still to seek out their simplicity and their eccentricity.

The Keys have been largely ignored until recently, the lack of fresh water being the real inhibitor to development. The

Navy had built an 18-inch pipeline in 1942 that ran the 130 miles from the Everglades wells in Florida City to Key West. The water took a week to travel the route. In 1982 the old pipe was replaced with a 36-inch pipe, increasing the quantity fourfold, providing indeed an oversupply of water and accelerating building and population growth. Oddly, the pipeline, as well as the construction of new bridges and wider roads, took place seven years after the state had designated Monroe County, which is the Keys, an "area of critical state concern" in an attempt to slow development (a perfectly nice word that unfortunately has been stolen away—undoubtedly while we were not looking—by the developers). A peculiar event occurred recently. Realtors dressed up in wood rat costumes and organized motorcades and rallies to protest new state guidelines that would restrict development in the Keys. It is true. People who felt themselves endangered by environmental laws dressed up like the cotton mouse and the wood rat—present inhabitants of mangrove swamp and hammock—and, aroused by lawyers and politicians, made a long, noisy trip down the highway to Key West where the governor was speaking, picking up additional incensed rat- and mouse-garbed people along the way. This is typical oddball Keys, but in this case, peculiarity has a threateningly modern and consumptive edge, which is familiarly Floridian.

W. C. Barron, the founder of Wall Street's *Barron's* magazine, said early in this century that the only values in the state of Florida are the values created by man. This was how the state was perceived by the wealthy who came from elsewhere to exploit it. Florida, that splendid, subtle, once fabulous state, has been exploited, miscomprehended and misused, drained and diked, filled in and paved over. The values of man have been imposed with a vengeance.

"Keys" comes from the Spanish word *cayos,* for "little islands." The Keys are little, and they are fragile. They cannot sustain any more "dream houses" or "dream resorts." The sustaining dream is in the natural world—the world that each of us should respect, enjoy, and protect so that it may be enjoyed again—the world to which one can return and be refreshed.

Time passes. There are more of the many, and they want too much. What the traveler wants, of course, is not development but adventure, and this is still possible in the Keys. The Keys have always been different. May they remain that way. Here's to them.

THE
UPPER KEYS
Key Largo
to Long Key

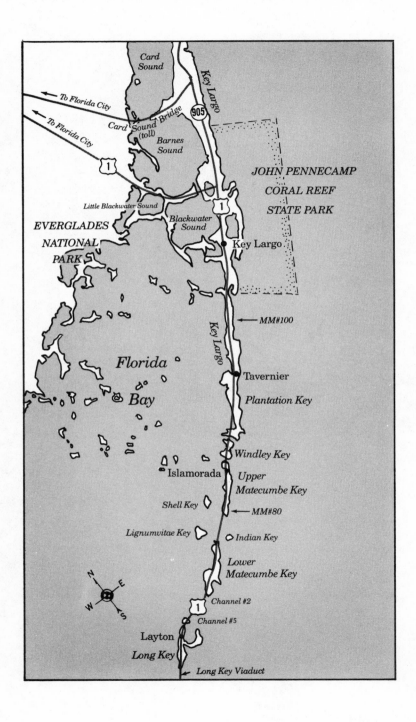

THE Spanish first found the Keys in Ponce de León's 1513 expedition and promptly called them, with inquisitional flair, *Los Martires*—the martyrs—because they seemed twisted and tortured. They logged out the mahogany that grew here early on, and probably enslaved the native Caloosa Indians, but they were indifferent to exploring or settling these stony islands. There was no gold, no fresh water, and many, many bugs. They mapped and named the Keys principally as an aid to their ships, which, laden with gold and silver, used the Florida Straits as their route from the New World back to the Old.

The first settlement in the Keys was at *Cayo Hueso,* or Key West, in 1822, more than two decades before Florida became a state. The other keys remained pretty much deserted until 1874, when the government surveyed them and plotted land for homesteading. The early homes were primitive, built from the local "coastal store"—the beach—with wood and materials washed up from shipwrecks. The biggest plague of the settlers was mosquitoes. The mosquito was king of the Keys. Mosquitoes blackened the sides of houses and obscured the shapes of animals. Mosquitoes blackened the cheesecloth which people swathed their heads in as they slept. If you swung a pint cup, the saying went, you'd come up with a quart full of mosquitoes. Smudgepots burned constantly inside and outside the driftwood houses. Burlap bags filled with wood chips soaked in old engine oil were hung to drip over stagnant water holes in an attempt to kill mosquito larvae. With mosquitoes gnawing on them day and night, a few pioneering families nevertheless managed to claw a living from what one writer of the time referred to as "worthless, chaotic fragments of coral reef, limestone and mangrove swamp."

The people who first made their homes in the Upper Keys were hardworking Methodist fishermen and farmers. They spoke with a Cockney accent, were closely interrelated, and bore the names Albury, Pinder, Johnson, Russell, and Lowe. Their more flamboyant wrecking neighbors were in Key West, but life in the "outside keys" was earnestly drab, farming rock being somewhat Sisyphian in nature. But farm the rock they did, burning and clearing the land and planting coconuts, citrus, pineapple, and melons in the ashy interstices between the coral. They homesteaded on the Atlantic, and transportation between the scattered houses was by shallow-draft boat. These boats also took the produce out to deeper waters, where it was off-loaded onto schooners which sailed to Key West as well as to northern ports.

In 1905, Henry Flagler, a former partner of John D. Rockefeller in Standard Oil and president of the Florida East Coast Railroad, began extending the train track from Homestead, through the Everglades to Key Largo. Flagler was always pushing southward, legend has it, because his wives were forever wanting to be warmer. That is why he pushed down from St. Augustine to Palm Beach. (Flagler also altered Florida history by having the state's strict divorce laws changed when an early wife of his went mad.) But the reason he desired the terminus of his Florida railroad to be in Key West was because it was a fine deep-water port. Shipping out of Miami was limited by the 12-foot depth of Biscayne Bay. Flagler was seventy-five years old when construction started and died only a few months after the project was completed in 1912.

For seven years, the track and train, freighted with peril and mishap, inched their way down the Keys to Key West. Settlers in the Upper Keys longed for the railroad to be completed, believing that it would put them in closer touch with their markets and make them wealthy. But eventually the railroad meant the end of their little coastal communities and their large fruit farms. Key West became a receiving center for produce from all over the Caribbean and South America, and cheaper fruit was introduced to the mainland. Too, the few inches of Keys' topsoil that had supported such exotics as Porto Rico, Abbakka Queen, and Sugar Loaf pineapples was soon robbed of all nutrients, and the plantations failed. Towns like Planter, which once shipped out a million crates of limes, pineapples, tomatoes, and melons a year by schooner, simply disappeared, a victim of sporadic hurricanes and the railroad. Other communities that sprang up along the track vanished too, when the 1935 hurricane blew the train away.

It was this hurricane—*the* hurricane, the nameless one—that made the history of the Upper Keys. It swept across the Matecumbe Keys on September 2, 1935, with an 18-foot tidal wave and 200-mph winds. Matecumbe is a name of obscure origins, but it may be a corruption of the Spanish *mata hombre*—"kill man"—which was also the meaning of Cuchiyaga, the Indian name for the island. In any case, it was a fated place. More than eight hundred people died in the hurricane, many of them members of the second "Bonus Army" of World War I veterans who, seeking early military benefits, had been hired instead by the Federal Emergency Relief Administration for work projects across the country. In this instance, they were building a road from Lower Matecumbe to Grassy Key so that the ferry route could be eliminated. Most of them died when the train sent down to rescue them was blown off the tracks in Islamorada. Of the eleven cars, only the 106-ton locomotive "Old 447" remained upright, saving the lives of the engineer and the fireman. Many of the dead were burned in funeral pyres overseen by the National Guard in the sunny days after the storm, while others were buried in a common crypt marked by a monument in Islamorada.

Besides winds, the history here is in the waters—in the wrecks and reefs. The waters off the Upper Keys conceal a remarkable number of wrecks, from Spanish galleons to British frigates to World War II freighters. Cannon from the HMS *Winchester*, a 60-gun British frigate which went down in a hurricane in 1695, are displayed on dry ground at Pennecamp Park, and the adventurous diver can frequently see less restored and considerably wetter and blurrier artifacts. A wreck that is not present but that has left its contemporary and eternal mark is that of the *Wellwood*, a 400-foot Turkish freighter which ran aground within the park's boundaries in the fall of 1984. The *Wellwood*, filled with chicken feed, and captained, it would certainly seem, with some incompetence by a C. H. Vickers, ignored the 45-foot flashing light that marks Molasses Reef on the southernmost boundary of the park and ploughed into the reef,

CONCHS

Englishmen, descendants of the "Eleuthera Adventurers" who settled Eleuthera and the Great Abaco Islands in the Bahamas, explored the good fishing and turtling grounds off the Keys in the late 1700's but did not settle on the land, preferring instead to wait offshore for ships to founder on the reef. Particularly popular were the waters of the Upper Keys, where ships foundered regularly. "Wrecking," which occasionally bordered on piracy, was much practiced by the Bahamians, who would salvage the cargo from sinking ships and sell the goods in the port of Nassau. Shortly after Spain ceded Florida to the United States in 1821, however, the Bahamians were forced to become residents of this country if they wanted to continue to engage in wrecking. They began to move their families to the new town of Key West, where an admiralty court had been established to legalize and regulate what had become a major industry. These Bahamians were called "Conchs," after the large sea snails they ate in considerable amounts and perhaps because they used the conch shell as a trumpet. With a hole correctly placed at the tip, the shell could produce a plaintive wail heard for up to half a mile, a way of announcing, "Wreck ashore." The strange collective nickname may have been used disparagingly at first, but today a Conch, a lifelong resident of the Keys, descendant of Conchs, is proud of the shrewd and stubborn individuality the name represents. Key West will maintain that the only true Conch is a person born on the "Rock" of Key West, where the birth of a baby was once announced by putting a conch shell on a stick in the front yard. It should be remembered, on the other hand, that until well into the 1900's *all* Keys' babies "went to Key West to be born," there being no doctors or midwives elsewhere. The creature that began all this associative lore—the conch—has been mindlessly overharvested and, almost gone, is at last protected in the Keys' waters. Restaurant conch is not local. Even though conchs mate and lay eggs at the same time, they just can't keep up with our "demands" on them.

annihilating four acres of living coral. It made a portion of that fabulous tract, all the peaks and valleys and colorful caves bright with life, as flat and as grey as a parking lot.

The reef that runs along the Atlantic coast of the Keys, close to the great Gulf Stream, is fantastically fragile. All reefs are complex and highly particular life-forms, requiring lots of sunlight and clear, warm water. The Florida Keys tract (the only reef in the continental United States) exists at the northernmost limit of tropical reef development. It is threatened by this potentially chilly location. It is threatened by its own wonderful accessibility. It is threatened by development on land, by boat bilge, by silt dredged up from marinas, by the effluent and rainwater runoff from condo complexes and parking lots. It is threatened by overuse and misuse. With all this close at hand, it seems cruel and unnecessary for fate to bring tons of chicken feed blundering out of the darkness for the singular purpose of extinguishing part of beautiful Molasses Reef, but blunder out of the darkness the chicken feed did. The Park Service has marked off the damaged tract with yellow cone-shaped buoys and are monitoring it for signs of regeneration, which they do not expect to occur. The part of the reef visited by the wayward *Wellwood* has ceased to exist. It has become part of Keys history, as gone as the Caloosa Indians, the railroad, and the green turtle.

KEY LARGO

By car there are two approaches to the Keys. The most commonly traveled is Route 1, which skirts the savannah of the Everglades, crosses Jewfish Creek (which is part of the Intracoastal Waterway) and broad Lake Surprise, so named by the first railroad survey party in 1902, who apparently had not anticipated its existence. The other, slightly longer way of entering the Keys is over the Card Sound Bridge—a toll that will deposit you farther up in the mangrove and hardwood hammock land of North Key Largo.

Sometimes it's nice to contemplate things that *aren't* there.

The 11-mile strip between the wealthy and very private Ocean Reef Club (considered by the FBI to be "the most secure resort in the country," for those of you who know what that signifies) and Card Sound Road's convergence with Route 1 is empty, but grandiose projects have long been planned for this area. In 1955, speculators bought up 1500 acres of virgin land here and incorporated it as the city of North Key Largo Beach. It was a phantom city with a phantom government but with very large intentions. It would be a city of 100,000 people to begin with, which would have increased the population of the Keys by 150 percent. It would be a super-city, of course, with much modern gadgetry, like monorails. The land was rescued from this ghastly inspiration when the Nature Conservancy and the Fish and Wildlife Service purchased it for their Crocodile Lake National Wildlife Refuge. Construction of the notorious "Port Bougainvillea"—described by its developers as "an imitation Mediterranean coastal village" of almost 3000 units, pocked with "baylets" and man-made lakes—was halted because the very enormity of the project bankrupted its backers. Many other condos and hotels have been planned for the Card Sound Road, but so far three homely beasts have prevented them from being built—the alligator, the wood rat, and the cotton mouse. Modest and much-maligned, but all federally protected endangered species, these three have kept bulldozers from overrunning the Keys.

The Card Sound Road and Route 1 converge just after MM # 109 at Lake Surprise, and one enters the Florida Keys. A sign with a leaping sailfish says so on your right. Following quickly on your left is another sign. This one says, "Hell Is Truth Seen Too Late."

Key Largo Key was once a series of barely connected keys with a few high ridges. Railroad construction filled in the channels between the islets, leaving us with what we now experience as a single long key which stretches all the way down to Tavernier. A four-lane road runs the length of the key, divided from MM # 100 down to MM # 92 by a wooded median.

The town of Key Largo was originally known as Rock Harbor. Real estate promoters sought to cash in on the publicity given the 1948 Bogart-Bacall movie and circulated a petition to have the name changed. The request was granted by postal authorities in 1952, and Rock Harbor became Key Largo.

The movie *Key Largo,* with the exception of a few interior set scenes shot inside the bar The Caribbean Club, was filmed entirely on a soundstage in Hollywood. The film itself may be drenched with Bogart charisma, but it certainly is counterfeit Keys, with director John Huston ornamenting the script with California touches such as fog and kelp. However, the fact that the actors never came to Key Largo, and that the film was not shot here, did not faze the town's boosters. Key West had Hemingway, why shouldn't Largo have Bogie? To compound matters, the owner of the Holiday Inn, maintaining that "Key Largo is laden with memories of the great actor," bought the riverboat used in the Bogart movie *The African Queen* (which was filmed mostly in England) and now offers "excursions" in it from his dock. As a random touch, he has the original Chris-Craft boat that was used in the movie *On Golden Pond* there as well.

What Key Largo is far more justifiably known for is the reef, for here is the beautiful and unique **John Pennecamp Coral Reef State Park.** The coral reef is one of the world's most ancient and involved life-forms, and the easy availability of this spectacular other world is what makes a trip to the Florida Keys so special. The reef, lying between four and seven miles offshore, runs parallel to the Keys from Largo to the Dry Tor-

The queen conch

tugas. It protects the Keys from storms and is also the reason why there are no sandy beaches on these islands—the reef absorbs the roll of waves which, if they came ashore, would gradually wear away rock to sand. The depths at which the most variety of life and geological relief occur is between fifteen and thirty-five feet of water. At greater depths there is not as much diversity, but the corals, sponges, and fish are larger. The living animals that form and build the reef are coral polyps that feed on plankton—the tiny organism that float past on ocean currents—which is also the food of great whales. There are both hard and soft corals. The hard ones have a flexible skeletal structure which undulates in the moving waters. These are the *gorgonians,* named for the snake-haired sisters of Greek myth, and they come in shapes of tubes, plumes, whips, and fans and in a multitude of colors. One of the most beautiful and easily recognizable is the common sea fan, the color of which is the most spectacular peacock blue. The hard corals are the castle builders. They are the brain, the staghorn and elkhorn, the pillar, the star and flower corals. Other hard corals have descriptive names like sheet, leaf, saucer, scroll, ribbon, tree, tube, and bush. Some colonies of polyps create massive spiraling structures that can rise as high as thirty-five feet from the ocean floor or spread out as boulders with deep, swirling convolutions. These coral polyps, building on the dead skeletons of former colonies, have a life span of centuries, but the reef grows with exceptional slowness. Staghorn and elkhorn corals grow only scant inches a year, and a good-sized brain coral may be hundreds of years old. The reef is perhaps the most complicated of all ecosystems, for nowhere else in the animal kingdom do so many organisms live together and participate in such interdependent relationships. More than five hundred species of fish live, feed, and are protected in its coraline caves. Some fish, like the dramatically streaked neon gobie, and crustaceans, like the banded coral shrimp, enjoy freedom from predation by grooming other fish of parasites. The gobie inhabits the deep grooves of brain corals, which other fish seem to regard as cleaning stations, while the coral shrimp actually lives within the jaws of the toothy moray eel.

Before marine sanctuaries were established and federal and

state laws passed, commercial collectors were dynamiting the reef for coral, as well as removing it with crowbars and even cranes. It's remarkable that there's anything left of the living reef at all. But there is some left and it's enchanting. It's also irreplaceable and unrenewable.

Peculiarly enough, one of the first establishments that greets you as you enter Key Largo is **Shell Man** at MM #106, a "decor" emporium filled with corals yanked out of the peaceful and astounding depths and lined up on dusted shelves beneath fluorescent lights. Mystery has been transformed into mere novelty. (Does someone back home desire a toilet seat with seashells laminated deep within? This is the place to get it, perhaps the only place to get it.) The corals have been imported from the Philippines, since the taking of coral is prohibited in the Keys, but there are no signs posted to tell you of this fact. Instead, the place is almost an invitation to the unaware to go diving, discover a pretty piece of coral, break it off, and take it home. *All* corals, including the "soft" sea fans and whips, are protected all along the Keys' 150-mile reef tract. If you see anyone taking coral or harming or molesting other protected marine species —turtles, rays and manatees—contact the Marine Patrol (743-6542) or, in Pennecamp, the park ranger.

DIVING

The first of the many dive shops you will see on the Key is **Capt. Slate's Atlantis Dive Center** at MM #106.5 (Phone: 451-3020). Those who dive with Capt. Slate, at least according to the pictures in his brochure, like to put largish dead fish in their mouths and feed them to even larger fish. If this is not to your fancy, however, Capt. Slate offers the usual—snorkel and scuba charters, instruction, and night dives.

As well, there are **American Diving Headquarters**, MM #106 (451-0037); **Quiescence** MM #103.2 (451-2440); **Sea Dwellers** MM #100 (451-3640); **Ocean Divers** MM #100 (451-1113); and **Divers' World** MM #99.5 (451-3200).

Dive shops all along Key Largo Key down to Tavernier dive

Pennecamp Park. There is an extensive dive concession within the park itself, but in general you have the potential of visiting a wider variety of reef sites with shops located on Route 1. Make sure you know how many will be aboard so you won't have the disappointment of ending up on a "cattleboat." There are heavily dived reefs and there are areas that aren't even named, yet are beautiful and exciting. Many shops offer multi-day dive packages, and some will even arrange for motel or camping accommodations. (Conversely, most of the larger motels in the area offer dive packages.) Rates usually run $15–$20 for a snorkeling trip, with about one and a half hours of diving time. Scuba trips are usually $25, with rental equipment running around $20. Wet suits can be rented for $15, not a bad idea in the winter, when even first-felt–warm waters can turn chilly after an hour. Other equipment, such as underwater cameras, can also be rented. Boats leave early in the morning and early in the afternoon. Call for reservations. Inquire as to advanced instruction classes and certification.

For experienced scuba divers, a dive at night is an especially remarkable experience. The coral polyps open like flowers to feed on the plankton floating by, and the water is lit by luminescent organisms corkscrewing through the blackness. Some fish, like the triggerfish and the big blue and green parrotfish, snuggle into crevices and seem to sleep at night. Others, like the bizarrely beaked filefish, come out to eat their favorite foods, stinging fire-coral and black long-spined sea urchins. Many fish change or lose their colors at night, while sea fans seem veined in fire. Big-eyed squid appear. And octopuses, those boneless, enigmatic forms which, because of their highly developed nervous systems, are believed to be more intelligent than anything in the sea, except for mammals.

The new fad in Key Largo is **Jules' Undersea Lodge,** a two-room "hotel" at the bottom of the lagoon. "Through this wonderful experience of sub-surface habitation, we open to the public one of the planet's last frontiers," one of the owners says. This particular frontier is only one hundred feet from shore and thirty feet below the surface, and has air-conditioning, television, a VCR, telephones, and "bathroom facilities." Perhaps you'll feel that this is not much of a creative step. It's $300 per

The coral reef

person per night and you're provided with hookah-type diving gear for when you venture outside. If you're not a certified diver you can learn how to use this equipment in a "Resort Course" that costs another $50–$75. You can have lobster, steak or chicken for dinner (just like on an airplane) and Belgian waffles for breakfast, but no alcohol is permitted unless you're on your honeymoon. Then you're allowed some champagne. There are plans to create a 6-acre "undersea leisure park" here—sort of a Snorkel World. Jules' is located at the Koblick Marine Center at MM #103.2 (phone: 451-2353).

JOHN PENNECAMP CORAL REEF STATE PARK

America's first underwater state park was established in 1960 and named for one of its most dedicated and determined advocates, John Pennecamp, a Miami newspaper editor who was also instrumental in creating Everglades National Park. Park waters stretch more than 21 miles from Carysfort Reef to Molasses Reef and inshore to the coastline. With the additional protected waters of the Key Largo National Marine Sanctuary, the preserve extends more than 8 miles into the ocean and encompasses 178 square miles. There are two small beaches on park grounds (in the shallow waters off one of them, the state has reconstructed a galleon wreck) and two nature trails, one winding by boardwalk through the mangroves. But the real meaning of the place is all beneath the water's surface.

If this is your first time out to see the reef (remember, the reef lies several miles offshore—you can't just wade out, dip your face down and see it), your first glimpse of the fanciful, lacy, undulating terrain and the beautiful bright fishes in the clear water will be startling. You will first be amazed. Then may follow, fleetingly, suspicion. Has the place been stocked? Have the fish been placed here by the concessionaire? Have these fish somehow, even, been *hired*? But your suspicions are unfounded. They fade away and wonder returns.

The park's concession stand does stock a good number of informational booklets about the reef. For an even more extensive selection of bird, coral, and fish identification guides, go to **The Book Nook** at MM #100 in the Waldorf Plaza Shopping Center, which has an excellent offering of Florida books in general as well as NOAA (National Oceanic and Atmospheric Administration) charts. These charts are absolutely necessary to the boater. They cost about $5 each.

The entrance to Pennecamp is at MM #102.5. For camping reservations and information, call the park at 451-1202. For information on snorkeling and scuba tours and boat and equipment rental, call 451-1621. Entry fees at Pennecamp and all

state recreation areas are $1.50 a car, $1 per person if you're a
Florida resident, $2.50 and $1.50 if you're not.

The park offers several types of diving trips and programs (for
example, a full-day introductory course in scuba diving, held
every Friday from 8:30 A.M. to 5:30 P.M. costs $70). A snorkeling
tour leaves at 9 A.M., noon, and 3 P.M. and costs $22 per person.
(A family plan is available on the 9 A.M. trip.) A snorkeling and
sailing tour on a 32-foot trimaran costs $38 a person for half a
day. Scuba trips cost $32.50 per person and leave at 9:30 A.M. and
1:30 P.M. The dive shop rents all equipment as well as a variety
of boats, including houseboats and 20-foot motorboats.* High
deposits are required on boat rentals. If you do decide to go out
on your own, it's important that you be able to read charts well.
The park service has white mooring buoys scattered around the
most frequently dived sites. Tie up to these. If you must anchor,
do so on a sandy spot. *Never* anchor on the coral itself. Careless
anchoring is highly destructive to the reef, for when coral is
broken, the wound invites invasion by algae and other organisms which spread rapidly and can destroy an entire colony.
When diving, always display the red and white "diver down"
flag and stay within one hundred feet of your boat. A lot of boats
are cruising around these waters, and the flag speaks of your
presence.

There are nine diving sites in the park, each distinguished by
some fascinating peculiarity. Park-based dive boats usually go
to White Bank Dry Rocks, French Reef, and Molasses Reef. The
Benwood wreck, a mile and a half north of French Reef, is a
popular scuba destination. The luckless freighter was first tor-
pedoed by a German submarine during World War II and, while
limping home, was then accidentally rammed by another boat.
Her hull was used for bombing practice for a while, and then she
was dynamited and sunk. Her battered and scattered remains
are now host to large schools of fish, and home, too, to the
secretive and commandingly repellent moray eel.

White Bank Dry Rocks is the largest of the snorkeling reefs.

---

*Houseboats $100 a day, $425 a week. A Hobie Cat is $24 an hour. Reef boats
with 90-hp motor $25 an hour.

It is a shallow garden wealthy with staghorn and elkhorn beds and star and brain coral heads, and full of the brilliant flitting movement of small tropical fish of dots and stripes and bands and bars, tiny wrasses—fish so darkly purple their bones are blue—curious and fearless angelfish, rock beauties, triggerfish, and damselfish (these last being the most aggressive fish on the reef and the ones most likely to bite you—this dismaying prospect tempered, however, by the fact that they are no more than two inches long). This is a perfect reef for the novice diver to explore. **French Reef** is primarily a scuba site, noted for its caves, winding canyons, and large fish. **Molasses** is the biggest reef in the park and has what many divers consider the greatest variety of both terrain and fish. There are shipwrecks, and sandy channels winding through towering coral wells. It's very likely you'll see beautiful manta rays here.

Dive shops on Route 1 visit the middle and more northern areas of the park. If you have a particular site or wreck that you are interested in exploring, inquire, remembering that trips are dependent on visibility and weather and that visibility in winter can sometimes be disappointing. **Carysfort Reef** (named, with an inexplicable alteration of the last letter, for the HMS *Carysford,* a frigate which had run aground there in 1770) is located at the extreme northern end of the park and is marked by a 100-foot lighthouse. This is a nice diving area and not a particularly busy one. The **Elbow**, marked by a navigational light, is the closest of the reefs to the cleansing and swift Gulf Stream, making visibility there almost always excellent. There are more shipwrecks located around here than almost anywhere else, and the fish have been fed so frequently by divers that they seem actually expectant of handouts. **Key Largo Dry Rocks** is the site of the 9-foot **Christ of the Deep Statue**, a duplicate of the Christ of the Abysses Statue in the Mediterranean off Genoa. The bronze Christ with upraised arms placed here in twenty feet of water was donated to the park by an Italian industrialist and sports spearfisherman, and much flowery rhetoric swirls about it. A park bulletin, reprinting the original dedication of the Abysses statue, says, "The dead shall no longer be lonely . . . Ships and phantoms of ships will crowd around Him; living men and dead men. The shadows of all those

THE GLASS-BOTTOM BOAT

The **Discovery** leaves three times a day from the park, at 9 A.M., at noon, and at 3 P.M. The 2 1/2-hour trip costs $14 for adults and $7.50 for children. It is rather like going from Hyannis to Nantucket on the Hi-Line, except that at the end of 2 1/2 hours you are not in Nantucket. *Discovery* trips are very popular, and reservations should be made in advance by calling 451-1621. The vessel winds through South Sound Creek and out six miles to Molasses Reef, which is the only reef it visits. Many people are disappointed that they do not see the Christ of the Deep Statue, but that is miles to the northeast. There is about a half hour of viewing time through the glass panels in the ship's hull while the *Discovery* wiggles and churns about. The trip is most enjoyable if undertaken with a large group of children, who will be highly vocal in their enthusiasm for what they do and do not see. They will invariably spot the seasickness bags in the shelf above the panels and yell *look at the barf bags* while the guide is pointing out a parrotfish. They will always insist that they have seen a shark, and they will have a very good time. Actually, it is not likely that you will see a shark, a turtle, or any of the larger or shyer inhabitants of the reef with all the bustling about the *Discovery* does, idling, then scooting sideways with a grand flourish of bubbles, leaving sea fans waving frantically in the propeller wash like shipwrecked maidens. What you will see are big basket sponges, a good variety of corals, and schools of porkfish and grunts. And you will frequently see barracuda wearing their customary peevish expressions. The 'cuda is enjoying a period of revisionist thinking at present. He is no longer considered the aggressive man-mauler he was once believed to be. The new attitude is that if he does blunder into you with his razory teeth it will be because of poor visibility or because you were wearing something shiny. In any case, it will be a mistake. Another mistake—this time one that people make—is eating barracuda. The fish shows his considerable resentment at being eaten by infecting the eater with ciguatera, or violent fish poisoning, although folk wisdom claims that if you cook a dime with a 'cuda and the dime stays shiny, it's safe to eat him. If the dime turns black, though, you'd better not.

A *Discovery* trip is undeniably the driest way to see the reef, but it is probably the least satisfying. If you're able to swim at all, it's far more enjoyable to take one of the dive boats out and snorkel the reef. The reef is another world which you can enter, and to be able to do so with the rudiments of a glass mask and a plastic tube is almost miraculous. Besides having that silly name, snorkelers *look* silly to the non-snorkeler, floating flatly around, making occasional rude noises through their tubes. But a snorkeler is not what he appears to others. He is what he sees. He has a magic glass wrapped around his eyes and he is in a world of beauty and color. Graceful movement. Silence.

who lost their lives in the sea will be present, without discrimination of nationality, blood or color. With His liberal gesture of invitation, He will welcome everybody . . ." And so on. The statue's liberal and equitable invitation is blurred frequently by algae. "It's real pretty when it's all scrubbed up," a park ranger says. "We've got to get out there more and scrub her up." What can't be scrubbed up is algae-smothered coral and this is becoming an increasing problem throughout the park and sanctuary. A large area near the Dry Rocks is covered with green-brown coats of algae that look like fur and stringy yellow strands of algae that look like hair. *Wherever does this gross stuff come from?* you might ask, even though it's not what you've come to see at all. (See **Caveat Auditor,** pg. 171.)

Not far from the Christ of the Deep, is **Grecian Rocks**, a good reef for snorkelers because it has shallow waters and very little current. Close by is the intriguing **Cannon Patch**, where a number of cannon from unknown ships lie scattered about. Farther south, beyond the park's boundaries, is pretty **Conch Reef** and the site of three Spanish galleons, the *Capitana,* the *El Infante,* and the *San Jose y las Animas,* all shipwrecked here in a 1733 hurricane. Even the ballast stones—mere stones, after all—are fascinating here. **Conch Reef** drops off to a depth of 115 feet, but close to the surface is a large stand of elkhorn coral, and there are stumpy remnants of formerly large colonies of pillar coral. (It was the devastation of Conch Reef by collectors that prompted state legislators to prohibit the taking of coral.)

WHERE TO STAY

Exploring the reef and taking advantage of the different packages the dive shops offer take days at the very least. Many places to stay are completely booked in the winter season and on weekends. Reservations are always a good idea. The motels are clustered in two areas—just south of the entrance to Pennecamp, and below MM #100, just beyond where the four-lane road divides. Most of them are on the bay side. The area code for all the keys, including Key West, is 305.

There's a **Howard Johnson's** at MM #102 beside the splendid monolith of Southern Bell, and the aforementioned **Holiday Inn** at MM #100, recently renovated with a jungle theme —lots of zebra-patterned area rugs. Best of the chains is the **Sheraton** at MM #97 (bay side), not far from the Wynken, Blynken and Nod Trailer Park, where ancient immobile homes reside on streets such as Tweety Pie Terrace, Thumper Thoroughfare, and Little Miss Muffet Lane. The Sheraton is trying to give a new resort feeling to Key Largo, and a standard room here runs $160 in season, $125 in summer. It's a well-laid-out luxurious place, concealed from the road by a buttonwood grove. Suites overlooking the bay are $230 in season; over the

Basket sponges and a barracuda

trees $160–$195. Good discounts are available. And there's tennis too (852-5553).

Although there are many more chains and deluxe resorts in the
Keys than there used to be, small cottages and more eccentri-
cally personalized lodgings can still be found. Many people stay
in these places for weeks, bringing their own coffeepots, broiling
up the fish they catch, eating from the mismatched plates
stacked in the cupboard (ant motel tin discreetly tucked in the
corner), shaking the scatter rugs out each day, and sitting outside on the dock at twilight with their compeers, sipping martinis they have mixed exactly to their taste. There's always a
little boat tied up that the kids can use, and the swimming pool
is usually part of the bay itself, set off by flaking cement walls,
its depth dictated by the tides.

   Largo Lodge, less than a mile south of the park at MM #102,
is a cool, jungly enclave—very refreshing after a day on and
under the bright water. The grounds, though not extensive, are
unique for their lushness. The palms are towering, the orchids
profuse, and every healthy leaf shines. The cottages are large,
with screened porches and separate kitchens, and can sleep
four. There is a boat ramp and a little dock on the bay, on what
is here called Tarpon Basin. The place is very pleasant, the
landlady jolly, but the rule in this Eden is that no one under the
age of sixteen is allowed. Prices are $85 a night for two, $5 for
each additional person. Telephone: 451-0424.

   Tarpon Basin (451-1661), close by, is typical of the small cottage complexes scattered along the Keys—a little sand beach
willfully created, a few palm trees, set quietly back from the
highway with moderate rates.

   Rock Reef (852-2401) and **The Seafarer** (852-5349) at MM
#98.5 both have cottages on tree-dotted grounds and little man-
made beaches. Rooms and efficiencies range from $58 to $108 in
winter; a cabin on the water is $91. **Popp's** (852-5201) and **Stone-
ledge** (852-8114), farther down at MM #96 and MM #95, are
similar in style and rates.

   In a class by itself is the **Blue Lagoon Resort** (451-2908) at
MM #99.5. This is an intense little jumble of trailers and cottages, the office manned by clerks of many nations. You can get

a small room in a trailer here for $25, if you don't mind sharing
it with an enormous TV. Fantasize that you are in a fifties
movie. You are on the lam. You are attempting to escape from
something terrible. You sit on the green plaid bedspread and
listen to your breathing. No one will ever find you here. Reservations are not de rigueur.

WHERE TO EAT

Key Largo has four great funky places to eat, several places
there's no need to write home about, and **Snook's Bayside
Club.**

Tiny **Harriet's,** close to Popp's around MM #95, is good for
breakfast as is **The Hideout** at MM #103.5 on the water at the
end of a street peculiarly named Transylvania Avenue. In a
humble house, very much unrestored (close to Jule's, "one of the
planet's last frontiers"), you can have fish and grits and biscuits
for breakfast. It is common knowledge that nothing beats fish
and grits and biscuits for breakfast. You can have it for lunch
too. Open 7–2 seven days a week. Telephone 451-0128. **Mrs.
Mac's Kitchen** (451-3722) has basic burgers and good chilli as
well as cold Key-lime pie that will make your teeth sing. Authentic license-plate decor. Open Monday–Saturday 7 A.M.–9:30
P.M. Then there's **Tugboat's** on Seagate Boulevard (just after
the shopping center before Route 1 becomes a divided highway,
take a left). Tugboat's is casual, cheap and cash only. You can
have a good fried-fish basket—try the shark—on a screened
porch that overlooks a crumpled yard with little plastic Japanese lanterns hanging in the trees and rotted wicker settees
now hosting flowers. Santy Claus beams out of one of the tug-
boats at you all year long.

Just around the corner, for those who prefer cocktails is **The
Pilot House,** which is on a marina and thus is popular with
weekend boaters who frequently do not make impressive landings. Or departures, for that matter. A tiki-bar is open in season
and the restaurant is open all year from 11 A.M. to 10 P.M. "Har-
vey's Fish Sandwich" is fussy and forgettable, although mem-

ory recalls a rather orange color. Shrimp and lobster dishes are more straightforward (451-3142).

The Italian Fisherman at MM #104 is large and open with big white statues gleaming nakedly in the parking lot and lots of outside dining on extended terraces. The place has a sprawling free-form quality—it's been expanding now for twenty years. The bar is the place to watch Key Largo sunsets. The ambience here is better than the food, which is, however, reasonably priced. The portions are large. They seem to worry about the conch dishes somewhat. ("Have you ever had conch before?" the waitress asks. "Maybe you should have it parmigiana.") It is the beginning of the Keys up here, but if you're

---

A BAR

Right beside The Italian Fisherman is **The Caribbean Club Bar**, the bar of movie myth. A sign inside says Absolutely No Dogs Allowed. Outside, there's a bit of littered waterfront and some benches and beer bottles scattered about. Inside, in the morning, there are men drinking shots and playing pool, and women sliding off their stools. It certainly doesn't look like the kind of place where a dog wouldn't be welcome.

But there is an explanation for the sign. Once dogs wandered in and out of here freely. They slept, snarled, scratched, and drank beer here. It was a democratic place. One man who frequented The Caribbean Club would often bring his pit bull bitch in. She was a champion pit bull, and she had a litter of puppies. So the man brought her in one day with a few of her puppies. While the man drank, the dogs went for a dip. One of the puppies, frightened of the water, climbed on the bitch's back and would not let go, and managed to drown its very own mother. The bitch was a champion pit bull who had been worth a great deal of money, and the owner, as well as being upset, was disbelieving. He gave the drowned dog mouth-to-mouth rescucitation and pounded on her heart, but the dog remained drowned. He was so mad at the puppy he kicked it to death. The management decided that dogs hanging out in the bar were a potential problem. Now dogs are not allowed. Absolutely.

---

trying conch, try it the simplest way possible. The more elaborate the preparation sounds, the tougher it's going to be. Open from 11:30 A.M. until 11 P.M. (451-4471).

Snook's at MM #99.5 (heading south, it's a right at the light down a narrow road to the bay) is a clubby place with elegant inside dining as well as patio dining on the water. If you eat inside you don't have to listen to the keyboardist. Probably the most sophisticated food for the next hundred miles. The fish is prepared six different ways, the fine cuts of meat, four. All the desserts have won awards—apparently pies and chocolate bombs have their own little contests each year. Even so, the menu is a model of classic simplicity. An excellent wine list. A bar too, of course, serving all the exotics—the Yellow Bird, the Pineapple Paradise, the Miami Vice, the Hurricane. Open 5:30–10:30 (451-3847).

TAVERNIER

At the end of Key Largo Key at MM #92.5, just north of the community of **Tavernier**, is the turn to the Keys' original settlement of Planter, which was homesteaded in 1866. **Harry Harris County Park** occupies the ocean site today. At the turn of the century, Planter had the only post office between Miami and Key West, but the town was abandoned when the railroad came through and people moved inland to be around the station, founding the new town of Tavernier, named for a small key offshore which the Spaniards had previously named *Cayo Tabona,* or Horsefly Key. If you want to go to the park, take a left on Burton Drive, wind your way past many streets filled with houses and trailers all festooned with Styrofoam lobster pot markers, and you will eventually reach it. There is a sandy beach and many concrete picnic tables that look like small temples dedicated to hibachi gods. Before you advance to the beach, picnic temples, and playgrounds, however, a great many signs will place grave demands on your sense of freedom and delight. Stop, they say. No Dogs, they say. No Parking. Stop. Slow. No Sports Or Games, they say. Perhaps you will find it more congenial to turn back to Route 1 and drive down to **Harry's Place** at MM #91. Harry's Place (it's the same Harry Harris actually, an early restaurateur and saloon keeper, later a county commissioner) is friendly and inexpensive, with weekend buffets and breakfast served as early as 6 A.M. The bar stays open until 4 A.M.

The development of Tavernier was inhibited by the depression of 1929 and the almost constant arrival of hurricanes, the most severe of all being the storm of September 1935, which devastated most of Tavernier's structures and erased all signs of habitation eight miles south on Matecumbe Key. A peculiar result of the hurricane for Tavernier was the subsequent construction of "Red Cross houses," built with the help of the Federal Emergency Relief Administration and the Red Cross. These were four-room houses built of reinforced concrete containing 80,000 pounds of steel, with steel rods anchoring the house to bedrock. The floors and roof were also made of concrete, and the walls were a foot thick. The window sashes were made of steel and contained double-strength glass. The houses were ugly as sin, of course, but built to withstand anything short of the Apocalypse. Unfortunately, seawater was used in the mixing of the cement, which rusted the steel reinforcing rods so that all the structures cracked.

But Tavernier is proud of these oddities, proud indeed of anything that dates at all, for the Keys, with the exception of Key West, are scant on old buildings. The town plans to establish a historical district that will include these hurricane houses as well as the simple wooden structures that remain from the days of the railroad, when Tavernier was the first station stop in the Keys. Tavernier was once considered an outpost—subdued, but an outpost nonetheless. No longer an outpost, the town remains subdued, hugging the road in a mannerly fashion. It has a new shopping center, **Tavernier Towne**, (complete with dignified *e*), at MM #91.5 and the only movie theater in the Upper Keys. It's a modest, rather dusty community and seems far removed from the water, although the water is there, of course, and along the ocean where the early settlers built their lonely little homes, situated to catch the breezes and keep the mosquitoes away, are the large weekend retreats of Miamians, each

CUCO BOBO

In the Depression, a round-trip ticket from Miami to Key West on the railroad cost a dollar. When the train stopped for water just south of Tavernier, passengers would dash into the lime groves and gather Key limes to liven up their rum drinks. In Key West, a Cuban called Cuco Bobo made a living in bars by imitating the railroad as it chugged down the Keys. Cuco was attired somewhat militarily, with a dazzling array of medals and ribbons. He would stand on the bar, move his arms like an engine gathering steam, shuffle his feet, and make toot-tooting noises. Several drinks were purchased for him during this process. He'd blow a whistle, eliciting further drinks. Then he'd start to call out the stops—*Tavernier! Islamorada! Matecumbe!* Oh, it was a long, dry trip. *Grassy Key!* Very seldom was Key West reached before Cuco Bobo fell off the bar.

equipped with a slick car and a motorboat. Hurricane bunkers, these houses are not.

PLANTATION KEY

Across Tavernier Creek at MM #90 and running down to Snake Creek at MM #87 is **Plantation Key**. Centuries ago it was inhabited by the Caloosa Indians. Remnants of a considerably large midden can be found on the bay on the northernmost end of the key. As you are probably aware, however, Indian mounds and middens are very boring, consisting of dirt, small grimy shells, and once-useful stones—dumps of non-acquisition. These middens are of most interest to enterprising gardeners, who can be seen carting away buckets of the old, rich soil for their own flowery purposes.

At the turn of the century, the first large schooner in the Upper Keys was built on Plantation Key by "Brush" Pinder. It was built "by the idea," without plans, the same way it was done in the Bahamas. Pinder named the 60-foot, 40-ton schooner, which was made of Everglades mahogany, *Island Home,* and she sailed Keys' waters for fifteen years, carrying ice, pineapples, passengers, and mail before the coming of the railroad.

Plantation Key boasts the restaurant **Marker 88** (located helpfully at MM #88), often described as "a destination of gourmets." Open for dinner only, it is attractive, expensive, requires reservations, and is quietly placed among trees on the bay. Inside, however, it is anything but quiet. The tables are set very close together and the noise within is beyond discordance, beyond clamor, beyond din or hubbub. It is not that the waitresses scream at one another or drop trays—it is the shrieking, babbling, crowing uproar of the patrons themselves. The kitchen may create inspired bisques and sauces and stuffings, but it is difficult not to be more impressed by the surrounding cacophony. Marker 88 is open from 5 P.M. For reservations, call 852-9315. (**The Naughty and Nice Gag Shop** has recently appeared just across the highway hoping to get some of the gourmet trade too.)

A mile away, at MM #87, is the **Plantation Yacht Harbor Resort**, with its big marina and its candlelit Commodore Room for those who regret ever having left Ft. Lauderdale. Reservations: 852-2381. Open 6–11 P.M. Adjacent is the more casual El Capitain Room, open 8 A.M. to 3 P.M. and 5 to 10 P.M. when the children are screaming for nachos or potato skins. Rooms are available at the Resort, most of them overlooking extensive areas of denuded land, faintly green, which appears to be waiting for a golf course to happen to it. Telephone: 852-2381. Rooms $60–$75 in season, $50–$60 May 1–November 30.

A bit of old Keys funk is a half mile away on your left, in the shape of a small and startling perma-stone castle—the former home of McKee's Museum of Sunken Treasure. When you toured the Keys in the 1950's, you'd do some fishing, eat some fish, and visit Art McKee's museum. McKee was a well-known local treasure diver of the 1940's and 50's who built his miniaturized version of a Spanish fort in 1949 and filled it with the things he'd found in nearby waters—cannons, muskets, swords, and gold coins. The museum has been closed since 1976, and the "castle" for sale for just about that long. Once zanily solitary, it's now banked by houses. Across the road at MM #86.5 is **The Rain Barrel**, a cluster of crafts shops in a garden setting. This is not the place to buy the armadillo pocketbook you've always wanted, or coconuts with spangled, painted faces. There are artful things back here, where printmakers, potters, jewelsmiths, sculptors, and wood and leather workers all exercise their talents. It's as though the entire graduating class of the Putney School in Vermont had come down to Plantation Key.

If you want to explore the reef off Plantation, local dive shops will take you to a variety of areas, usually visiting the reefs of **Inner and Outer Conch** and the ledges and drop-offs of **Davis Reef** and **Crocker Wall**. Outer Conch has a zigzag maze of ridges separated by long, winding valleys of sand, where huge rays can often be seen gracefully swimming. Sometimes captains bring bags of bread crumbs and chopped sea urchins to feed the fish. Other trips concentrate on spearfishing, shell collecting, or lobstering. Dive boats make morning and afternoon trips, and the costs usually run about $30 for a two-tank scuba trip, $35 for night dives, $20 for snorkelers. Make reservations and inquire as to location and group intention. You don't want to be happily feeding a fish and have your dive companion nail it right before your eyes.

Lady Cyana, MM #86 (664-8717)
Treasure Divers, MM #85.5, just behind **The Sandbar**, which offers Nashville music, pool, and barbecue (664-5111)
Holiday Isle, MM #84.5 (664-4145)

An in-shore patch reef, easily accessible if you're just poking about in a rental boat, is **Hens and Chickens Reef**. This reef, originally named by the Spanish, lies three miles offshore and is marked by a navigational light. Large star coral heads once grew here, but the reef was killed in 1970 when a particularly cold winter brought cold water laden with sediment out of the bay through Snake Creek into the Gulf. The living coral is gone but the structures remain and are being repopulated by soft corals. Fish and lobsters still live among the rocky remains, and many moray eels also lurk about here. As is often the case with reefs close to shore, visibility at Hens and Chickens is frequently cloudy.

THE BACK COUNTRY

To the west of Plantation Key are the waters of Florida Bay, the "back country" which, once you pass the Intracoastal Waterway, which roughly and rather closely parallels the Upper Keys, is the Everglades National Park. These uninhabited islands of the upper and central bay have names like Caloosa, Buttonwood, Triplet, Tern, Eagle, Black Betsy, and Manatee. All are mangrove, red and black, the red the pioneer, its roots graceful as hooped skirts, clumping forward, building land. There are primitive campsites on some of the keys in the bay, including Nest in the eastern portion and Rabbit and Man of War Keys in the Dildo Key Bank (there is a modest explanation for this name, one is certain) in the western bay. For the interest of etymologists, the grim name of Arsenic Bank nearby is a distortion of Arsenicker in turn a mispronunciation of these keys' *real* name, Marsh Sneaker.

The back country is unique and mysterious, both subtle and grand. It's a silent wilderness of extravagant rushing clouds, shallow waters brightened by sun and darkened by the shapes of fishes, green islands appearing as if by magic on the horizon and 360-degree sunsets. The northwestern part of the bay is home to the secretive slender-snouted crocodile, rarer than the freshwater alligator. Crocs are said to have five distinct calls, all to do with love and warning. Poachers say that their red eyes look just like dollar bills. In the warmer months, the beleaguered manatee grazes on the succulent grasses of these flats. A docile, dallying creature, its biggest enemy is, of course, man, this time piloting the motorboat that churns thoughtlessly across its great, browsing bulk.

The grass beds of the back country support large numbers of redfish, trout, snook, mangrove snapper, tarpon, and the small, fast, hard-fighting gamefish jack crevalles, and provide a nursery for lobsters and crabs. And this is where the bird rookeries are, the nesting islands and feeding grounds, the resting areas for those who make long migrations. Brown pelicans nest in great numbers, favoring a new key each season. The American Bald Eagle, too, nests here, usually raising his young on one key and fishing and hunting on another, perhaps not liking to dispose of his most immediate neighbors. There are a multitude of herons who work these waters—Louisiana, Little, Green, White, and Blue. And egrets, terns, turnstones, plovers, skimmers. Some stalk or spear. Some glide and scoop. Others sprint through shallow water, striking right and left. Others dabble and probe or are masters of the surprise attack. One of the most beautiful birds that live and breed here, though not in great numbers, is the roseate spoonbill. No one who sees the brilliant colors of this bird against the dark green mangroves and blue back country sky will ever forget it.

These are fabulous waters to explore in a small boat, although the back country takes years to know, and voyaging into its quiet wonders should not be undertaken lightly by the casual

A Keys' gator

boater. Channels are complex, usually little more than a tortured winding through mangroves and hammocks which suddenly open out to basins and flats. Always stay in channels and do not stray into the shallows where prop damage can wreck havoc on fragile seagrass meadows. The time of high and low tides can differ several hours between locations only a few miles apart. Basically, you can tell water depth by color. If it's brown, you're going to run aground. If it's white, you might. In the winter, the bay can be whipped by winds into choppy foam. In the summer, the waters can be flat as glass, with faraway boats seemingly floating in the air, and the sticks that mark channels turning into long-legged herons that fly away. At any time of the year you should be prepared for very rapid weather changes —waterspouts in the summer, brisk squalls, and sudden wind shifts. Your boat should be equipped with binoculars, good charts, a compass, and a push pole (a 10-foot pole with a spatulate end, which you use to push yourself off mud banks, pole across the flats, and anchor in the marl). The marly bottom of the bay is alarming to the uninitiated who, hopping over the side of the boat, will promptly proceed to sink. Visions of

---

THE ROSEATE SPOONBILL

"It is as though an orchid had spread its lovely wings and flown," an enthusiast once described the spoonbill.

The spoonbill had almost been exterminated by plume hunters at the turn of the century. The feathers were not as popular as those of the egret for ladies' hats, but the wings were torn off and made into fans, though the buyer was often disappointed when the brilliant colors quickly faded. Knowledge of the horrors of avian carnage gives reading Edith Wharton a new dimension.

Julian Huxley once noted that the "bird mind is not yet complicated by reason." The roseate spoonbill is a simple and shy creature of many troubles, yet garbed in glory. The young are an immaculate white and only gradually become suffused with pink. Three years must pass and three moltings occur before the bird achieves its full brilliance of nuptial plu-

Roseate spoonbills

mage—in rose and carmine and orange—and will mate. The drawing of the spoonbill in John Audubon's *Birds of America,* considered not to be by Audubon, does not reflect the true radiance of the bird's colors. It is not likely that Audubon saw many of them. In his remarks, he noted that their flesh was oily and poor eating, and that they were difficult to kill. (Some years later, in 1874, a man named Frederick Tingley Jencks, realizing that the species was growing scarce, visited two nesting colonies in the Lake Okeechobee region of Florida. He found eradicating the birds time-consuming but not impossible. He returned day after day, shooting all the birds in both colonies until no spoonbill remained. He "collected" a total of twenty-six skins.)

By 1939, the only nesting site for the birds in the state of Florida was on Bottlepoint (now called Bottle) Key, off Tavernier in Florida Bay. Robert Porter Allen, an ornithologist working for the National Audubon Society, made an intensive study of the colony in 1939 and 1940, camping on the far end of the key away from the birds and on a skiff offshore, observing their courtship, breeding, and feeding habits, and writing a charming book, *The Flame Birds.* The spoonbill favors the little killifishes of the marly flats of shallow man-

grove pools, grazing the opaque water, swinging their sensitive bills to and fro, feeling through the water as "one might
with the fingers of the hand." Mating between the birds is
decorous, the female showing her willingness by isolating
herself upon a pleasant bush and shaking convenient twigs or
branches with her bill. After a seemly amount of bill-clashing
and twig-rattling—which usually goes on for two weeks—the
male perches behind the female, reaching across her back
and grasping the twig she is fiddling with in his bill. Together
they grip the twig. Then the twig is dropped, and the male
grasps firmly the slender middle portion of the female's bill
with his own. Progression progresses . . . and so are baby
spoonbills begun!

Roseate spoonbills now nest in April and May on several of
the islands in Florida Bay, including the keys named for
Allen himself and the Audubon sanctuary, Cowpens, through
which the Inland Waterway cuts a swath. They remain far
from common, so to see them is indeed an event—their bright
existence making the beautiful back country of the Keys even
more beautiful.

Amazonian quicksand movies flash through one's head, but it
is not quicksand, and it will not devour you, although it is sucky,
sticky stuff. Always wear sneakers when tramping around either Bay or Gulf waters, for protection against coral, spiny sea
urchins, and other skittering, perhaps stinging, perhaps slimy
things.

Duly informed, but not unduly alarmed about squalls and
slither, make an effort to get "out back." The experience of
birding, fishing, and exploring in the bay is something you
should not miss in the Keys.

If you've had experience in handling a sailboat, contact **Key
Largo Shoal Water Cruises** and bareboat charter one of their
nifty wooden boats. They have several 25-foot Black Skimmer
cat yawls—a type of shallow draft sharpie perfect for traversing
the thin waters of Florida Bay. These pretty boats with the

tanbark-colored sails sail beautifully, and you'll have a memorable time with them. The sharpie's cabin can accommodate two. Also available is a 34-foot Gauntlet, a shoal draft cruiser which can sleep four to six. You can charter the boats for up to two weeks—there are five hundred square miles out there after all. The sharpies are $150 a day, $895 a week. In the summer, when you'll be sharing the magnificent solitude with more mosquitoes, the costs are $100 and $700. One of the finest months to cruise is November. The larger yawl is $165 a day, $975 a week in season. Write to Key Largo Shoal Water Cruises, P.O. Box 1180, Key Largo, FL 33037 (451-0083). They're located at MM #99.5, down the first right past Mrs. Mac's Kitchen.

WINDLEY KEY

Just across the Snake Creek Bridge at MM #86.5 is **Eric's Floating Restaurant**, an establishment which is gourmet undefinable. It *is* floating, because it's a houseboat. Within, it is ambiguously decorated with large wild animal skins and heads, and lace tablecloths. Without, naked maiden statuary crouches over the waters of a little lagoon. There is also a vague Viking ship motif. Locals love it when they want to get dressed up and spend an arm and a leg and another arm, which they just feel like doing sometimes. Dinner 5–10. Telephone: 664-9141.

The bridge at Snake Creek got stuck during Spring Break in March of 1988. A gust of wind misaligned the spans when they were in their highest open position—a gust that bartenders for ten miles in each direction considered "an act of God." People were stranded for seventeen hours. Beer was delivered in iced-up wheelbarrows. It was the wheelbarrows that made the moment "Conch."

Holiday Isle is one of the best-known pleasure and partying meccas in the Keys, but if you want a smaller, quieter place to lay your head, there is a cluster of little motels here on the ocean. The **Drop Anchor** is pretty and relaxing, with a palm-studded beach and a resident great white heron. In season (December 15 to mid-April), rooms are $50, two-room suites $115, kitchenettes $65. Summer and fall, prices drop $10 to $20. Telephone: 664-4863.

Windley Key was once two separate islands named the Umbrella Keys, but they were joined with fill by railroad construction. The key was quarried extensively for bridge and causeway fill, and after the railroad was completed, various companies continued to quarry the beautifully patterned fossilized coral rock for use as decorative veneer on buildings. The rock was known as keystone. The living reef runs along the Keys. The dead reef is the foundation of the Upper Keys. The exposed rock of the quarry walls shows the patterns and borings of polyps, gorgonians, and other inhabitants of the ancient reef. Three of the old quarries can be found on the bay side of the highway shortly after the Snake Creek Bridge, and there are hopes of acquiring this area, which spans more than thirty acres, as a state geological site and park. As well as the fascinating quarries, there is a dense hardwood hammock running along the high land above the walls with large mahogany, torchwood, joewood, and white ironwood, all rare native trees of the Florida Keys.

Theater of the Sea at MM # 84.5 was created from one of the old quarries the railroad crews dug in 1907. It was flooded with seawater and stocked with fish as a tourist attraction in the 1940's, which makes it one of the oldest marine parks in the world. There are some very amorous sea lions here, and a number of more locally grown cheerful and acrobatic dolphins. They put on a very nice show for children. Shows are continuous from 9:30 A.M. to 4 P.M. Admission is $8.50 for adults, $5.50 for children 5–12; under 5, free. There are also some gloomy sharks and a blind crocodile. They do not put on shows.

Holiday Isle (MM # 84.5) is big and brassy, with the mood of a speeded-up film. From the road it looks as though something tumultuous—even disastrous—involving a great many people has just occurred, and it usually has. On winter weekends five to six thousand people ready to fish and rock out crowd this complex, which is said to include ten bars—even taking double-vision into account a considerable number. (You will see a lot

HURRICANES

Reading about hurricanes and having hurricane parties are, naturally, much more enjoyable than evacuating for a hurricane, preparing for a hurricane, or assessing the damage from a hurricane. The Keys haven't had a hurricane in a very long while. Most people have never experienced one, and many think that those who voice their fears about hurricanes are just trying to put their bad mouth around the Keys. A hurricane is a monster whirlwind. It has a name and massive amounts of rain. It has winds of between 74 and 200 mph and stirs up giant waves and strong tides. It is born of blazing sun, still water, and warm, wet air in either the Atlantic Ocean, the Gulf of Mexico, or the Caribbean Sea any time between June and November, although it's most likely to occur in the autumn equinox between mid-August and mid-October. It begins life as a vacuum, a *beckoning* vacuum, attracting faraway breezes which approach it in a clockwise-twisting curve, only to reverse and swirl excitedly in ever-tightening counterclockwise gyres. Cool air arrives, is sucked up and made warm, everything climbs higher and faster, creating wind and rain, and then this thing starts to *move,* gorged with water power, fatally attracted to land (which will weaken and eventually extinguish it)—a real 3-D monster. Conchs know that a hurricane is coming when the poinciana loses its leaves or doesn't blossom, or when land crabs move to higher ground or ants climb straight up the walls or dogs and birds start acting peculiar. Scientists know that a hurricane is coming by reading their satellites, radar, and computers. But no one can forecast with true accuracy where a hurricane's point of landfall will be. A computer's reliability for predicting where a hurricane will hit ranges from 10 percent at 72 hours to almost 75 percent within 12 hours. Even with half a day's notice, the margin of error on a hurricane with a breadth of 150 miles remains at 65 miles in either direction. If the Hurricane Center in Miami forecasts 12 hours in advance that a storm will hit Marathon, it could strike anywhere from Key West to Key Largo, requiring total evacuation of the Keys. But the feasibility of complete over-the-road evacuation is nil, and if it were possible, it would take at least 35 hours. Besides, behavioral studies have shown that 25 percent of the population in a hurricane's path wouldn't leave their homes even if ordered to.

So, what to do! According to a NOAA Coastal Hazards Program booklet, if you're at home you should stock up on candles, masking tape, and radio batteries, fill your bathtub and washing machine with water, and throw your aluminum furniture in the swimming pool. You should secure your boat in a safe harbor or tie it up in the mangroves. You should keep your ear pasted to NOAA weather radio. If you go to a Red Cross Shelter, you should bring food and bedding. You should not bring intoxicating beverages, pets, or firearms. You should probably not bring John D. MacDonald's *Condominium* for reading material, either.

Some people feel that the Florida coastline is a disaster waiting to happen, and project 20-foot tidal waves sweeping over the Keys. Others trust in the offshore reefs to break up any mass of water before it reaches land or don't even trouble themselves to think of hurricanes at all, believing them to be obsolete, rather like kerosene lamps. Whatever, almost everyone would agree that trying to determine which direction the wind is going to blow is like trying to chart the course of a leaf on a giant river.

of pliers in these bars, and in fact in all the bars scattered along the intensive fishing grounds of Islamorada and Marathon—machismo being measured by the size of the pliers sticking in belts or jeans pockets, as pliers are used for wrenching the hooks from the mouths of huge fish.) The resort sponsors offshore power boat races and windsurfing and fishing tournaments throughout the year. For these special events and all holidays, minimum stay requirements apply. Languid, it's not. December 15 to May 1, economy rooms $105, ocean view $130, suites $195–$325. Rates drop $20 to $25 between May 2 and Labor Day and drop slightly again between September and mid-December. All rates, however, go up between $10 and $25 each year. Telephone: 664-2321.

Within dueling distance, at MM #83.5, is the **Whale Harbor Restaurant and Marina** with the adjacent **Chesapeake Motel,** marked by a shell-plastered toy lighthouse. Hurricane

Donna struck here vigorously in 1960—the area seems a popular landfall for storms. There's a good upstairs tiki-bar here over the charter boat docks, and an extensive seafood buffet served daily from 4:30 P.M. for $12.95. Sunday the buffet begins at noon and costs $9.95. The Chesapeake is quieter and less wildly sociable than Holiday Isle, yet close enough to make one's indulgences and then retreat to roomy villas and nicely landscaped grounds. Again, there's a three-day minimum stay during holidays and special events. Motel rooms are $104 a night; a nice room on the water is $145. Villas range from $110 to $210 in season, $10 or so less at other times. Telephone: 664-4662 or 664-4663. Reservations are important during the season.

UPPER MATECUMBE KEY

September 2, 1935. On this Labor Day morning, half a century ago, large red and black hurricane warning flags were flying along the Keys. The foremen for the hundreds of workmen who were building a road here telephoned the Overseas Railroad headquarters in Miami and begged for an evacuation train to be sent down for them. A rescue train left Miami late in the afternoon, stopping at Homestead, the last mainland stop, to shift the locomotive from the front to the rear of the train, the engineer planning on pulling out of the storm rather than backing out of it. When the train stopped at Snake Creek at 7 P.M. to take on evacuees, a cable, torn loose by winds that were blowing over 150 mph, snagged on the engine cab, and more than an hour's effort was required to free it. By the time the train had backed down to Islamorada, winds had reached 200 mph. Hundreds of people were on board when a tidal wave engulfed the train and tore it from the tracks.

After the hurricane, one could stand in the middle of the key and see from ocean to bay and from one end of the island to the other. Nothing remained standing except the angel that marked a grave in a tiny cemetery on the beach in Islamorada. The angel can be seen today on the grounds of the Cheeca Lodge

Hurricane!

(of all places) between the Cheeca's Ocean Front Villas south
and the golf driving range and heliport pad—a bit of *memento
mori* in the midst of the good and fancy life.

> *This lovely bud so young so fair*
> *Called home to early doom*
> *Just called to show how sweet a flower*
> *In Paradise would bloom*

The angel is missing a hand and part of one wing, but she is
still there, watching over the grave of Etta Dolores Pinder, who
was born in 1899 and died in 1914, the only child of one of the
early homesteading families of the Upper Keys.

Just beyond Cheeca, around MM #81.5, is a hurricane monument that marks the mass grave of many of those killed in the
storm. The monument is constructed of locally quarried limestone and bears a striking art nouveau impression of palm trees
bending in the wind.

ISLAMORADA

Most of the restaurants, resorts, and shops on Plantation, Windley, and Matecumbe Keys running from MM #88 down to MM #73 and Channel #2 use **Islamorada** as their address, for that is the community and post office which serves these keys.

For many people, this area is easily comprehended by its attractions **(Theater of the Sea)**, the concentration of good restaurants **(Ziggie's, Marker 88, The Green Turtle)**, and its accommodations (which range from the calm and dignified **Cheeca Lodge** to the playful, disorderly **Holiday Isle**) and is their ultimate destination in the Keys. Here, within a few miles, are the big marinas at **Holiday Isle, Whale Harbor**, and **Bud 'n' Mary's**, these three providing the largest concentration of charter fishing boats in the entire island chain, a fact which allows Islamorada to claim for itself the title "Sport Fishing Capital of the World."

People come here to fish, eat, drink, fish, drink, and fish. From December to May there is the annual South Florida Fishing Tournament. In February, there's the Ladies Sailfish Tournament. There's the Bonefish Fly Tournament in April, and the Ladies Invitational Tarpon Tournament. In the summer there are Shark Tournaments which allow, even urge, the use of shotguns, and baseball bats. There are Great Grunt Rodeos and Dolphin Scrambles. In the fall there are more bonefish tournaments and billfish tournaments and sailfish tournaments. Tournaments are usually sponsored by breweries and resorts, and there are cash prizes and trophies and patches and plaques and citations. Prizes are given for the biggest fish, the smallest fish, the weirdest fish, and the most fish.

For tournament and charter information, contact:

Whale Harbor Marina, MM #84 (664-4511)
Holiday Isle, MM # 84.5 (664-2321)
Bud 'n' Mary's, MM #80 (664-2461)
Abel's Tackle Box, MM #84 (664-2521)

For a brochure containing the names, addresses, telephone numbers and specialties of members of the **Florida Keys Fishing Guides Association,** write Box 936, Islamorada, FL 33036.

WHERE TO EAT

Ziggie's Conch at MM #83 is small, crowded, and plain, with some of the best and most innovative cooking around. The list of specials takes the owner—or, when exhaustion sets in, the waitress—a good ten minutes to recite. It is all a production of the highest, most eccentric order. Open 5 P.M. Closed Thursdays. Reservations are almost always necessary. Telephone: 664-4590 or 664-3391.

Lorelei (MM #82 at the Islamorada Yacht Basin). The tiki-bar outside is friendly, the gathering place at the end of the day for back country guides. The restaurant has lots of glass and lovely bay views, although you may be seated by a large mermaid with a tail of glued-on tarpon scales which occupies one wall. Lorelei has many steak, lobster, and rich seafood casserole offerings. Their snapper stuffed with crabmeat is good, but expensive even by Key West standards. Open 11 A.M. to 3 P.M. for lunch, 5:30 to 9:30 P.M. for dinner; Saturdays 11 A.M. to 9:30 P.M. Telephone: 664-4656.

Green Turtle Inn (MM #81). Popular, crowded, cluttered, the Green Turtle has been around since 1947, when patrons really tucked in the turtle steaks. In 1970, just before the government passed laws prohibiting the killing and selling of green turtle, the owner of Sid and Roxie's Cannery across the street was processing over a thousand pounds of turtle meat weekly. The turtle steaks and chowders you now get at the inn are from freshwater turtles raised in farms around Lake Okeechobee. Several old cottages have been joined to make up the restaurant, which is cozy and hearty, the walls covered with photographs of jolly, beaming patrons and framed newspaper headlines of puzzling relevance—*Another Jap Warlord Kills*

Self. Open from noon until 10 P.M. Closed Monday. Telephone: 664-4918.

Papa Joe's (MM #80). A nice old place at the end of Upper Matecumbe, overlooking Tea Table Channel. Italian dishes, fresh and inexpensive fish dinners. A tiki-bar is cantilevered over a bait shop in back. Open from 11 A.M. until 10 P.M. Closed Tuesdays. Telephone: 664-8109.

Manny and Isa's (MM #81.6). Manny has an orchard behind his tiny restaurant, and each summer he squeezes 9,000 Key limes for you. The pies are classic. $1.75 a slice, $10 for the whole statement. Open 11 A.M. to 9 P.M. Closed Tuesdays. Telephone: 664-5019. Don't expect ambience here, just good . . . pie.

WHERE TO STAY

The Cheeca Lodge (MM #82). Cheeca sounds like something meaningfully Indian, but in fact it's just a preppy nickname for Cynthia Twitchell, who with her husband ran the lodge as a private club in the fifties. Known for years as one of the Keys' few resorts, it had an understated, clubby atmosphere, a forgiving nine-hole golf course, a preppy white-sand beach, and a seemingly endless 525-foot fishing pier, down which all guests were obliged to trek. Everything went on in a low-key way until new owners decided they wanted to spend $40 million. Everyone thought that was a lot, so an expensive study was commissioned to see if it was possible to spend that much. The study determined that it was possible. Cheeca now has 203 rooms, more than double the original number, two more tennis courts, another pool, a date palm–lined courtyard, parrots burbling in cages, and a series of meandering lagoons. Cheeca's elegance isn't so low-key any more, but it is still a romantic and friendly resort. Rooms run $200–$300 in season, suites $260–$325. There are extensive activity programs for children. Telephone: 664-4651.

. . .

The Islander (MM #83) occupies almost the same amount of land as The Cheeca Lodge—25 acres—and has a nice beach and two pools (one salt water, one fresh), but lacks Cheeca's cachet. It is sparsely landscaped, with a large number of units arranged so that they look out upon the backs or beginnings of other large numbers of units, and rooms are decorated in garish colors. Ample spaces, however, and modest rates. In season (December 15 to mid-April), rooms $60; with kitchenettes, $73. A lanai of one's own is another $10. From mid-April to mid-December, rates drop $10 to $15. Telephone: 664-2031.

Breezy Palms (MM #80). Much smaller and very pleasant. Nicely furnished rooms and efficiencies on the ocean by the towering Ocean 80 resort. No beach really, but small, busy piers, assorted sunning spots, and a pool. Winter rates $75. An apartment by the pool $100. Telephone: 664-2361.

LIGNUMVITAE AND INDIAN KEYS

Between Upper and Lower Matecumbe Keys lie two unconnected, uninhabited keys of considerable historic and natural interest—Lignumvitae and Indian.

Lignumvitae, a 345-acre island, along with Shell Key and Indian Key, was purchased by the Nature Conservancy and the state in 1970. Arrangements can be made at **Long Key Recreation Area** for a two-hour interpretive tour, where small groups are escorted through the island by a ranger.

Of all the Keys, Lignumvitae is the highest—sixteen feet above sea level—and is a true island. Although the giant mahoganies were removed in the nineteenth century, and although some building and introduction of exotic plants and animals took place in the 1920's, Lignumvitae is considered to be virgin hammock, the last untouched bit of tropical forest in Florida. Botanists say that to enter Lignumvitae is to enter the primeval past. Certainly, it is to see a portion of the wonder that Florida once was.

The history of the Keys is a harsh one of dynamiting, burning, collecting, and developing. Lignumvitae has miraculously escaped all that. Its last owner, a Miami dentist, wanted to build a bridge from Lower Matecumbe Key and develop a resort there. He liked golf, so there would have been a golf course. Restaurants. The works. Amazingly, this didn't happen. Lignumvitae was saved. Perhaps it's blessed. It has never been burned like the other keys; fire has never destroyed the organic humus that takes centuries to form over the coral rock. Farmers never cleared and seared the land to get a year or two of good fruit production. Snail collectors never discovered it and burned the hammock when they left, as was their habit. (All of Florida's tropical hammocks were home to varieties of tree snails, which with their varied markings were astonishingly popular with collectors throughout the world. The snails of each area had evolved distinct color patterns on their shells. It was common for a collector to go to a hammock, collect a few snails, then set the land on fire to increase the rarity and value of the variety he had collected. The snail peculiar to Lignumvitae has a shell neatly circled with fine bands of red and green on a base of cream.)

Lignum vitae is a tree noted for the extreme density of its wood. Because of the rich resins which keep it from drying out, it has been used in boat outfitting, outlasting even steel and bronze. *Lignum vitae* was first described in *Ortus Sanitatis,* one of the major botanical works of the fifteenth century, as a tree in the Garden of Eden. Whoever consumed it was said to be strengthened with perpetual health, clothed in immortality, and protected from anxiety, weakness, and infirmity. It was described as being not only nonflammable, but purified by fire, and it was the wood from which the Holy Grail was created. In the Bahamas today, lignum vitae is called holywood or broke-iron tree and is used as a cure for impotence.

The Matheson family, which owned Lignumvitae from 1919 to 1953, built the large limestone house visible from the dock, as well as the windmill and cistern. They decorated the lawn with six cannons from the wrecked HMS *Winchester,* which ran aground on Carysfort Reef in 1695 and was discovered in 1939. They built an airstrip, brought in a bulldozer to maintain a trail, and imported burros, Galapagos tortoises, Angora goats, round-eared brown rabbits, Indian geese, ducks, and peafowl. They also made extensive plantings of exotics with the assistance of their friend, the famous botanist David Fairchild.

The strange species are gone, along with the other disturbances. The house remains, the only interruption in the mangrove shoreline, facing east away from the sea, untouched by the 1935 hurricane that cut such a narrow and ferocious swath between Tavernier and Marathon. Around the house are huge mastics and banyans and sapodilla trees, and beyond is the forest of the hammock. There are 133 varieties of trees here, including the thorny plants of the low, hot woods on the western shore—prickly ash, cockspur, hog plum, and cat's claw. There is also an enigmatic 3,000-foot coral rock wall built no one knows when, or why, as well as a Caloosa burial ground.

For years before the state purchased the key, the caretakers of the property were the remarkable Russel and Charlotte Niedhauk. *Charlotte's Story,* a 1930's diary of the Niedhauks' caretaking of Elliott Key, north of Key Largo, is available in local bookstores and is a charming and guileless account of risk, ingenuity, and adventure in a primitive Florida.

Tours of Lignumvitae are conducted daily except Tuesday and Wednesday. A ferry operated by the park service leaves Indian Key fill at MM #79 at 8:30 A.M., returning at noon, and at 1:30 P.M., returning at 5. The price is $6 for adults, children 6–12 $3. Call the Long Key State Recreation Area (664-4815) for reservations. Boat rentals are available at **Robbie's** (MM #77.5) or **Bud 'n' Mary's Marina** (MM #80). Small motorboats cost $30 for half a day. If you bring your own boat, tours cost 50¢ and are conducted at 10:30 A.M., 1:00 P.M., and 2:30.

A nice time to visit Lignumvitae is during the first two weeks in April, when the trees are in bloom.

The Spanish named **Indian Key** *Matanzas,* which means slaughter, purportedly because four hundred shipwrecked Frenchmen were killed by the Caloosa Indians here. The slaughter seems more legend than fact and may just be another example of the Spaniard's gloomy penchant for bloody place names. Once again, however, the name proved historically fateful.

In the 1830's, the tiny 11-acre island was a flourishing town, the personal kingdom of a wrecker named Jacob Housman, who established a salvaging station here so that he would not have to obey the rules and pay the fees set by Key West courts. Indian Key had a post office, three streets, twenty houses, wharves, warehouses, and a resort hotel called The Tropical. There was even a bowling alley in this best of all possible worlds, the bowling balls probably made of lignum vitae wood.

Audubon anchored offshore on the revenue cutter *Marion* for a week in the spring of 1832 and discovered birds there which were entirely new to him, including the roseate tern, the double-breasted cormorant, and the reddish egret. He extensively used the services of one of Housman's pilots, a man named Egan. Egan took him along the channels and through the maze of mangrove unerringly to the objects of his desire. "Not a Cormorant or Pelican, a Flamingo, an Ibis, or Heron, had ever in his days formed its nest without his having marked the spot," Audubon wrote. While George Lehman, his background artist, drew the key itself, Audubon sketched the birds.

Audubon was not a precociously gifted draftsman. Even after he had perfected his method, in which freshly killed specimens were run through with wires and arranged in lifelike positions, he still had to keep shooting the same species over and over, so that he could sketch them in different positions. In *The Birds of America,* he wrote of the brown pelican, "This superb male whose portrait is before you . . . was selected from a great number . . ." In his writings he also shares with us a disappointment he suffered:

Lo, I came in sight of several pelicans, perched on the branches of the mangrove trees, seated in comfortable harmony, as near each other as the strength of the boughs would allow. I ordered to back water gently. I waded to the shore under cover of the rushes along it, saw the pelicans fast asleep, examined their countenances and deportment well and leisurely, and after all, levelled, fired my piece and dropped two of the finest specimens I ever saw. I really believe I would have shot one hundred of these reverend sirs, had not a mistake taken place in the reloading of my gun. A mistake, however, did take place, and to my utmost disappointment, I saw each pelican, young and old, leave his perch and take to wing.

Audubon loved the singular plants, the gorgeous flowers, and the "salubrious" air of Indian Key. He gives an account of a raucous party the islanders threw, complete with fiddles and diluted claret for the ladies.

Jacob Housman was a wealthy man and a law unto himself, but he still had to worry about the Indians. He arranged to have the Navy's Florida Squadron, a fleet of seven ships based on nearby Tea Table Key, to protect his holdings, but the squadron, known for spending more money on "medicines," primarily rum, than all the other units of the Navy combined, were to be of little use to the townspeople of Indian Key.

By 1840, Housman's town had fifty-five inhabitants, including a physician-botanist, Dr. Henry Perrine, and his family. Perrine established a nursery on the northeast end of Lower Mate-cumbe and did plant research on Indian Key. All in all, he introduced more than two hundred plants to tropical Florida. He had many interests, including silkworms and stingless bees, but his true obsession was *agave*—a plant cultivated for its sturdy sisal, a durable fiber, and also, less prosaically, as a source of hashish. Dr. Perrine also treated the sick, including Seminole Indians. Housman, on the other hand, ever enterprising, was trying to negotiate a contract with the government which would permit him to hunt and kill the Indians at two hundred dollars a head.

On August 7, 1840, with the Naval squadron away, the Seminoles, no doubt having heard of Housman's income-producing scheme, attacked the island, burning every building except the home of the postman, Charles Howe. Howe was a Mason, and his Masonic apron with its all-seeing eye and other mystic symbols was found spread upon the table. The eye may have given the Indians pause, but they went on anyway to kill sixteen people, one of whom was Dr. Perrine. Those who escaped the massacre hid in turtle kraals near the houses or in the cisterns beneath them, although gruesome popular history claims that some who sought safety there were boiled alive. Housman and his family survived, but he never reestablished his empire. He returned to Key West and worked on a former rival's salvage vessel, dying in a ship accident six months later. His body was buried on Indian Key, and there is a historical plaque identifying the site. Someone has stolen the skeleton, to say nothing of the tombstone, although fragments of the stone were recovered and taken to Lignumvitae for safekeeping. Other markers identify the house site, the hotel cistern, and so on.

A new community was formed on the island in the 1870's, when the key became a site for building schooners and sloops. It was also on this tiny key that the construction workers for the Alligator Reef lighthouse, built in 1873, lived, and where the iron pile structure, built and dismantled in a northern foundry, then shipped to Florida, was stored before being transported to the reef.

Indian Key is certainly not the unblemished paradise that Lignumvitae is. It seems ironic that it ended up as a historic site rather than a botanical one, when one considers Dr. Perrine's extensive introduction of exotic plants here. Damage was done in the 1930's and 1940's, when treasure hunters dynamited it to search for valuables they thought had been buried there. Tourists were even brought over at $5 a day and furnished with shovels so that they could dig. Today the landscape seems almost Mexican, with its sisal plants and prickly pear, descendants of the doctor's plants, but there is also a restful wild tamarind grove, the delicate, feathery foliage of the leaves softening the glare of the sun.

As with Lignumvitae, you must acquire or hire a boat to get over to Indian Key, but then you're on your own. You may explore from 8 A.M. to sunset.

A mile south of Indian Key is the *San Pedro* wreck, a ship that went down in 1733. It lies in eighteen feet of water and consists mostly of ballast stones although it has recently been enhanced by replicas of timbers, anchors and cannons.

LOWER MATECUMBE KEY

Judging from the amount of tangled monofilament around the power lines, some of the worst fishermen in the Keys frequent the catwalks over Indian Key and Lignumvitae Channels. Fishing here and along the bridges that span Channel #2 and Channel #5 between Lower Matecumbe and Long Key is very good, offering catches of snapper, grouper, and, in the spring and early summer, snook. In the winter, after a cold snap and the ensuing nor'wester, shrimp leave the cooler waters of the bay and can be netted from the bridges at night.

Alligator Lighthouse, the most beautiful on the reef, white and stately, is visible off the Matecumbe Keys. Over five hundred species of fish have been found on the reef the light marks. **Buddy's Dive Shop** at MM #79.5 makes trips to Alligator. Buddy's also takes experienced divers to an artificial deep-water reef, water created when a 65-foot trawler loaded with marijuana was deliberately scuttled. The "Cannabis Cruiser" sits upright on the bottom, still loaded with its ruined bales, and makes an interesting wreck dive.

Lower Matecumbe has a number of troubled time-shares, most of which would be thrilled if you rented a room for the night. Developers went into a greed frenzy in the early 1980's, when they came up with the idea of selling both space *and* time. The new structures are circular, erected on pedestals with an ambience of early space station. The old ones are old motels. **Caloosa Cove** at MM #73.8 covers all bases—it's a time-share condominium resort with a full marina, charters, room and boat rentals, tennis courts, and a bar which is inexplicably called The Safari and filled with African "artifacts." The establishment leaps into the void of hyperbole with its billboard slogan, Paradise At Your Command. Telephone: 664-8811.

A far lovelier sight is the watery stretch between Lower Matecumbe and tiny Craig Key at MM #72. This area has some very pretty picnicking spots and some of the most beautiful views to be had from the highway in the Keys. You will see many birds feeding here—little blue herons, which when young

PELICANS: COLORS AND A LEGEND

Brown pelicans can be seen everywhere, all year long, in the Keys. The white pelican breeds in the summer near the mountain lakes of Montana and Utah and is only a winter visitor to the islands in Florida Bay. (Unlike brown pelicans, white pelicans don't dive for fish. Instead, their fishing is a communal effort, with ten to fifteen birds forming a semicircle and herding the fish to shore, where they can then scoop them up with their bills.) Many of the brown pelicans you see begging for fish off docks and bridges are young birds. A pelican in his first year has a brown neck and wings and a very white belly. In the second year, his body is more grey than brown. By the third year, his belly is quite dark. In the summertime, the adult pelican's head is white with a dark brown stripe on the back of the neck. In early fall, the brown stripe molts to white, and yellow courting plumage appears.

The pelican is a bird of myth as well as droll actuality. His image is common on ecclesiastical heraldry and was often engraved on chalices. Many medieval bestiaries include a story in which the mother pelican caresses her offspring with such devotion that she kills them. When the father returns to the nest, he so despairs over the death of his young that he tears at his breast with his bill, and the blood from his wounds revives the dead birds. Dante, in the *Paradiso* (Canto XXV, line 113) calls Jesus Christ *nostro Pellicano*—mankind's pelican.

Pelicans feeding

are pure white; white ibis, with their bright orange, curved bills; white egrets, with their black legs and beautiful long breeding feathers, which are called "aigrettes"; and great white herons, the largest of the herons—over four feet in height, with a wingspan of seven feet—readily distinguished from the egrets by their much greater size and their light-colored legs. The great white is rare except in the Keys, where it is frequently seen. This very limited range, however, indicates few total numbers, and their small population is devastated by storms and hurricanes.

Craig Key once had several fishing shacks built out over the water and even a post office, established in the late 1920's because President Herbert Hoover had once anchored his yacht close by and it was thought that he might want to mail something. Storms blew everything away, but in the 1960's, a concrete-block mansion was built on the bay side by the Twitchell family, the original owners of the Cheeca Lodge. Concealed behind a stone wall and a grove of pine, the manse has five bedrooms, two full kitchens, eight baths, and a mirrored bar modeled after Cheeca's. Mrs. Twitchell was an A&P heiress who was known for her sense of humor. Mrs. Twitchell's sense of humor is responsible, it is said, for the air jets in the front door jamb that would blast air up ladies' dresses.

The road curves sharply after Craig, crossing Channel #5 and the Intracoastal Waterway, which links the ocean and the bay at MM #70. The next key, **Fiesta**, is a fill, as is Craig. Fiesta was originally called Jewfish Key, then Greyhound when the Greyhound Corporation built a post house there for its bus passengers, shortly after the highway was pushed down to Grassy Key in 1937. Now it's the site of a KOA (Kampgrounds of America) campground.

Layton is a city, incorporated in 1963, but certainly a modest one. Once, two locked black and white police cars (actually, one of them was only painted to *look* like a police car) were parked on either side of the highway near MM #68 and people thought they were somewhere and slowed down, but these were recently hauled away, one of Layton's biggest events in years. Nevertheless, the city has what every city should have—an Italian res-

taurant, sailboats, and sharks. Rather, it used to have sharks at
the Sea World Shark Institute, once open to the public, but
recently closed to the public so that the facility, now known as
Sea World Marine Science and Conservation Center, could get
research grants while it continued to collect and provide Sea
World's Orlando ocean aquarium with Keys' fish, turtles, and
dolphins. Who knows what takes place back here in the specimen holding tanks and on the wet tables? More blood chemistry
and blood gas level tests one would imagine. More sea urchin
studies. Passing through these gates is more difficult than a rich
man's getting into heaven. The secretary who guards the place
will tell you she believes there's a cute manatee back there, a
manatee you are most certainly not allowed to see.

Dive shops in this area visit **Tennessee Reef**, one of the least-
dived reefs in the Keys because of its rather remote location.
Much of the collecting undertaken by the Sea World facility
takes place here. There's a lot of variety on Tennessee. Tall
walls and drop-offs support large corals and fish. There are lots
of shells and conchs hopping across the sandy patches. And
around the 1930's wreck of the USS *Tennessee* herself, which
lies in twenty feet of water, many brilliant tropicals dart singly
or in schools.

Lime Tree Bay Resort at MM #68.5 (664-4740) has the eccentric quality of old-time Keys accommodations. A zoo, a paperback library, a shuffleboard court, and a postage-stamp beach on
a grassy bay. Rooms and efficiencies run $75 to $80 in winter.
Each room is decorated in a different motif. You might be given
the bullfight room, for example—toreadors everywhere!—or the
mounted fish room. There's a simple restaurant that serves
breakfast and burgers, and someone may be banging away on
a musical instrument in the beer and wine bar at night. Close
by is **Lewis Rents Boats** (664-8060), where you can rent well-
maintained daysailers, Hobie Cats, Windsurfers, or canoes.

LONG KEY

Long Key State Recreation Area at MM #67.5 is one of the three state parks on the Keys. The swimming here is poor—you see people far, far from shore and they're still only up to their knees—but the rangers offer a variety of interesting programs, including a guided overnight canoe trip on the second Saturday of each month. You must provide your own tent, sleeping bag, and food, as well as bring your own canoe. (A minimum of three canoes and six people is required for a trip.) The expedition leaves at noon and you paddle to the extreme eastern end of the park. The snorkeling is fun—you'll see lobsters and octopuses —and the beachcombing can be interesting if you're able to block out the astonishing amount of discarded plastic. Always there seem to be dolls' heads on remote beaches, and Long Key is no exception. Here, too, scattered amidst the plastic, can be found the rubbery, flattened egg cases of turtles.

There's quite a bit of bird activity on the flats. The best show is put on by the reddish egret as he attempts to acquire lunch.

Reddish egret

This is a gangly, charming bird—a two-toned heron, the head and neck reddish brown, the body slate grey. He also goes through a white phase, when you could easily confuse him with a variety of herons and egrets, including even the immature little blue. But what distinguishes the reddish egret is his peculiar eating habits. Other wading birds have dignity. They stalk. They stand motionless. They are patient and aloof. The red selects the minnow he wants and chases it until he gets it, in a frenzy of running, lurching, splashing, and zigzagging, flapping his wings and clacking his bill until the minnow, exhausted, surrenders in a blur of foam.

The seaweed that coats the beach here is a kitchen cupboard for the birds, jumping and crawling with tasty amphipods. But for you, the adventurous camper, the seaweed after the sun goes down becomes a jumping, crawling hell. You cannot imagine how many bugs creep, crawl, and fly on a Keys' beach after dark. So don't just undertake this overnighter lightly, with a beach towel and a can of Coke. Bring lots of insect repellent and cover-ups, so that you can enjoy the enormous sky and the glittering ocean phosphorescent with life.

Reservations for the canoe trip should be made by calling Long Key State Recreation Area at 664-4815.

Campgrounds in the Keys are very popular places, in both the winter and summer months. The state parks have an ingenious system of reserving 50 percent of the campsites, leaving the other half available on a first-come, first-served basis. You have

---

BUGS

Mosquitoes are big here. They have been called the most reliable defenders of wilderness in the state. Sandflys are big. They're called "flying teeth." Palmetto bugs, the southern cockroach, are very big, and shiny, too. You'll see them in the best of places as well as in the wilds. At a pool party at an elegant home, a guest was heard to exclaim, "Oh, look at the little turtles!" as a family of these creepies lumbered across the patio. If you crush them, there is a terrible smell of almonds.

to make reservations early, though not *too* early—not more than sixty days in advance, and by telephone, not mail. Checkout time is 2 P.M., and there's a two-week maximum stay, with a fee of $21 a night.

One nature trail in the park winds around a lagoon and is called the Golden Orb, after the spectacular spiders that weave their webs there. The webs are heavy and huge, the female spider a royal red and gold. The males are tiny little things in the corners, or not around at all. They spend so much time searching for females, courting them, and mating with them that they neglect eating, and often drop dead from exhaustion.

By 1906, construction of the railroad had come as far as Long Key. Henry Flagler built screened cottages for his workers while they labored on the Long Key Viaduct. Other workers were housed on large covered barges called quarterboats. When a hurricane struck Long Key in the fall of 1906, one of these quarterboats broke its moorings and was swept out to sea, drowning more than a hundred men.

After the viaduct was completed, Flagler turned the construction camp into a fishing camp, The Long Key Fishing Club, for the wealthy who arrived by yacht and rail. He supplemented the bungalows with a luxury lodge on a white sand beach on the ocean side, and even built a narrow-gauge railroad that ran through a tunnel beneath the tracks for the convenience of his guests.

Zane Grey, the well-known writer of westerns, was one of the camp's most famous guests. He first visited here in 1913 and organized the club's fishing contests, established "to develop the best and finest traits of sport, to restrict the killing of fish, to educate the inexperienced angler by helping him and to promote good fellowship." Grey brought sailfishing into vogue. At that time, sailfish were considered pests and were called spikefish or "boohoo" because of the disappointment they often caused by slicing through lines intended for more popular quarry, such as kingfish. Grey introduced light tackle methods, and taking sailfish became an art. He found the fish the gamest and most beautiful fish to catch on light tackle, with its pirouetting leaps and its great sail spread. Grey visited the fishing camp frequently over the years, in January and February, adhering to a schedule of rising early, writing for one hour, fishing for ten, then writing for another hour or two in the evenings. He worked on books such as *Code of the West* and *The Light of Western Stars* here as well as doing a great deal of exploring and photography. "So much beauty and wildlife," he wrote, "so wild it was tame." Grey was also known for releasing trophy-sized catches and not mourning the ones that got away. He wrote of a lost tarpon, "Into my memory had been burned indelibly a picture of a sunlit, cloud-mirroring, green and gold bordered cove, above the center of which shone a glorious fish-creature in the air."

The Long Key Fishing Club was completely destroyed in the 1935 hurricane. Just south of the boat rentals in Layton, there is a historical tablet commemorating the site if not accurately marking it.

THE
MIDDLE KEYS
Long Key Viaduct
to Bahia Honda

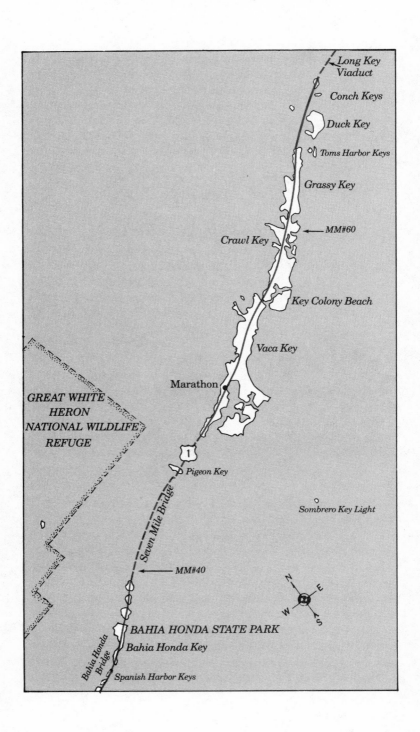

FORTY-TWO bridges link the Keys, but it is in the Middle Keys where the three longest and most impressive ones stand. Beside them are their shadows, the bridges recently built. The road now traverses these shadows—the strong old bridges run emptily alongside. Everywhere there is water, water that becomes sky, the shadows of rays like clouds moving across the blue. Water loves light. The light changes. Dawn and sunset break. Thunderclouds mass. The water is black, emerald, azure, sheer, and the vault of sky becomes the vault of water. Flocks of egrets fly bone-white across that impossible interstice. The Keys are lovely litanies of colors and creatures, fishes and birds.

If one were to know the Keys only by car, this passage over the bridges of the Middle Keys is the most impressive. The trip by train must have been astonishing. John Dos Passos in a letter to Hemingway called it a "dreamlike journey." The trains crept across the bridges no faster than fifteen miles an hour and seldom exceeded forty miles an hour over the mostly deserted Keys. The dreamlike journey made possible by the railroad was created with swarms of vessels, workboats, dredges, seagoing cranes, pile drivers, quarterboats, and floating cement mixers. At one point, Flagler's general manager, Joseph Parrott, had every freight steamer on the Atlantic coast that flew the American flag under charter to bring in materials.

Before the railroad, there were few people on any of these keys. There were salt-works on Duck Key in the early 1800's, but they had been abandoned by 1837. A few Bahamian families lived along Key Vaca, but they had deserted it by 1860. In 1926, the population of Marathon was only seventeen. It was not until the 1940's that sportfishing created a reason for the town's existence. Other, now highly populated areas are of even more recent invention. In the 1950's, causeways were built to islands such as Duck Key, and even islands that weren't, such as Key Colony Beach. One best perceives the beauty of this area—its remaining wilderness—from the great bridges, even though, as in the case of the newly installed utility poles which run the distance of the Seven-Mile Bridge, modernization has reduced the awesome effect.

People remember traveling on the old bridges with fondness, even though delays were common. Accidents and breakdowns would jam up the narrow lanes. The drawspan on the Seven-Mile Bridge would stick. Small airplanes would sometimes make emergency landings. These were usually occasions for a party. People would abandon their cars, throw out a fishing line, set up the cooler and the radio, become tight friends with complete strangers, and socialize in the sunshine, beneath the merging seas and the sky.

The beautiful **Long Key Viaduct** at MM #65.5 was Flagler's favorite bridge, and the one he used in photographs advertising the railroad. One hundred eighty arches span two and one half miles of water, making it the second largest span in the Keys. Be sure to pull off the road to the left just before crossing the new Long Key Bridge built close alongside. Walk down the embankment, where in spring there will be a profusion of flowering vines and stacked crayfish traps, and look at the graceful old arches, darkly Roman against the green tropical waters and far nobler than the sensible modern piers.

Stacked crayfish traps are once again in evidence on the other side of the bridge during the closed season, April 1 to July 25. Here at MM #63 is **Conch Key**. Conch Key consists of sixteen acres, every inch of which is covered with houses and crayfish traps. The crayfish, or "bug," or Florida spiny lobster has long antennae, many legs, and no claws. All the meat is in the muscles of the tail, which is used for backward propulsion. Fishermen, lobstermen, and retirees inhabit Conch Key, along with hundreds of crayfish traps.

Crossing the bridge over Tom's Harbor Cut at MM #61, you will see on your left **Duck Key**, dominated by the striking green and pink **Hawk's Cay Resort**. The colors, according to the designer, are actually seafoam green, salmon, cabbage green, and paper bag brown. This is no place to bag your lunch, however. For luxury, this is *the* place in the Middle Keys—awash

in Jacuzzis, chefs in white hats, chaise lounges, linen tablecloths, and fresh cans of tennis balls. Hawk's Cay used to be the
Indies Inn before the Indies became ramshackle and slipped
into receivership. Fifteen million dollars' worth of renovations
later, it is now ready to receive you. It's very tasteful, very
comfortable, very elegant, with lots of French doors, wicker
furniture, and gleaming tiles, but there is the flavor of the
Board Room in some of its larger pavilions and terraces. The
clay tennis courts are called gardens here, for they are set
amidst some sea grape and palm, and there is a marina a short
distance away that offers fishing charters, and a nightclub with
a dance floor. Many are the planned activities at Hawk's Cay,
and adult guests are treated rather like shy campers who must
gently be introduced to fishing rods and tiny sailboats and even,
behind and beyond the mannered affluence of the place, Nature.
A bizarrely named "Scratch 'n' Sniff" tour will take you by
rubber raft past the canals and expensive stuccoed homes of
Duck Key and encourage you to observe starfish bumbling
across the flats or herons clinging to a bit of undisturbed mangrove. And it will bring you back to the resort in time for lunch.

In season (mid-December to mid-April), large suites are $400
a night, smaller suites range from $220 to $340. Rooms run from
$135 to $200. Through the summer and fall, suites cost between
$170 and $300 a night, rooms $85 to $145. A three-nights' deposit
is required at Christmas, New Year's, and Easter. A lavish
breakfast buffet is complimentary daily. Telephone: 743-7000.

Below elaborate Duck Key lies **Grassy Key**, where Flipper's
Sea School used to be the big attraction: Flipper, the movie star,
whose real name was Mitzi, is buried here and a 30-foot-tall
monument to a dolphin mother and baby still stands on the bay
side of the highway at MM #59. Flipper's moved to a new and
more elaborate site in Key West, invested a fortune in advertising, and promptly went out of business. The facility on Grassy
Key became the **Dolphin Research Center** and is open to the
public on a limited walking-tour basis. The inquisitive dolphins
rise to greet you as you stand on the rickety causeways between
the pools. They chatter and click and turn to be patted and
stroked and fix you with their marvelous eyes. There is modest

research and training done here, but it's so relaxing on Grassy Key that dolphins from more high-pressured attractions and institutions come here for R&R. (Recently, two dolphins were flown down for a vacation from the National Aquarium in Baltimore. Because of poor lighting and a bad tank design, the dolphins had been constantly seeing their own reflections and with no privacy from each other or themselves, they had become anxious and eventually developed ulcers.)

Dolphins are curious, playful, social, and very sexy. They're bisexual. They have complex brains which are larger than man's. They have several stomachs and no sense of smell. They have an incredibly refined capacity to form auditory images and "hear" the texture of objects around them, suggesting that they can look into each other in eerie ways and read emotional states. They once lived on land, and gradually, for unknown reasons, took to the seas. One story, and why not believe it, is that they approached man around the time of Plato and Aristotle but that philosophers and religious men rebuffed them, so they retreated into the depths of the sea to await a better time for communication and understanding. They have remarkable memories and can comprehend simple sonic sentences. They become bored easily. When they give birth, there is frequently another female close by acting as midwife, assisting the new mother in bringing the baby to the surface for his first breath of air. Dolphins breathe through their blowholes, emitting occasional whiffs of sweet-smelling air, almost like chlorophyll. (Japanese fishermen, complaining that dolphins compete with them in catching cuttlefish and yellowtail, herd them ashore and club them to death.) Dolphins have their own legend. It is said that they believe that one day a few humans will break through to a new, transhuman level of consciousness and make contact with them. There are several versions of this legend. One is that these humans, true philosophers who comprehend the whole in all its parts, will join the dolphins and never return. Another is that they will return to the world of men and be locked up as lunatics. A third has them join forces with the dolphins, stage a bloodless coup d'état and establish a peaceful and paradisiacal rule over all man and animal kind. The last version is that the philosophers and the dolphins will lead a bloody insurrection of all the beasts, smash the machines and eliminate the human race because of the grave threat they pose to the planet.

There was once a sanctuary for injured birds here—hawks, herons and pelicans harmed intentionally or unintentionally by man. Most of the injuries to pelicans are the result of fish hooks and monofilament. (Never discard old fishing line for a bird to become entangled in. Don't toss away those eternal six-pack grippers either. A pelican looks like a large bird, but it weighs only six pounds. Its bones are hollow and usually can't be set.) Unfortunately this particular sanctuary no longer exists, but if you do find an injured bird call the Florida Keys Wild Bird Rehab Center in Islamorada at 852-4486. The Dolphin Research Center offers something new more geared to the tourist—you can partake of the latest craze and swim with the dolphins here—though you don't just swim with them, you "encounter and interact" with them, but by appointment only. It costs $50 for twenty minutes. Call 289-1121 for reservations. (These programs may be canceled as it's questionable whether they comply with the intents and purposes of the Marine Mammal Act.) For the more serious devotee of the divine dolphin, there is Dolphinlab, a seven-day course of lectures, films and field trips to the reef and back country. Write to P.O. Box Dolphin, Marathon Shores, Florida 33052, or call 289-0002.

The difference between dolphins and dolphins

THE DIFFERENCE BETWEEN DOLPHINS AND DOLPHINS

Dolphins are spiny-finned gamefish of flamboyant colors, the brilliance of which fades instantly with death. They are of the genus *Coryphaena,* family *Coryphaenidae.* People catch them and eat them because they taste very good. Dolphins are also the smart and friendly mammals who nurse their young, speak in "clicks," and like to play around boats. They have little teeth and big smiles. Hemingway once remarked that he would shoot his own mother "if she flew in coveys and had a good strong flight," but most people would feel that dining on these individuals was rude, if not cannibalistic. These dolphins are small-toothed whales, genus *Delphinus,* family *Delphinidae,* and have a distinct and easily recognizable snout. The name *porpoise* can be applied only to a few species of *Phocoenidae* that lack this pronounced beak and have spade-shaped rather than conical teeth. However, most fishermen, restaurant owners, and even some scientists call mammalian dolphins porpoises to distinguish them from the gamefish dolphins. The best-known of the mammals is the bottle-nose dolphin—the one seen in "shows"—which you can refer to as a porpoise if it will make you feel more comfortable while you're chowing down the dolphin fish, which perhaps should be called what it is in other parts of the world—*dorado* or *maki-maki.* Dolphin sounds so pretty, though. Most fish have such goofy epithets—jewfish, mullet, turbo, snapper. Bonefish. Permit. Grunt.

For eating out, the **Grassy Key Dairy Bar** at MM #58.5 is *the* place to go. The name is strange, but the food is the best for miles. There are two squat cement ice-cream cones in front. A good breakfast place, it also serves lunch until 2 P.M. and seafood and beef dinners, with wine and beer, from 5 to 10 P.M. Closed Sundays and Mondays.

Rainbow Bend Fishing Club at MM #58 is a relaxing alternative to the hustle and sprawl of Marathon eight miles farther down the road. The Cheeca Lodge was the last of the great old fishing clubs. Places that go by that name today are, for the most part, time-shares that have taken over a failing motel and have failed in turn. There's a shaggy, desperate, deserted quality to these places. The people you see look as though they feel they should be enjoying a different vacation —snow-skiing, perhaps. This is not the case with the small, well-run Rainbow Bend. Most of the rooms here are efficiencies or suites and are nicely and lightly furnished in rattan. Prices run between $120–$155 and do not go down so you'd notice in the summer. Oceanfront suites and apartments are $160–$185. Prices include breakfast as well as the use of motorboats. Fish the flats off Duck Key or explore the reef at Coffins Patch, once called "Atlantis" because of the tall pillar coral that made exotic fishy cities there, before collectors and shell shops hauled off the larger specimens. (Pillar coral grows approximately one inch every forty years, so it's unlikely you will ever see what the "collectors" did.) The airy, second-story restaurant here is called the **Hideaway** and the food is so fancy that they say people come all the way down from Miami to eat it. (That is, they don't do anything else here. They eat it and go back.) Prime rib, filet medallions, seafood delmonico. Cognacs and creams, special sauces and bouquetieres. Amaretto frequently figures. There's a good wine list. **Rainbow Bend** (289-1505).

Just beyond, on Crawl Key at MM #56.5, is a road to the left that leads to **Valhalla Beach Motel**. On the road maps, a town named Ecstasy is mentioned, but Ecstasy is hard to find. You might, in fact, spend a very long time hunting around for Ecstasy. Valhalla Beach Motel, however, can be attained, and it's a nice little place with a sand beach on a tidal creek and bird-busy mangroves all around. You should make reservations (289-0616), for there are only a dozen rooms. Most of these are efficiencies that run about $65 a night. No credit cards. It's a return to a simpler, sweeter Keys back here, a sleepy exception to the wired development of so much of the area. The beautiful views seem almost illusory, a scrim before the pumped-up, pumped-out communities of Coco Plum Beach and Key Colony Beach beyond.

The next several miles are empty of all but mangroves. The water pipe that runs the length of the Keys is clearly visible here on the right. Activity begins just beyond the old Pull-and-Be-Damned Creek—the scourge of railroad workers who had to row supplies across its strong currents—a part of Vaca Cut now filled in. Here is **Adventure Island**, a feverish dream for the highly active, where there are sailboat, catamaran, sunfish, and jet-ski rentals. You can also have the thrilling rackety fun of a helicopter ride. There was ambition here once—there are twenty-seven picnic tables behind the tiki-bar—but excited intentions have given way to exhausted somnolence. A bored Rottweiler is tied beneath a broken barbecue stand by the helicopter pad, and parrotfish with toothy smiles graze in the waters off the dock.

Opposite Adventure Island is a **Howard Johnson's** with its comforts, and the **Marathon Inn**, once the Holiday Inn, soon to be the Saratoga Inn, behind which you will find many of Marathon's charter boats. To your left at the traffic light and over the causeway is the city of **Key Colony Beach**, created in 1959 by dredging up bay-bottom and adding it to low-lying offshore Shelter Key. It has houses, condos, time-shares, boatels, tennis courts, a golf course, a marina, three miles of canals, and earnestly cared-for lawns. And there it is. Key Colony Beach is notorious for sponsoring, in 1969, a sailfish tournament in which 553 sailfish were caught in four days of fish horror. The tournament continues to be held each November.

A bit farther south on Route 1 is **The Diving Site**, a dive shop behind which is **Coral Lagoon**, a motel with bright, spacious efficiencies on a canal. It's a bit Florida-suburban but it's quiet and sunny (289-0121). The rooms are $65 a night in the fall, $80 in the summer, $95 in the season. There are tennis courts and a pool, the good pool close to the bad pool, a deep, dark, unappetizing thing which seems to be connected to the dive shop. *Whatever was this for?* you might ask. . . . *Ahhh, I think they kept turtles in it or something* . . . someone will say, . . .*but there's nothing in there now.* . . . You peer at the slick sad water and can't imagine . . . turtles.

Diving in the Marathon area is generally based more on the grimmer activities of spearfishing than on reef exploration. Spearfishing is not allowed in the Upper Keys down to Long up to three miles from shore. Below Long, it is permitted at distances of more than one mile from Route 1. Because of the configuration of the Keys, speargunning often takes place close to shore, particularly under the bridges. The fish in Pennecamp are practically tame, plump with cracker crumbs and popcorn and used to having divers swim among them. There are giant grouper in the reefs off Largo that are routinely petted and hand-fed by divers. The reefs off Marathon, however, are combat zones, and the dumb fish that expects to be pampered here will end up skewered.

Divers hunt fish around **Delta Shoal** and **East and West Turtle Shoals** and search the coral heads of the **Content Keys** for lobsters and stone crabs. The shallow Content Keys are on the Gulf side, southwest of Marathon, a good snorkeling area for windy days. The areas most dived are **East Washerwoman Shoal** and the lighthouse at **Sombrero Reef**. Sombrero has nice coral formations and impressively gaudy colonies of tiny fish safe from everything but aquarium collectors, for all tiny tropicals are poisonous if eaten.

The only wreck dive in the Marathon area is the *Thunderbolt*, an old Army cable-laying vessel, intentionally sunk for divers, five miles south of Key Colony Beach.

For fishing information hang out at **Hall's Bait and Tackle**, at MM #48 (743-9474) and keep your ears tuned to advice, suggestion and rumor. Hall's can give you information about local guides and their specialties.

The bridge over Vaca Cut brings you into the Marathon area. **Captain Hook's Marina**, on your left at MM #53, is worth a stop. There are live fish pools and a complete and helpful tackle shop. Both a party boat, *Marathon Lady,* and a charter boat operate from here. The charter is a 25-foot open boat with bimini top which offers a variety of fishing trips, including night shark-fishing expeditions, and Everglades trips.

KEY VACA

The Spaniards might have originally called this key *Cayos de Bacas,* which means "berries," or *Cayos de Vaccas,* which means "cows." If it was cows, they were referring to the manatees that once thickly browsed on the vegetation offshore. Or they may have named it for one of their own conquistadors named de Vaca. The name's obscure, to be sure. Key Vaca runs from Vaca Cut at MM #53 to Knight's Key at MM #41, the terminus of Henry Flagler's railroad from 1908 to 1911, while workers constructed the Seven-Mile Bridge.

Marathon and its remoralike subdivision, Marathon Shores, have consumed Key Vaca. There is simply nothing of Key Vaca which is not Marathon.

Optimistic travelers have for years harbored the hope that there is more to Marathon than what they see, but unremarkably this is not the case. Marathon is exactly what they see and what you will see as well—a careless, unrespectable town who presents her homely face to you without a bit of a blush—although under more demanding perusal she will turn a bit defensive, for she lacks panache, although she can show you a good time. Old football stars love her.

Sunset and a Beach

Marathon offers a very nice sunset, you'll be relieved to know. In the winter, go to the tiki-bar at **Bacchus**, which gives good food as well as view. It's down 11th Street just before the Seven-Mile Bridge. Sitting or strolling on the old bridge is the thing to do at dusk too. **The Sunset Cafe** at **Buccaneer** (pg. 72) also does rampant sunset. They even shoot off a cannon.

The beach is **Sombrero Beach**, down Sombrero Road at MM #50. The swimming is good, for the water is deep, the beach is immaculate, and the carefully mowed grass of the adjacent park offers not one single sandspur. The park, which is on Hawk Channel and the Atlantic, also has a little playground and a softball diamond with a burrowing owl who stubbornly makes his home behind second base. The island off the southwest boundary of the park is Boot Key, joined by a costly bridge to the highway in 1959. The bridge, complete with drawspan and bridge tender, is maintained by the county, and in the finest tradition of mystery bridges leads absolutely nowhere, a developer's scam having failed to produce anything on the key except access to it. There is a radio tower, and a road that wanders nervously about until it vanishes.

Crane Point Hammock

In the middle of Marathon, opposite the Gulfside Shopping Center, the typical paved wasteland that K Mart and McDonald's like to discreate from nature and call home, lies the lovely Crane Point Hammock, recently acquired by the Florida Keys Land and Sea Trust. This is a true tropical forest, a magnificent 64-acre hardwood and thatch palm hammock on the Gulf. It's a different world back here—a glimpse of the real Florida. But, too, there's a rather retro and over-designed museum, **The Museum of the Florida Keys**. There are dioramas with stuffed birds, and one room depicts the reef as it might appear inside a very peculiar person's head—stuffed fish suspended from the ceiling and a clicking, whispering, gurgling soundtrack. The trail through the hammock, as it is now designed, is only a quarter of a mile loop. There is a brochure that informs you about the trees. Try to avoid the woman behind you reading from it. " '. . . Stop five. If you are lucky and quiet you might encounter a raccoon or rosy rat snake. . . .' Ichhhh, let's make noise." The museum is open 9–5, 12 to 5 on Sundays and costs $3.50.

MARATHON

Marathon is a strip, heavily developed. Residents do live here very happily, it is assumed, off the highway, in subdivisions and along long canals that accommodate their boats, but to the traveler, inching along the congested road, this community (for Marathon is not a town and has no form of local government, being more or less run by the Chamber of Commerce) appears a soiled servicing station for those enjoying the abstraction of "The Heart of the Keys." It's prettiest at night, when the neon lights, appearing after the blackness of Crawl Key, suggest a jackpot possibility.

Marathon's history is that of the railroad that virtually created it. It began as a base camp for thousands of railroad workers, the most reliable of them being men from the Caymans and from Spain. The rest were derelicts from Philadelphia and New York, shanghaied by railroad recruiters. After the 1906 hurricane, Flagler housed the men in wooden barracks on land rather than on quarterboats. The camp on Key Vaca consisted of not only tents and barracks, but cottages, a hospital, a power plant, and repair shops for the locomotives. Railroad workers named their new settlement Marathon—legend has it—after their own endurance, and built gyms and basketball courts for themselves.

Eighty-six miles of the Overseas Railroad had been completed by 1906, and miles of open water remained. A long trestle and dock were built on the southernmost end of Key Vaca at **Knight's Key** so that steamships could meet the train. Nothing today remains of this port, where ships from Cuba unloaded pineapples, sugar, and oranges, and vacationers set off on the six-hour trip to Havana. Just before the bridge today, a railroad car painted in Flagler's favorite colors, yellow and brown, is on display. It is unlikely that this particular car ever made the journey, if you're a stickler for things like that. (Flagler's luxurious private car Rambler, which he rode in elderly triumph into Key West, was discovered in the 1950's sitting in a field in Virginia, where it was being used by a tenant farmer. It is now at the Flagler Museum in Palm Beach.)

Flagler took soundings for a deep-water harbor at the tip of Key Vaca, and Key West feared that the railroad would go no farther, that Knight's Key would become the port of entry and Key West would remain remote and unlinked. But work began on "the great one"—the Seven-Mile Bridge—and was interrupted only by a 1909 hurricane that washed out forty miles of embankment and track in the Upper Keys, convincing the engineers that more small bridges were needed, instead of filled embankments that dammed up hurricane tides. Eighteen miles of bridges replaced the originally planned six to provide a freer flow of water.

When the Seven-Mile Bridge was completed in 1911, the workers moved on. No more boats filled with girls and liquor (followed by other boats filled with preachers) plied the waters between Key West and Marathon. The population plummeted. The town became known to train passengers as a place where they were often sold colored water through the windows instead of whiskey.

Marathon remained a sprawling wide-open outpost throughout the 1940's, when it was large enough to contain thirteen bars and restaurants but still no churches or schools. During World War II, an airstrip was installed as a training base for B-17's, or "Flying Fortresses." The 8,000-foot airstrip runs along the highway through Marathon Shores and is today home to a variety of private planes and charters. There are also regularly scheduled flights to Miami several times a day.

During the 1950's, a Detroit developer, Phil Sandowski, whose later gift to the planet was the City of Key Colony Beach, created the "instant" canals of Marathon and brought subdivisions to Key Vaca. The streets run from 126th Street down to 11th Street at MM #47.5, where the fishing and crayfish boat docks are.

Marathon has Cuban food at **Castillito** (MM #48); a breakfast hangout where an early-bird beer and big, bad biscuits are a favored combination (**Vernon's Iron Skillet** at MM #48); a big dance floor that rocks until 4 A.M. (**The Side Door Lounge** at MM #50); several liquor stores that are open all night long; and a hospital with a twenty-four-hour emergency room (**The Fisherman's Hospital**, close to MM #49). It *used* to have Fanny's, a strip joint whose sign read Whatsa Matter, You Scared? Marathon is known for historical drinking. The first fatality of the completed Overseas Railroad was a local man, Tom Jones, who, when he saw Flagler's special train pass through at 9 A.M. on January 22, 1912, began celebrating and didn't stop until seven days later when he was pronounced dead of alcohol poisoning.

WHERE TO STAY

Marathon has an astonishing turnover in motel and resort ownership, with places continually going in and out of receivership. Mushroomlike "villas" sprout up overnight with realtor flags flapping beseechingly for your attention. The prettier, palmier places are up-Keys a way. **The Gulf View** at MM #58.5 (289-1414) is bright and pleasant as is **The Golden Grouper** with its little beach at MM #57.5 (743-5285). Rates are about $50 a night in season. Particularly charming are **Conch Key Cottages**, off the road at MM #62.3. Pine walls, big porches, hammocks on the secluded beach. All the cottages have full kitchens and are $125 a night (289-1377). There is also an assortment of apartments and efficiencies that go for $65–$75. Many people like to settle in for the week in this cozy place.

In Marathon, one of the oldest and most established resorts is **Faro Blanco** at MM #48. Built in the 1940's, it has a four-story lighthouse that once could be rented but now is privately owned. The pleasant cottages on the grounds run from $70 to $100 a night. The cottages take kids; the condos ($225 a night) do not. There's an Olympic-size pool, a bar, and a big marina. There are also permanently moored houseboats that cost $85; $95 with a kitchen. Telephone: 743-9018. People are fond of the restaurant here, **Kelsey's**, which serves up expensive portions of chateaubriand, rack of lamb, and shrimp scampi. They'll also cook your catch for you for $10, but only if you fillet it yourself.

The **Buccaneer** at MM #48.5, which cannot decide if it wants to be a "resort" or a "lodge," is the new brute on the block. There are older cottages on the grounds as well as new round "villas" with Singapore hat–like roofs and Jacuzzis and microwaves. There are also tennis courts, pools, charter boats, and a circular bar facing inward, away from the water and its array of rental craft. A wandering crooner with a guitar sings Elvis Presley ballads, and there are a great many large guests wearing many gold chains and drinking triple Red Labels lounging about. Dinner in the restaurant is served by waiters and waitresses in pirates' garb, plumes and frills and so forth —a Miami fantasia of pirates. Maybe it's *just* what you want.

Cottages in season $75 a night. Villas (two-bedroom, two-bath) are $200. Telephone: 743-9071.

The **Coral Lagoon** (pg. 66) at MM#53 is a reasonable and comfortable find with its plantings and hammocks and **The Coconut Grove** MM#50 (743-5312) is simplicity itself with its shuffleboard and outdoor grilles. Rooms at the latter run about $50.

WHERE TO EAT

Most people drive up to the Grassy Key Dairy Bar (see page 64), particularly on Tuesday night, which is "Mexican Night," but it must be faced that every night cannot be Mexican Night. If you're flush, try the **Hideaway** (see page 65). You don't have to drive as far as the people from Miami. It's open from 5 to 11 and requires reservations.

In Marathon, try **Castaway**, down 15th Street, just before the Seven-Mile Bridge. Shrimp, shrimp, shrimp—a crustacean's personal nightmare. Beer and wine. A popular spot. Open 5–10. Telephone: 743-6247.

The Quay at MM #54 is prettily lit and formal, with nice views of the water. The menu is elaborate and reaches for the extraordinary, like the alligator steak, which is seldom available to the chef. If it were made available to the chef it might be for reasons you would prefer not to know about—for example, the occasion of a marine patrol officer being recently called upon to dispose of a gator for swallowing someone's dog. Open every day from 4 P.M. Telephone: 289-1810.

The **Cracked Conch Cafe** at MM #50 has a bar and serves breakfast and lunch all day long, from 8 A.M. until midnight. Casual, with a little outside patio and reasonable, well-prepared soups and dinners. Telephone: 743-2233.

Herbie's at MM #50.5 is an old-time, breezy place of screens and picnic tables. Inexpensive. Lots of fish, draft beer, and badinage. It is so popular that you are often discomfited by the hordes waiting outside, balefully regarding you as you eat. Open 11 A.M.–10 P.M. Closed Sundays. Telephone: 743-6373.

The **7-Mile Grille** at MM #47 is another favorite open-air restaurant, although it's not open early and it's not open late and it's closed Wednesday and Thursday. Very authentic it appears, set back on the dusty access strip a little below the highway. Beer, grouper chowder, and uncomplicated fish baskets. Open 11:30 A.M.–8:30 P.M. Telephone: 743-4481.

At **Bacchus by the Sea** at MM #47.6, down 11th Street, you can eat either inside or out on the dock with one of Marathon's nicest views. Good Italian food and, of course, fresh seafood. Lively bar. "Celebrities" are sometimes seen here forking down the mussels marinara. Food is served from 11 A.M. to 10 P.M. Telephone: 743-6106.

FISHING

Marathon is obsessed with fish. It has been said that there are 450 species of fish in the waters off the Keys, and Marathon is desirous of every single one of them. Here, too, there are tournaments—tarpon tournaments, sailfish tournaments, dolphin tournaments, and bonefish tournaments. There is no kingfish

A marlin

tournament, that variety having been virtually wiped out by commercial netters. Occasionally the severe depletion of a species is noted, and bureaucracy lumbers into action, but gross overfishing of certain varieties can go on for years with the only complaint being that there aren't as many fish as there used to be.

Stone crabs and Florida lobsters have diminished greatly in number—there are three million crayfish traps between Key Largo and the Dry Tortugas, according to *National Fisherman* —and there is also a decline in the once abounding populations of grouper and snapper, fishes taken intensively commercially, as well as being the staple of party boats.

Tournament fishing is now encouraging releases, but a visit to the charter boat docks or a glance at local tabloids, particularly the monthly *Florida Keys Angler* published in Islamorada, will show you that many visitors have a deep desire to be seen standing beside large dead fish hanging from hooks, touching possessively the thing they have hauled up from the deep—a thing of once-remarkable colors turned grey, a thing with poundage numbers scrawled in white paint upon its sides. Deep-sea hunters will say that the killing of a big fish after a long battle is an emotional necessity (although battle time has been shortened considerably by the handling capabilities of modern sportsfishing boats, which can back up and maneuver quickly). Otherwise, anglers kill gamefish apparently for two reasons —photographic confirmation (although dead fish of a given species tend to bear an uncanny resemblance to one another) and possession of a mount or "trophy" (a trophy being a painted replica of the caught fish that can be hung in the living room or wherever). It is now known, and even grudgingly acknowledged by taxidermists themselves, that there is very little fish in a mounted fish. The taxidermist is a colorist who works with a little skin and a lot of plastic. But what is reality, after all? Reality is a tricky business, one which, as Audubon remarked about the love of turtles, is complexly conducted and perhaps not a fitting object of discussion here.

Reality aside, this is Marathon, and Marathon intently fishes.

Tarpon fishing is popular here in the spring and through July —a little too popular for the beleaguered dolphin—particularly

under the bridges where schools of "silver king" congregate to
run through the deep channels back into the shallow flats
where they spawn and feed. You can't eat tarpon, but people
love to catch them because of the fish's extraordinary perform-
ance when hooked. For the first five minutes, before they sound
and "dog it out," a hooked tarpon jumps, shakes, and tailwalks.
He then, it is said, feels to the fisherman like a falling piano.

The terms you will hear used to describe types of fishing are
Gulf Stream, back country, reef or *wreck,* and *flats* or *bonefish-
ing.* For a brochure on local guides, write to the Marathon
Guides Association, Box 65, Marathon, FL 33050.

Gulf Stream fishing is done by charter. The fighting chairs
are for marlin and sailfish, and the bait is constantly trolled.
Dolphin is also found in deep water in the summer. Usually four
or fewer people make up a charter, and the cost runs around
$300 a day. Cobia, shark, wahoo, and bonito are often caught.

Back country fishing is done bay-side and is for "bottom fish"
—trout, grouper, snapper, and jewfish. Grouper is the fish that
most unerringly finds his way into your fish sandwich or your
"all you can eat" fish fry. A fish of fickle history, the grouper
begins life as an egg-producing female, then changes sex later
on. It also completely changes color when frightened. Jewfish
are its speckled, obese, large-mouthed cousins, a type of giant
sea bass that can weigh up to seven hundred pounds. Shark and
barracuda are also fished for in the back country.

Reef and *wreck* fishing are done most often by party boats.
These large boats take out fifty to seventy-five people at a time
and charge around $25 a day per person, usually less for chil-
dren. All bait and tackle are provided. Again, grouper and snapper are called upon and frequently answer. Some boats take
two- and three-day trips to the Tortugas for even more extensive
catches of bottom-feeding fish, returning to port with ice chests
full of fish, floorboards covered with fish, fish blood, fish slime,
gaping fish mouths, and staring fish eyes. Fish lust is a definite
requirement for these Tortuga trips. Prices from Marathon are
around $150, slightly more with rod rental, and the coveted
stern spots are extra. Party boats can be found at the **Winner-
Sombrero Docks** down Sombrero Road at MM #50 by bearing
right at the golf course. Charter boats can be found farther

down this road or behind the big motels such as **Faro Blanco** and **The Buccaneer**, as well as at the big marina at Key Colony Beach, where bareboat charters and sailing trips are also offered. Or, again, ask around. Some charter boat captains work out of their backyards.

Flats-fishing for bonefish and permit has more mystique connected to it than any other type of fishing in the Keys. This is not a blood-riot of hauling up creatures from the black depths, but a ghostly stalking through crystal-clear sands and turtle-grass flats. Zane Grey called the bonefish "the wisest, shyest, strangest, wariest fish," possessing "baffling cunning." The bonefish comes into the flats when the tide is low to feed on clams buried in the bottom, at which time it is prone to sharks, barracuda, and clever bonefishermen. It is a slim, furtive fish built for speed. It never leaps when hooked, but makes a long and astonishingly powerful run. Three to five pounds is the average size, eight to nine pounds is a big one, and anything larger is a trophy catch. The world record is twenty-three

---

LIGHTHOUSES

From the Seven-Mile Bridge, four miles south of Marathon, you will see **Sombrero light**, one of six spidery, graceful lighthouses that mark the reef off the Keys. All were built between 1852 and 1880 and have an iron-pile construction, the pilings of the foundations driven deep within the coral on which they stand. They are the **Fowey Rocks light**, the "Eyes of Miami," which replaced the ineffectual Cape Florida light on the mainland; the **Carysfort Reef lighthouse** off Key Largo; **Alligator Reef light** off Lower Matecumbe Key; **Sombrero** off Marathon and the tallest of the reef lights at 140 feet; **American Shoal light** off Cudjoe Key and six miles west of Looe Key; and **Sand Key light**, eight miles southwest of Key West.

Vessels once ran aground regularly on the reef—there was at least one "good" wreck a week—supporting a flourishing salvage industry that made Key West, where the admiralty court was located, a very wealthy little town. "Everything that the commerce of the world afforded reached Key West," Jefferson Browne wrote in his 1912 book, *Key West the Old and the New*. "The wrecks not only threw on these shores rich cargoes, but many valuable citizens were thus furnished. . . . Several of our prominent families owe their residence here to the fact that their ancestors were wrecked on the Florida Reef."

Keys' people relished their wrecks, certainly, but however beneficial wrecks were to Key West, they did not appeal to ship owners, who demanded that the government erect navigational aids along this treacherous and much-traveled route. It seemed impossible at first to build lighthouses on the reefs, so lightships were used. The lightships were a dismal failure. They were unseaworthy, they blew off course and were sometimes grounded on the very reefs they were supposed to warn about, and their lights were scarcely discernible, erratically lit, and badly placed, so that mariners were deceived more often than assisted. Open-skeleton wrought-iron lighthouses were originally designed by Alexander Mitchell in 1836. The Carysfort Reef light was designed by I. W. P. Lewis and was built in 1852, the first of its kind. The lighthouses were erected on as few pilings as possible, in order not to obstruct the free flow of water, and their webby, open construction offered less resistance to wind and water during hurricanes. Another benefit of the iron-pile design was that it could be manufactured, assembled to make sure that all the parts fit, then broken down again and shipped to open water. The Carysfort Reef light was manned until 1960, but now a solar panel charges the battery powering the flashing light.

The second light to be built on the Keys was Sand Key, off Key West. There was originally a 60-foot brick lighthouse here which was destroyed in an 1846 hurricane, killing the woman tender and her children. The new structure was the first of the reef lights to be installed with a Fresnel lens, named for its inventor, the French physicist Augustin Fresnel, a lens which increased by many times the ability of lamp light to be concentrated and magnified. Hurricanes and storms have rearranged the sandy beach here or made it disappear altogether, but the rust-red, square, pyramidal tower, screw-piled into the coral beneath, has been unharmed. The Fresnel lens was recently removed and replaced with a flash-tube array, the battery again powered by solar energy, which projects the light for nineteen miles.

Caribbean destinations, on one of our splendid ships. Explore the Bahamas, Barbados, Jamaica, Martinique, San Juan, the Virgin Islands...or relax in Labadee and CocoCay, Royal Caribbean's own treasure islands, with their unspoiled beauty.

7-NIGHT CARIBBEAN
Starting From
$**649***
Cruise Only
3rd & 4th
Passenger $99*

SOUTHERN CARIBBEAN/SONG OF AMERICA

What better way to see the pristine U.S. Virgin Islands (along with elegant St. Kitts, St. Maarten and exotic Guadeloupe) than from our refined Song of America? Three times named Ship of the Year, she certainly takes no liberties when it comes to serving you, November through April.

7-NIGHT SOUTHERN CARIBBEAN
From
$**699***
Cruise Only
3rd & 4th
Passenger $99*

SPECIAL FALL SAVINGS

It pays to read between the lines. Royal Caribbean is also now offering special fall fares, including air from select gateways. Call us to find out more about these reduced rates. Choose any of our destinations the Caribbean over: from St. Thomas, Cozumel, St. Maarten, Antigua, Martinique and San Juan, Barbados, Playa Del Carmen, Ocho Rios (among many others). And cruise aboard one of our remarkable ships ~ which take you where you want to be, in a style to which you can easily become accustomed.

Of course, don't get caught poring over the fine print too long ~ these special rates won't last forever.

Call us for more details. Because now you can go anywhere on Royal Caribbean. Anywhere, but wrong.

Victorian house-turned-inn offers beachfront in Key West

By CHERYL BLACKERBY
Cox News Service

KEY WEST, Fla. — Even Ernest Hemingway didn't have it this good. His house on Whitehead Street had a huge pool — the island's first — but La Mer, a Victorian inn six blocks from Hemingway's house, sits next to a shady, sandy beach.

The inn is the island's only guest house with a beach. Most of Key West's many inns are in Old Town near the gulf end of Duval Street. La Mer is a half-block from the other end of Duval, next to the ocean.

Not only is the inn next to a beach — it's next to the island's prettiest and least-known beach, South Beach. Most people go to the rocky Smathers Beach, a crowded public stretch of sand on the edge of town.

The inn, a turn-of-the-century two-story mansion with a wraparound porch on the first floor and balconies in back, would be a nice weekend choice even if it didn't occupy such a choice spot.

A private home until it opened as a guest house eight years ago, the mansion regained its original Victorian elegance during a restoration that included marble bathroom floors, armoires and wicker furniture in its 11 guest rooms.

The Dewey House, a Victorian mansion next door, is undergoing a renovation by the owners of La Mer, Old Town Resorts. The house's 19 guest rooms will be finished by Christmas. A Jacuzzi will go in back and all bathrooms will have Jacuzzi tubs. The house is next to the South Beach Raw Bar.

The two inns and newly renovated motels are transforming the South Beach area — until recently a quiet neighborhood of private mansions and a few 1950s-era motels popular with families.

The formerly lackluster Southernmost Motel, which attracted film stars including Spencer Tracy in the mid-1950s, was renovated Key West-style and now has gingerbread trim, tin roofs and lush landscaping around its two pools. The South Beach Oceanfront Motel, built in 1956, has renovated rooms that overlook the ocean. The motel is next to South Beach and has a pier and a pool.

Cayo Hueso Cottages, 509-515 United St., a half-block from Duval and one block from South Beach, is a collection of six 19th-century cigar-makers' cottages centered around a pool and connected by wood walkways. The complex, opened eight months ago, includes a three-bedroom, two-bath house with a private pool.

Atlantic Shores Motel, 510 South St., is a newly refurbished art deco hotel, and has a restaurant called Diner Shores, an open-air cinema and a clothing-optional pool. The clientele is mixed — gay and straight.

If you go

For information about La Mer, the Southernmost Motel and South Beach Oceanfront Motel, call (800) 354-4455. Summer rates (until Dec. 22) at La Mer for two people range from $115 to $150. At the South Beach Motel, $94-$138; the Southernmost, $79-$125. — Cayo Hueso Cottages, (800) 654-2781, summer rates for two people range from $99-$375 for two people. Rooms have TVs, VCRs, CD players, full kitchens and private decks. — Atlantic Shores Motel (800) 526-3559, summer rates for two people range from $55-$70.

Sombrero reef was first charted and named by the Spanish, and a light was placed here because it was midway between the Carysfort and Sand Key lights. Like the earlier lights, it was built under the direction of George Gordon Meade, who later became a major general during the Civil War, commanding the Army of the Potomac which defeated Robert E. Lee at Gettysburg. The octagonal, pyramidal skeleton tower of Sombrero was completed in 1858; its original Fresnel lens is displayed at the Lighthouse Museum in Key West.

Ships continued to run aground in the dark interstices between the lights, but the Civil War delayed further construction of lighthouses. It was not until 1873 that Alligator Reef light was constructed off the Matecumbe Keys, on what was considered the long reef's "elbow." This beautiful black and white structure, considered by lighthouse historians to be one of the finest iron lighthouses in the world, was named for the USS *Alligator,* one of the eight schooners of the West India Squadron, which hunted pirates off the coast of Florida and went aground on the reef in 1821. She was blown up by her own crew so that pirates wouldn't salvage her. Alligator Reef light survived the 1935 hurricane, undamaged by the 20-foot tidal wave that surged past the light on its way to annihilate the shore.

The northernmost of the reef lights was built in 1878 on Fowey Rocks off Key Biscayne. During its construction, workmen were often terrified by ships bearing down on them and wrecking on the reefs only yards away.

American Shoal lighthouse was the last to be built, completing the system of reef lights in July 1880. Again, it was a pyramidal skeleton tower enclosing a lightkeeper's dwelling. Looe Key and the Sambos were reefs upon which ships continued to wreck in the cavernous darkness between the Sombrero and Sand Key lights. American Shoal realized the Keys' "band of light" and brought to an end the days of the wreckers.

All the lighthouses are automated now, the lights powered by batteries that store solar energy. No keepers are needed to trim the wicks and keep the lamps clean and full of oil, nor to draw curtains over the lens at sunrise to protect it from the glare of day. The structures are massively graceful, and through their skeletal forms, the reef waters glitter and dance. They seem abandoned and improbable by day, vaguely stirring the spirit, beneficent and speechless icons that at night send messages of warning and comfort.

pounds. Its Latin name is *albula vulpes*—"white fox." Permits are easier to see than bonefish. They are larger and more vertical—like large silver dimes with black fins. Their eyes are the most sentient of any fish and their bodies are clean and silken. Flats-fishing for bonefish and permit is done in an outboard with the engine stilled, the guide standing on a spotting platform and poling across the flats. It is a silent sport of considerable skill and even delicacy. There are guides who specialize in the flats, and most of them are booked solid in the bonefish months—May is considered the best month—the season runs until November. Almost all guides require the release of these fish caught during a charter. Costs run around $250 a day. When the president comes to the Keys to fish, he stays at Cheeca and goes bonefishing with guide George Hommell, who runs the tackle shop **World Wide Sportsman** in Islamorada. George, the guide, describes actually hooking a bonefish as "happiness." He also says that George, the president, "often gets quiet when he fishes," and that when he catches a fish, "he gets excited."

THE SEVEN-MILE BRIDGE

It is said that Henry Flagler loved concrete with a passion. He was seventy-eight years old when his workmen began construction on the Seven-Mile Bridge (MM #47 to MM #40), which, when finished, was considered the Eighth Wonder of the world. His young construction engineer, J. C. Meredith, literally worked himself to death on the project, collapsing a year after work on the span began.

The bridge was built in four parts. The first three spans —Knights Key Bridge, Pigeon Key Bridge, and Moser Channel Bridge—were made of steel-girder sections laid on top of concrete foundation piers. The entire bridge had 546 of these piers, more than any other bridge in the world. The piers, all made of a special cement that was imported from Germany, were secured to bedrock that in some cases was 28 feet under water. The Moser Channel swing span was 253 feet long and opened for any boat that required more than a 23-foot clearance. The last,

The beach at Bahia Honda Key

westernmost part of the bridge consisted of 210 concrete arches similar to those used on the Long Key Viaduct.

The Seven-Mile Bridge, like all the bridges of the Keys, withstood all hurricanes, even the 1935 one that meant the end of the railroad. A year after that disaster, work began on converting the railway into a highway, and the 14-foot width of the bridge was widened to twenty-two feet with I-beams. Much of the old track was used as guardrails for the road. This highway served travelers, often harrowingly, for more than forty years, until a new bridge was constructed and completed in 1982. The new bridge is wider and higher than the old and has eliminated the need for a drawspan by rising 40 feet higher over Moser Channel at MM #43.5, providing a 65-foot clearance.

A portion of the old bridge runs to **Pigeon Key**, once a community of railroad workers and their families. There was a school and even dairy cows. Later it became headquarters for the toll district operation when the highway was briefly a toll road in the 1930's. During World War II, it was used as a tropic zone GI training center and is now leased by the University of Miami which uses it sporadically for marine research.

The old bridge is now used by fishermen, campers, runners

A bull shark with pilot fish

and roller skaters. Each April, there's a seven mile sponsored run on the new bridge while in the waters below, "superboats" race, sponsored by the American Power Boat Association. Beneath the waters, in the spring, the tarpon make their far more silent, silvery run, frequently followed by large sharks, including the bizarre and voracious hammerhead.

Beyond the Seven-Mile Bridge—the "great one"—at MM #40 is **Little Duck Key,** a filled area with a public boat ramp and several cement picnic shelters. This little duck is many, many miles away from the big Duck (once touted as a fairyland playground for millionaires at MM #61). Then come **Missouri** and **Ohio** keys, named by homesick railroad workers one would imagine, but they are more filled causeway than island. An elaborately appointed campground follows Sunshine Key, for those campers who don't want to get away from it all, and then there is **Bahia Honda,** a state park which has the finest beach on the Keys.

BAHIA HONDA KEY

The Spanish name is "Deep Bay" and this marks the geologic transition from the Upper Keys, which are coral, to the Lower, which are limestone. As it is transitional, it is unique in many ways, its coral skeleton supporting sand beaches, dunes, and a coastal strand hammock in which a number of rare plants grow, including the yellow satinwood, the only tree of its kind in the

SHARKS

When men catch sharks, they do not simply kill them, they mutilate them as though in the grip of an ancient rite. They hatchet fins, chop out jaws, pry out teeth, slit open bellies and grind up claspers or ovaries beneath the heels of their boots. Scientists and fishermen alike seem to be always stomping and skidding around in the blood and viscera of a ruined shark.

This is how you go shark fishing: You usually go out at night. You chum the waters heavily with garbage, offal, the bloody remains of fish. You fish with very heavy tackle, stout leaders, large hooks. When a shark hits the line, lights are struck and when the shark is reeled in alongside the boat your companions blast at him with shotguns, taking care not to strike each other or the boat. Winched up, the shark is then battered with clubs for a time for a prevalent belief is that dead sharks often come back to life. Hauled aboard, the belly is then cut open and the contents of the stomach examined and marvelled at. Shark can be eaten, but most people don't bother, for acids build up in the flesh if it is not cleaned and iced immediately, and the meat spoils quickly. Those who go shark fishing usually just go for the ambience.

Men hate sharks. They hate them a lot. But what does it matter? The creature's existence cannot truly be confronted. The shark is not in the Tarot. It is not in the signs of Heaven. Its strict reality remains beneath the waters of the world. The shark is deft and original and very ancient. Dead or alive, it inhabits impossible depths and will inhabit them forever.

Keys, and the Jamaica morning glory. The seeds have all been brought here from the Caribbean and the West Indies by birds, wind, and water. There is a nature trail that winds around a lagoon at the northeastern end of the park where you can wander through this subdued exotica—you will see quite a number of the slender Silver Palm, pale as the silvery raccoons that forage here under the hot sky.

The beach sand is fine and the swimming excellent here. There is a boat ramp for trailered boats as well as a marina and small dive shop. You can also rent Windsurfers. Bahia Honda costs $1.50 for the driver of the car, $1 for passengers. Camping runs around $25 a night. Phone number at the park is 872-2353. As with other state parks, half the sites are unreserved on a first-come first-served basis. Stop by in the morning and have your name put on a waiting list. Names are called at 3 in the afternoon. Some handsome rental cottages on stilts have been built by the park service on the bay side which can be seen from the highway at MM #37. The access road is only available through the park. These are $125 a night. Mid-September through mid-December they're $97 a night.

To read the histories of the Overseas Railroad, engineers and workers were in a continual state of amazement. Here, it seemed, they did not realize the significance of the Spanish name for the channel. Bahia Honda was far more difficult to build than the Seven-Mile Bridge because the waters were so deep. When trying to locate bedrock for the foundation of the center span, workmen found only water, more and more water in a hole that seemed, for weeks, to be bottomless. Since the water was so deep, tide surges would be higher in a storm, so the bridge, as well as being the hardest to build, was the highest. When the Overseas Highway came in 1936 to remodel it as a road, they could not widen its enclosed structure so they built their road over the top, and it resembles nothing less than a roller coaster. The four-lane bridge you're traveling on today is a recent construction, and, of course, not nearly as nice.

Diving is good near the bridge pilings which provide mini-reefs replete with corals, lobsters, sponges, and fish. However, bridge diving can be dangerous both because of rapid and

abrupt tide changes and a superabundance of sea urchins and
stinging fire coral which seems to flourish in areas of swift
currents. The current that flows through Bahia Honda Channel
is the fastest in all the Keys.

A phenomenon occurs here each year around the last full
moon of May. Small reddish palolo worms hatch from rocks and
sponges, and the tarpon come in great schools to slurp them up
at the surface. At this time, tarpon can be caught on a small fly
instead of the large live mullet they prefer as bait.

After the Bahia Honda Bridge come the **Spanish Harbor
Keys,** including **West Summerland** which is marked by a sign,
a sign that may bewilder you as **West Summerland** is 10 miles
east of **Summerland Key.** Two coral rock storage sheds for
dynamite from the time that the railroad was being pushed
through were found on West Summerland years ago but they
have been misplaced again in the overgrowth.

There are several places to pull off the road during these few
miles to rest or picnic or walk along the damp, curving shore.
You can sometimes find old bottles along the swampy shoreline
of both Summerlands, and farther down on Sugarloaf Key.

THE LOWER KEYS
Big Pine Key
to Key West

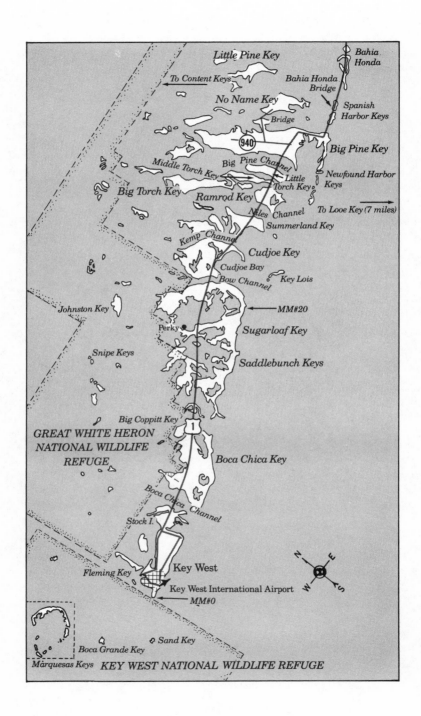

THE Lower Keys are dark and wooded, and though settled, seem lonely. They are not fabulous, nor are they lush or exotic or breathtaking. They are too modest for superlatives. They are subdued, sometimes eccentric, even secretive. And some dirt roads that lead farther and farther back into the mangroves toward unnamed flats and channels are better left unexplored. It's said that when Fat Albert, the Naval surveillance blimp, is brought down for a checkup or because of bad weather, the air springs alive with the chatter of drug runners, and the sound of outboards popping into action is heard far and wide across this watery and muddy frontier. There are those who live simply here and those who live well, and those whose privacy is the best known thing about them. The land is scrub, cactus, slash-pine. Big Pine has trees of uncommon size for the low-lying tropics and Cudjoe even has a stand of cabbage palms. In the old days, these keys seemed always to be burning. Settlers burned the trees to make charcoal and deliberately set other fires to flush out the tiny Key deer. Sparks from the passing railroad also set the Keys aflame. Even so, the land is low and wet which makes great tracts of it uninhabitable. When the old, iron, water pipeline was laid alongside the road it had to be raised on pilings so it wouldn't disappear into the muck. On a chart, the area is sprinkled with bays, bights, harbors, lakes, and sounds. Offshore, is **Looe Key,** a reef known for the clarity of its waters which are cleansed constantly by the waters of the Gulf Stream. The land moves back and forth upon itself, the woods rustle with palm warblers. Birds of prey like this landscape—eagles, falcons, red-tailed and red-shouldered hawks. A frequent sight along these keys is osprey nests on telephone poles on the south side of the highway. The osprey nests for life and the nest grows larger and larger over the years, an indication of how long the couple have flown and hunted together. In March and April, there's great activity around the nests and you'll probably see

A nesting osprey

an osprey returning, a fish hanging heavily from its talons, or perched hunched, carefully dissecting the meal for its young. These keys, too, seem to abound, even specialize in, quiet water trips, conducted leisurely by naturalists in a variety of craft ranging from canoes to Chinese junk-rigged trimarans to roomy wooden sailboats. The Great White Heron National Wildlife Refuge encompasses the waters of the Lower Keys and Key West and to explore these waters is to realize the essence of the Keys.

Take care in respecting this essence. You're going into nurseries back here. For the safety and survival of wild things, there are certain things you must do. Don't anchor within two hundred feet of islands and keep speed and noise to a minimum when passing. Some species and individuals don't seem to mind jets screaming overhead or cars tearing by on the highway, but most birds, particularly nesting ones, don't like noise and simply can't acclimate to it. The approach of a boat can frighten a bird from its nest, leaving the eggs or nestlings exposed to the frying sun. As well, avoid boat wakes around islands. Some ospreys nest low and a wake can wash right over the young. Jet

skis (their supporters call them "water bikes," their detractors
call them "thrillcraft") do not belong in the back country, and
you should not support the businesses that promote "mangrove
safaris" on them. If you see anyone behaving irresponsibly or
harassing wildlife, don't ignore them, report them. Call the
National Key Deer Refuge at 872-2239 or the marine patrol.

For a unique high-quality adventure, sail the back country with
Capt. Bill Schwicker on his beautiful 28-foot wooden boat, *Egret*.
He designed and built this boat himself in 1980 and with its
10-inch draft, it's a perfect vessel for the waters. No engine, it
glides over the meadows and among the mangroves. A nice day
for two at $185 (872-2607).

You can rent your own boat from **Bud Boats**, off Watson Boulevard on Big Pine, near the Old Wooden Bridge Fishing Camp
(which sounds much nicer than it appears) on the way to No
Name. They have a variety of craft from 13-foot Boston Whalers
to Makos and Aquasports. A 17-foot Whaler with sunroof and
VHF radio will cost $95 a day or $425 a week. If you have a dock
where you're staying, they'll deliver. Telephone: 743-6316.

Coming off the Spanish Harbor Bridge, **Big Pine Fishing
Lodge** with tent and trailer camping and a few motel efficiencies (872-2351) is to your left and the restaurant **Island Reef** is
to your right at MM #31, behind several gigantic date palms.
It's a harrowing turn in from either direction but once there,
you'll be happy. They have a variety of pot pies, steaks and a
few fish dishes. On Sundays they have roast lamb and chicken
and stuffing. They may be overly prideful of their homemade
breads but it's a nice place, casual, with the good Keys' "feel."
Wine and beer only. Open for breakfast and lunch from 6:30 to
2:30 and for dinner at 5. But they close early—9:30—and are
shut on Tuesdays (872-2170).

  Other good places to eat in the Lower Keys are the tiny **Big
Pine Coffee Shop** at MM #30, open from six in the morning
until nine at night and the seasonal **Mangrove Mama's** (open
at 5 P.M.).

Best places to stay are **The Sugarloaf Lodge** (745-3741) and the dive-oriented, canal-side motel **Looe Key Reef Resort** (872-2215).

BIG PINE KEY

Big Pine, eight miles long and two miles wide, is second in size only to Key Largo. It is known primarily for its herd of tiny Key deer, a distinct subspecies of the Virginia white-tailed or a full species, *dama clavia,* of its own, depending on which biologist you talk to. The deer stand only two and a half feet tall and weigh less than seventy-five pounds. Fawns weigh only two to four pounds at birth and their tiny hoof print is the size of a thumbnail. By the late 1940's, hunting had almost exterminated them and there were less than fifty animals left. The publicized

A Key deer

plight of the "toy" deer of Big Pine and that of the Ivory-Billed Woodpecker in Louisiana sparked concern over endangered species and began the conservation movement in this country. The efforts to save the woodpecker were unsuccessful when one of the last nesting areas of the Ivory-Billed was bulldozed to plant the magnificent soybean, but the habitat of the deer was saved and, through rigorous law enforcement their numbers increased. "Rigorous law enforcement" is a pseudonym for Jack Watson, a former hunter turned militant environmentalist, and the refuge manager through the 1960's and 70's. Watson's war on poachers is legend. He was known to have burned the cars and sunk the boats of those in that gross fraternity. He even made house calls on those he heard were jacking deer. One famous incident concerned a poacher who was out and up repairing his roof when Watson confronted him. "Sure," the man bawled, "I've been shooting 'em, and I'll keep shooting 'em if I want until there ain't any left!" So Watson shot him, unfatally I must unhappily add, right off the roof.

Big Pine Key doesn't look very Keys-like. It has pine trees and subdivisions and shopping centers. The Winn-Dixie's aisles are jammed with "moribundis" just like the rest of Florida. In the summer, the moribundis leave for the mountains, and the aisles are jammed with sweaty locals cooling off by the frozen foods. Big Pine has scant human history. It has always been sparsely settled, even in the railroad days, and though there were various schemes to make use of the land—dairy farming for one —the cows keeling over under the weight of mosquitoes—and a shark processing plant—nothing was profitable, and so the land was inevitably bought up for development. Now it has a vociferous go-growth population led by retired colonels who can't understand why wetlands shouldn't be filled, particularly if they're not near the shoreline, and why marinas can't be carved out of three-foot deep waters. They are determined to reap the monetary rewards from the land they bought for $200 an acre back in the 1950's.

Big Pine is formed of oolite, which means that the limestone cap rock is honeycombed with sinkholes. The sinkholes are caused by the underlying rock being dissolved by water causing the surface rock to form pockets. Small shallow sinkholes are called solution holes. Farmers called them "banana holes" and used them to plant what they could. Ferns take advantage of the moist soil that accumulates and they flourish in the rock. The larger sinkholes are dearly loved by gators who move along the labyrinthian corridors beneath. If you see a largish snout poking from a medium-sized hole, you'll know that a considerably large gator resides beneath.

There are two basic biogeographic rules concerning plants and animals. One is that islands have fewer species than a comparably sized piece of mainland, and the other is that peninsulas support less and less diversity the farther they are from the land mass. These are perfectly good rules in general as they apply to the rest of the state of Florida, which, of course, is a huge peninsula, but they have no relevance at all in the Keys. As well as being the only truly tropical area of the continental United States, the Keys have the most diverse terrestrial and marine ecosystem in the country. What this means on Big Pine is that you can enter the National Key Deer Refuge (passing churches, ball field, houses and for sale signs along the way, as well as many, many signs alerting you to the deers' presence —there appear to be more signs at this time than deer), walk through a pine and palm forest into a tropical hardwood hammock, and continue toward a tangled mangrove shoreline of small sandy beaches and coral outcroppings facing Big Pine Channel . . . which will lead you eventually into the deeper waters of the Straits of Florida, beyond which is the clear wild blue of the great Gulf Stream.

Fascinating to the biogeographer, and certainly interesting to anyone with a little time and some imagination, or even just the luck to see the gators, little deer, hawks, herons, and orchids of this place.

To get to the refuge, pass MM #31 and turn right at the light on Route 940, Key Deer Boulevard. Bear left toward the Big Pine Key Road Prison. Up a ways you'll see a sign to the refuge. About a mile and a half up the road, Watson Boulevard intersects. To the right is the road to No Name; to the left, the refuge headquarters. Continue on another mile and a half to the **Blue Hole,** a small fresh water sink which was blasted out to make larger and provide fill for a parking lot where you can park your

car and look at the Blue Hole. The pond ranges in depth from
a half foot to twelve feet and has a resident alligator, who, upon
occasion, exhibits himself. Until recently, the Big Pine Baptist
Church used the Blue Hole for baptisms, despite the alligator.
To the immediate left here is Higgs Lane. Walk down this road
until you see the refuge sign, then bear to the left and go around
a gate bar to take the trail that will go through pine lands to
Watson's Hammock. The neatly constructed cement canals
you see are mosquito ditches. These are connected to the Gulf
and filled with tiny fish—gambusia—who do nothing but eat
mosquito larvae night and day. This was the government-
approved mosquito control for the Keys for decades, and a slip-
pery concept to grasp. The back country is latticed with these
ditches in which the mosquito lay its eggs and the mosquito fish
eats them. Before the Navy built the water pipeline down the
Keys in the 1940's, the health authorities would come to individual homes and dump a handful of gambusia into private cisterns.

Watson's Hammock is a hardwood forest, dappled, lovely,
cool, and quiet, with a fifty-foot canopy. There's a huge gumbo-
limbo tree here. With its peeling red bark, it is lightly called the
"tourist tree" because the limbs look tortured with flaking sun-
burn. The tree is peculiar in a number of ways. Posts made of
the stout limbs sprout roots and become living fences. The sap
of the tree is very gummy and was once used to catch birds. The
Caloosa Indians (of which little is known except that they were
very tall and feared their dead), and later the white settlers,
boiled down the sap and spread it on the tree limbs. The birds
would alight and their little bird feet would *stick* to the
branches. Even in the 1930's and 1940's trapping wild birds on
the Keys was a lucrative business.

You'll also see the Jamaican dogwood, or fish-fuddle tree, the
branches of which those mysterious Indians scraped and lay on
the water, causing fish to rise, insensate. There are also century
plants, orchids, bromeliads, and the huge webs of the gigantic
Golden Orb spiders.

Another nice walk is a few hundred yards beyond the Blue
Hole. This is the **Jack Watson Nature Trail**, a well-marked
loop trail less than a mile in length. There should be pamphlets

available in a box at the beginning of the trail but usually the box is empty. The numbers on the trail direct your attention to various palms, including the thatch and the elegant silver; poisonwood trees, highly toxic but with fruit prized by the White-Crowned Pigeon; and sinkholes, large and small.

The best time to see the Key deer are at dusk or very early in the morning, in either the ferny parts of the forest or in the lower-lying buttonwood sloughs where there might be water. They also browse on the lawns of the burgeoning developments

---

BAD TREES

There are three trees that have really become pests in Florida —the punk, the pepper, and the Australian pine. Some people like all three because they're fast growing and good screening material, and they like the punk (the *melaleuca*) because it reminds them of the eucalyptus, and the pepper (euphemistically called "Florida holly") because of its little red berries, and the pine (*casuarina,* not a true pine at all) because of the pretty sound the wind makes coursing through its branches.

But *you* should not like any of them and should never plant the punk, the pepper, or the Australian pine. All three, of course, are easily seeded and require no care whatsoever and all grow like mad and crowd out indigenous trees. The punk is ugly with its thick, spongy, white shredding bark and many people are allergic to its blooms. Plus, bees make lousy honey from its blossoms. Unfortunately, bees make good honey from the blooms of the pepper, and beekeepers have been known to encourage the spread of this bad bush just to keep their bees busy. (Bees *are* terribly busy. Each lives but six weeks, works demoniacly, and gathers only half a teaspoon of honey.) The casuarina is the nicest with its susurrant voice, a pretty sight on a white sand beach swaying green against a perfect sky, but it too is a pushy pest. Its needles and roots put out a toxin in the soil that prevents other types of plants from growing around or beneath it. Also, with its shallow, spreading root system, it flops right over when a vigorous wind comes up.

Another bad tree is the poisonwood which is the Keys'

poison ivy except that it is a tropical hardwood which grows up to thirty feet tall. It has large, shiny, limp leaves. Its small, yellowish-green flowers are arranged in sprays and it bears an orange fruit in the fall. Its leaves and bark are often splotched with dried black sap. It has that *look* of being a no-good.

of Big Pine, their habitat being increasingly "shared" by humans. In May and June, you might see fawns feeding with their mothers on the mowed shoulders of the roads, in terrifying proximity to traffic. Slow down, slow down, slow down. At the beginning of 1991, it was estimated that less than three hundred deer remain and thirty-three of these were killed by cars and dogs six months later.

The most comfortable time to tramp around the back country is the dry, mosquito-free winter, but the trees are not in flower then and there is little bird activity. A good way to explore this area is by canoe.

NO NAME KEY

A Russian is said to have been No Name's first resident. He homesteaded almost two hundred acres, setting trip-wired guns in the underbrush so that visitors were offered the opportunity of being shot. Little was known about him except that he grew very large sapodillas. (The sapodilla is a large shade tree that provides brown, baseball-sized fruit in the spring. The fruit of the "dilly" is coarse and pink and tastes rather like candy that fine sand has been sprinkled over.)

A small village with a school and post office sprang up in 1922 when a car ferry ran between Marathon and No Name. The railroad had bridged the gap in 1912 but there was no land route. Automobile travelers had to take two ferries to traverse the Keys, the other running between Lower Matecumbe Key and Grassy Key. The ferries, *The Florida Keys, The Pilgrim,* and

The Key West operated until 1938 when the Seven-Mile Bridge and the Bahia Honda bridge were rebuilt to accommodate cars. The 15-mile trip to No Name took about two hours. At that time cars drove on a marl road to Big Pine, then south across Big Pine Channel to the north corner of Little Torch. Wooden bridges connected the Torches, Ramrod, and Summerland Keys. Once the ferry service was disbanded, the village by the landing disappeared.

During 1962, a Key Wester, sympathetic to the Cuban refugees, allowed a group training to be guerrilla fighters to use his shack as headquarters on No Name. The key was fairly inaccessible, the bridge leading between it and Big Pine having both rotted and burned. The revolutionary experiment ended when one guerrilla shot and killed another, mistaking him, he said, for a raccoon.

A new cement bridge crosses Bogie Channel and connects No Name to Big Pine today, used mostly by fishermen. The road runs straight to the vanished ferry landing and stops at some very impressive rocks. There is absolutely no way you can make the mistake of running off the road into the water without annihilating yourself on the boulders first. There is no electricity on No Name and consequently only a few houses. Deer appear at the end of the afternoon and congregate on the road. Drive slowly and never feed them. A deer who is fed from a car will eventually be run over by one.

The **No Name Pub** is on Big Pine just before the bridge and is open to midnight, serving beer and good pizza. Its only ambience is that it's hard to find.

THE TORCH KEYS

Big bad parties have been taking place on No Name and The Torches recently. Sometimes they get really bad and someone is found murdered after them. Three particularly gruesome murders remain unsolved. All that the police know is that the vultures didn't do it.

A REALLY BAD TREE

A really bad tree is the manchineel, one of the most poisonous trees in the world. It is not common, but does grow wild on the Keys, particularly Big Pine. It is a small, sprawling tree with a spreading rounded crown and alternate oval leaves that narrow to a sharp point. It produces green and yellow flowers and a crab-apple sized fruit which is deadly when eaten. Some people confuse the tree with a guava and it is said, although it's difficult to imagine by whom, that the fruit is sweet.

Poisonous apple aside, the tree itself is vitriolic. The copious sap is caustic and even rainwater runoff from the leaves can burn and sear the skin. Almost any kind of behavioral abnormality can be attributed to extinct tribes of Indians, which is why you should not be surprised when you hear that the Caloosas employed the manchineel as Grand Inquisitor, tying their luckless victims to the tree and letting the milky sap run where it wished over them, the sap pickling and flaying the flesh as it went.

The Torches have always been a little strange. Just beyond the bridge crossing Big Pine Channel and linking Big Pine with Little Torch was once the Island Woman Bar, known principally for its owner's global economic views (the world's problems began with the invention of money). It is now out of business, perhaps because he gave free beer today rather than tomorrow. A succession of restaurants followed but it would be chancy to stop by for a meal these days as it has become a Jehovah's Witnesses meeting hall.

Down this road half a mile is **Parmer's Place**, a friendly complex of apartments, cottages and trailers named after birds and fishes. You can stay in the Grunt, for example, for $55 a night, though you might prefer the more elegantly named Egret at $70. There's a boat basin and dockage here and many people trailer their boat down and rent by the week. Or you can rent from Bud Boats on Big Pine (they'll deliver) and cruise around these unparalleled fishing and diving waters. Weekly rates at Parmer's are around $500. Telephone: 872-2157.

The Torches, Middle, Little, and Big, got their names unsurprisingly from the resinous torchwood trees that grow there. The wood burns when green and was used for kindling by homesteaders. It may also have hallucinogenic properties. Woodcarvers working with torchwood admit to getting a kick out of it. The rare Schaus swallowtail butterfly, who might know something, feeds exclusively on it. The butterfly was thought to be extinct at the turn of the century but was found on Matecumbe Key only to disappear again after the 1940 hurricane. There are some on Lignumvitae.

Buttonwood trees, an upland mangrove, were also cut and burned to make charcoal for cooking fires. The habit in the Keys was to cut the hardwood and plant coconut palms, pineapples, and limes. None of these farming ventures was successful and all were abandoned. One can still find Key limes growing wild in the Torches. The trees, which are not indigenous, but were introduced from the West Indies, are fiercely thorny and bear a small tart and juicy fruit which is yellow when ripe and falls into your hands nicely at a touch. One of the reasons Key limes were never successful commercially was because they were too thin-skinned and therefore too fragile to ship.

The Torches were most populated in the 1920's when the old road ran down the western side of Little Torch. When the Overseas Highway was built after the 1935 hurricane, utilizing the railroad's bed and bridges, many of the old roads were abandoned, along with the communities that had flourished beside them.

There is little here now, certainly—houses, trailers . . . There is a biologist on Middle Torch who keeps his six acres as a "habitat for snakes" which sounds nice, at least it sounds natural, until you realize that because his specialty is snakes and he wants to find snakes when he's looking for them, his six acres is a "Dixie farm" covered with trash. Old boats and flattened gasoline tanks, rotting boards and fabric, rusted metal of all sorts. All the kinds of snakes that exist in the Keys from the

SNAKES

The Keys have all the varieties of snakes found in Florida. Yes. All the harmless snakes, the *rat,* the *water,* the *indigo,* the *black,* the *corn,* the *green* and the *king*—as well as the poisonous ones—the *cottonmouth,* the *rattlesnake,* and the *coral.*

You may understandably be interested in the poisonous snakes. The *cottonmouth* is rather difficult to identify because he changes color as he grows from a baby to an adult. He can even resemble the gentle, huge indigo snake. But the cottonmouth has a big thick triangular-shaped head which is flat on top and if you get very close he will probably show you what he is by opening his mouth to display the whiteness of his jaws. The *diamondback* is the heaviest poisonous snake in the world, although at eight feet, it is not the longest. It is found in piney and palmetto woods, sandy areas, and hammocks. *Coral snakes* are the most intriguing because they're small and pretty as well as being the most deadly. They grow only to a length of around two feet and their black bodies are brightly banded in orange and black. The harmless *scarlet king snake* is often mistaken for the *coral snake,* but the *scarlet king*'s nose is red, while the *coral*'s nose is black.

Proper snake identification depends upon considerable calm.

Snake experts tend to have three maxims:

In identifying the coral snake, they say, "If his nose is black, he's bad for Jack."

They say that all snakes are non-aggressive and will not go out of their way to bite you.

They say that snakes are where you find them.

black racer and endemic little ring-necked snake (weird in that it has no ring) to the huge indigo and diamondback rattler can be found here. Except they couldn't be found the hot winter morning we spent turning over the trash. Perhaps they had been dined on too vigorously by predators the previous fall. Or perhaps they were offended by their littered home. Or worse, they were tired of the old funky litter and wanted new funk! In any case, there were no snakes, in what had once been a lime grove.

A road that runs the length of Big Torch is called a "scenic drive." Historically, Monroe County has been madly successful in using taxpayers' money to build roads and bridges that go nowhere. Condos, marinas, and golf courses are but a gleam in a speculator's beady eye when these projects are pushed through and this "scenic drive" is no exception. There is nothing there. And after about eight miles of zigzagging blacktop over swampy land, it ends. Those who make the trip appear bewildered but they dutifully emerge from their cars and look. What is there is mangrove, and yet more mangrove—more and more of that splendid, hardworking, giving tree, nursery to nestlings and fishes, busily making land all the while it nourishes. Look upon it, this tangled swamp, and be both respectful and glad.

Off the humble Torches at the western end of the Newfound Harbor Keys is **Little Palm Island**, a 5-acre sand-covered rock owned by a succession of millionaires and now run as a precious thatch-topped luxury resort. A millionaire-style pool-lagoon conception runs through the island. Suites in the bungalows are $501 per couple per night. (Five hundred and one!) It's $621 per couple per night with meals. You can bring your own watercraft and yachts are welcome. If you feel you can't afford $501 for an evening at this time you can still go over to the restaurant for breakfast, lunch or dinner. There are certain regulations, however, involving lunch that might make you think twice. The minimum for lunch is $25 per person and this does not include taxes, tips, and whatever you would spend at the bar. Men must have "collars"—have to leave your Hog's Breath shirt at home. If you want to go swimming, you have to have a beach club membership, which is extra too. There are no children in your party, they hope. At night, entrees run between $18 and $25. The menu also offers *Les Desserts*—"(Desserts)" they add helpfully. *Les Chocolats* (Chocolate) and *Les Cafe et Thé* (Coffee and Tea). A launch leaves the **Dolphin Marina** at MM #28.5 every hour on the hour from 8 A.M. to 10 P.M. For dining reservations

Egrets in the mangroves

call 872-2551. Resort reservations 872-2524. (You're really going to do this??)

RAMROD KEY

This key bears no resemblance whatsoever to a ramrod—it is shaped more like a helmet. In the days when the railroad passed through, Ramrod claimed a post office, although the train never stopped here. It merely slowed down while mail was tossed on and off.

The most interesting thing about Ramrod is **Looe Key** which is seven miles offshore. Looe, named for a frigate that ran

aground here in 1774, is a National Marine Sanctuary and perhaps the most beautiful reef in the Keys, certainly the most
varied and interesting reef in the Lower Keys. The Sanctuary
covers 5 square miles, the reef itself is roughly Y-shaped, 200
yards wide and 800 yards long. Parts of the reef are awash.
Other sections have gullies plunging down to 35 feet between
the coral heads to a pristine sand base in what is called a "spur
and groove system." Looe is a lovely and lively community with
exceptionally clear waters, so it is wonderful for the snorkeler
as well as the diver. You'll see thousands of fish here, lobsters,
octopuses and rays. Long tongues of pillar coral rise within
three feet of the surface and there are massive brain corals as
well as an array of "soft" corals—the undulating gorgonians,
sea fans and sea whips. Looe, with its winding coral corridors,
its deeply carved caves, and diversity of life, is a spectacular
reef.

Never anchor on coral and when diving, never touch it or
stand on it. All life is protected in the sanctuary. Spearfishing

A brain coral gives lobsters shelter from a spotted eagle ray

and collecting are not allowed. Dive shops offer full and half-day reef trips and night dives.

Underseas Inc. MM #31 on Big Pine rents all equipment including cameras. A half day is $20 per person, a full day $30.

Sea Center Dive Shop MM #29.5 on Big Pine makes trips on its 35-foot dive boat *Innerspace 1*.

Reef Divers on Ramrod is located at the **Looe Key Reef Resort**, just past the Torch-Ramrod Channel at MM #27. The resort is a small motel on a canal with boat dockage. It's inexpensive and very popular. They seldom have rooms available during the season if you just drop in, so reservations are necessary. Rates are $65 a night, $50 after Easter. There's a pool, a crowded tiki bar, and an unhurried restaurant which serves an "early bird" special until two in the afternoon. Reef trips, as well as scuba lessons. Instruction, equipment, and two tank dives on Looe costs $75. (872-4154).

Crossing pretty Niles Channel where the generous sky allows you another opportunity to pick out a favorite cloud, you come to **Summerland Key**, where the outlines of some impressive housetops can be seen on the western shore. A road off to the right runs along the Channel and ends at a dismantled dock leading to a small island with a familiar sign Keep Out with a perturbing twist Be Aware Of Caretaker. Enigmatic Summerland is developed with a series of canals on the eastern end and it has a dusty main strip of billboards which is a tiny, hopeful version of something larger and even more dusty. The food in the restaurant at **Monte's Fish Market** at MM #25 is palatable enough, but **Jo-Jo's Diner** should only be attempted if starvation is imminent.

CUDJOE KEY

The best crayfish in the Keys are said to be found off Cudjoe. The second and last most interesting thing about Cudjoe is its name, about which there is much dispute. There is the slender "joewood" theory, the joewood being a common little tree with fragrant blossoms. There is the slenderer yet "Cousin Joe" theory —an early homesteader from Key West, Joe by name, cousin to someone, who first settled here. There is also the more thoughtful explanation that the name Cudjoe was a customary African name given to a male child born on the first day of the week. The Africans, brought to Florida as slaves, then freed, often went to live among the Seminoles by whom they were enslaved once more. It would not be unlikely for one of these men to leave the Everglades and migrate to an isolated key where he could lead an independent life. Nor would it be unusual for a freed

---

KEY LOIS

Off Cudjoe, in the Atlantic just before Hawk Channel, is Loggerhead Key, recently named Key Lois. Lois isn't visible from the highway, although it is, clearly, from haute Little Palm. Lois looks a little odd, as well it might since its only occupants are monkeys. One half of the key is grey as though in shadow, the other half is a healthy, mangrove-wooded green. A narrow tidal river separates the two, a river which, it is said by those who put the monkeys on the island in the first place, they could cross but prefer not to. The monkeys, several thousand of them, inhabit the grey half, which they have denuded with their climbing, scrambling, swinging, and clinging. They are 70-pound, dog-faced, Rhesus monkeys, bred and raised here for laboratory research. As with the cattle one sees grazing in green pastures, they probably lead a very happy life until they don't. There is no natural food for them on the island and no fresh water, so someone arrives daily by boat with water and hundreds of pounds of Purina Monkey Chow. At other times a boat will arrive, collect some of them to fill an order from a laboratory, and take them away. Boats also arrive upon occasion to lug off the monkey feces accumulating there. It's a very clean island and the monkeys are purportedly the biggest, blondest, and healthiest in the world. The original colony of 100 was captured in India in 1972.

The descendants are now a multimillion-dollar business for
the owners of the Massachusetts supplier of lab animals for
the U.S. Food and Drug Administration. The veterinarian
owner of the island, Dr. Henry Foster, wanted to rename
Loggerhead Key Key Lois, as a tribute to his wife, although
why Lois would want an island full of yowling, scratching,
gibbering monkeys named after her is not known. The state,
however, apparently not liking to have places renamed willy-
nilly for uxorial reasons, refused. The doctor got his way
nevertheless with the acronym *Laboratory Observing Island
Simians,* and Loggerhead Key became Key Lois, even though
it might be more accurately called Mon Key.

No Trespassing signs are posted around the island, but
there is no caretaker there, the monkeys apparently being
their own best protection. So one probably will not see them,
but if one did, it would be across a great distance. And the
monkeys would be watching from a great distance too
—across that far distance that separates monkeys from men.

Key Lois, like the holy, ruined, Indian city of Galta, but
with nothing sacred here—no temples, no priests, no pil-
grims. Just the monkeys, monkeys, monkeys.

black man to come up from Key West and, using the name he
was born with, work one of the "outside" keys.

Be that as it may, Cudjoe is rather an orphan. Since it has no
post office, it has no zip code, and since it has no zip, any person
or establishment thereon is considered part of Summerland
Key, which, as we recall, seems to the jaded eye to consist
primarily of real estate offices.

Cudjoe is damp and low for the most part. Most of the development is on the eastern side with small concrete-block houses
crouching on man-made canals.

Just over the bridge that crosses Bow Channel at MM #20 is
Mangrove Mama's, perhaps the most seasonal restaurant on
the Keys. Open 11–12:30 for lunch and 5–10 for dinner in the
winter until abruptly it is no longer, and the place looks as

---

FAT ALBERT

Fat Albert is a 1400-foot, ground-tethered blimp, a radar-stuffed aerostat that floats benignly over Cudjoe, keeping its eye and ear on everything, druggies mostly, with its millions of dollars worth of fancy electronics. Fat is a fine sight, but it crashes frequently, victim of storms and other mishaps. Once, it even had to be shot down deliberately because it had "escaped." What you see today is Son of Fat. Perhaps, even Son of the Son of Fat.

It required millions of very heavy bricks to construct Fort Jefferson, which was built to oversee all activities in the Florida Straits, Havana, Pensacola, Mobile, the mouth of the Mississippi—in short, all of the Gulf of Mexico. Now the dainty Fat, lighter than the air it bobs in, does the job, although he may not float forever. Cute Fat is expensive to maintain.

---

though it's been closed for years. But this place jumps! Classic tacky Keys. Fireplace, wine, and beer served in mason jars. The food isn't that good, but it doesn't seem to matter. On seasonal Sundays there's barbecue and a band. It's closed on Thursdays, it seems. Telephone: 745-3535.

SUGARLOAF KEY

Sugarloaf was settled at the turn of the century when a sponge raising station was built there. The farming venture consisted of cutting off bits of live, large sponges, attaching the bit to a piece of concrete and allowing it to grow in a pen in the water. Charles Chase, an Englishman, created the Florida Sponge and Fruit Company in 1912 and built a town, which he named for himself, complete with watchtower and guard to chase off sponge poachers. The company went bankrupt on the eve of the first World War when Chase's assets were frozen in a London bank. He sold his holdings, which comprised almost all of Sugar-loaf, to R.C. Perky, a Florida real estate salesman who quickly changed the town's name from Chase to Perky and set out to subdivide and develop it. Perky's town was never built, but the man is responsible for the key's weirdest and most winsome construction.

The Bat Tower

The bat tower, shingled brown and elegant, is about thirty-five feet tall and is to be found down a dirt road just past the Sugar-loaf Lodge, to the right of the road that leads to the Sugarloaf Airport. People bounce down the road to view it, circle it warily in their cars, then look a little embarrassed because they've gone out of their way to see it. The bat tower, standing there quietly batless, suffers these visitations with dignity.

Dr. Charles Campbell, a former health officer for the city of San Antonio, Texas, wrote a book in the 1920's entitled *Bats, Mosquitoes and Dollars*. It was Campbell's belief that the bat was one of man's best friends, both because of its insatiable appetite for mosquitoes and its valuable excrement which made great fertilizer. The bat towers or "roosts" of cypress lath which he designed were condos for thousands of bats, and the chute in the center of each structure collected guano, making each bat tower "a little gold mine."

It had not been that many years since malaria and yellow fever were found to be transmitted by the mosquito and that those diseases could be eliminated by mosquito eradication. Dr. Campbell's theories were well-received. San Antonio, upon his urging, even passed an ordinance which made it illegal to hurt a bat. Sixteen bat towers were built according to his plans which he did not charge for, charging only for the bait which cost $175. This secret formula was said to be indispensable in attracting bats. Campbell never disclosed the formula, but it almost cer-tainly consisted primarily of batshit. One of the towers built in Texas was called the Asylum Bat Roost and was built on the grounds of the Southwestern Insane Asylum. Six of the towers were built in Italy and many were adorned with a crucifix.

The Perky Bat Tower as envisioned by Mr. Perky

Perky, frustrated in his attempts to develop his key into a huge resort—he had already built a gambling casino, restaurant, and cottages—because of a considerable mosquito problem, read *Bats, Mosquitoes and Dollars* and grew hopeful. He sent away for the plans and bait, built his bat tower and dedicated it at a party on March 15, 1929, to "good health in Perky, Florida." The box of bait did not arrive in time for the party, but when it eventually did it was opened, water sprinkled upon it, and it was installed in the recesses of the tower. It was noted by someone attending that event that "a smell like that ought to attract something," but sadly the bats never came. Never did a bat visit the bat tower. After a year, when it was believed that perhaps fresh bait was needed, Perky sent away for another box, but Campbell had died, and with him the formula for success. Perky shortly afterwards went bankrupt. His fishing camp burned and he himself passed on. Only the bat tower remains, still pristine and expectant.

The **Sugarloaf Lodge** at MM #17 is the only lodging of note between Sugarloaf and Key West. Its gas station has the most expensive gas in the Keys and the attendant appears fairly smug about this fact. The lodge has tennis courts, a 3,000-foot airstrip, a swimming pool, and a marina with fishing guides and boat charters available. It also has a pond in front of the glass-walled restaurant where a porpoise named Sugar has lived for almost seventeen years. A faded sign by the pond mentions two dolphins, Sugar and Dolly, but it is best not to ask about Dolly as she has not been numbered among the living for quite some while. Sugar is fed Spanish mackerel three times a day and performs a few tricks with cups and saucers and dimes. She also has an inntertube and a palm frond that she's *very* fond of. The restaurant serves huge cuts of roast beef as well as a variety of fish dishes, the entrées running between $12 and $18. The rooms are pleasant and spacious and all have a view of water. Rates run about $100 in winter and drop to $60 during the summer. Efficiencies are $10 more. Telephone: 745-3211.

During the season, December to May, **Fantasy Dan's** at the Sugarloaf Airport gives sight-seeing airplane rides. A 10-minute trip costs $10 while a half-hour trip takes you around Key West for $20. Telephone: 745-2217.

One of the last vestiges of the old road is on Sugarloaf. The new road is built on the former railroad bed, but before the hurricane of 1935, automobiles traveled a meandering westerly route along the Atlantic. The road is overgrown and quiet, good for bicycling and bird watching.

Take Sugarloaf Boulevard, directly across from the lodge and follow it through a subdivision until it dead-ends. To the left are the "nude canals," an abandoned development which has been taken over by three rather distinct groups of sunbathers. There appears to be a rather overweight, if not obese, heterosexual section, a more comely heterosexual section, and a homosexual section. The water in the canal is a divine robin's-egg blue and is dotted with rafts and inner tubes. Pickups and vans are parked on the barren, platted lots beside it. The road used to curve northward up to the famous old fishing camp **pirate's cove**, a rich man's retreat which was wiped out by a hurricane in 1945, continuing to a wooden bridge which paralleled the railroad bridge to Cudjoe. This road is unpassable now, a small bridge which once crossed Tarpon Channel having been destroyed.

If you choose to avoid the nude canal, (and who could blame you) but still want to explore, take the right fork off 939. This, however, will only lead you after three miles to the wooden remains of another missing wooden bridge and a rusted Ford Landau with a Go Gators sticker which has toppled grille-forward into the warm, quiet waters bringing to mind the words of one of Thomas McGuane's characters—"I didn't know what I was, not a Southerner certainly. A Floridian. Drugs, alligators, macadam, the sea, sticky sex, laughter and sudden death. . . ."

It is customary to say good-bye to the bat tower before resuming the plunge to Key West, for now the pace picks up, the land crouches flatter. **The Saddlebunch Keys** are low and pale, the mangrove, growing on just a few inches of mud above coral rock, stunted. This is the "heavy dew" of the Keys, not quite land and not quite water.

Big Coppitt is the suburb for the Navy air base on **Boca Chica Key.** Boca Chica used to be Key West's favorite beach and there were fishing camps and restaurants there in the 1930's. The military condemned the property during World War II, the Army building airstrips there, and the Navy later taking it over to train pilots. The Navy has gradually closed off much of the area over the years (there's still a bit of abandoned beach road you can walk at the end of State Road #941), and now the glum sight of old missile silos (the *new* missile silos are on Fleming Key), complete with buzzards brooding on top, is affordable only by boat. Our own American vultures congregate on Boca Chica bunkers. It is a sight that certainly can be missed, but it wouldn't hurt to remember it.

You will probably be driving faster now for here the land turns ugly. Everyone is driving faster. Even the cormorants, those worried birds, fly hurriedly across the flats, or, appearing more worried still, stand on pilings or wires, drying their sodden wings. **Shark Key** is a brand-new creation for the rich, with a gate and big new palms for the instant "look," but **Rockland Key** is industrial, little more than a borrow pit, the mangroves all gone, steam shovels moving the marl around, a concrete factory to come—Flagler would have been smitten.

STOCK ISLAND AND APPROACHES TO KEY WEST

Stock Island has always been a service island. Originally cattle were penned there to fulfill the dietary desires of those sick of fish in Key West. Today on Stock Island there is the dump —popularly called Mount Trashmore, looming over the almost always bankrupt, but well-groomed Key West Resort Golf Course. The Florida Keys Hospital is here and the Tennessee Williams Fine Arts Center, which puts on a variety of plays and musicals and brings classical music and jazz ensembles to town. Call 294-6232 for their schedule. Florida Keys Community College, beside the Fine Arts Center, offers some interesting short-term courses for the long-term visitor—plant and bird identification, crash courses in Spanish, and the like. If you continue along this road, Junior College Road, looping back towards Route 1, you will also find the **Key West Seaplane Service** which has several flights a day to Fort Jefferson in the Dry Tortugas (see pages 224–28). On the other side of Stock, to the south of Route 1, at Junction 941 are trailer parks (which even the police take pains to avoid after dark); most of the shrimp fleet; **Oceanside Marina** where some excellent charter boat captains can be found (the marinas on Stock had previously been best known for the "mother ships" of cocaine that found safe harbor there); and the infamous, recently closed dog track. (Many people in the Keys have adopted greyhounds, well aware that otherwise these intelligent, elegant dogs would end up in the Gulf Stream or the landfill after their last race. Greyhounds make great pets and come in every color but grey . . . and why should that pose a problem?) Stock Islanders enjoy their sunsets, as capable of staring in crazed fascination at the clouds as anybody, and are fond of their beer—the down and dirty bar at the **Cow Key Marina** being held in special esteem by many.

But you do not dally on Stock Island, now you move on. Behind you now is the big billboard that says Paradise Welcomes The U.S. Armed Forces. You hang onto the wheel as pickups with huge tires and bumper stickers—I Love My Cockatoo, Fly

Navy, Easy Does It—and small fierce Hondas rush past you. You plunge over the Cow Key Channel at MM #4 where a tumultuous division greets you.

To the left is South Roosevelt Boulevard or A1A, the road that goes past little "Houseboat Row," the airport, the beaches, and the condominiums. The condos are all familiarly banal, a new one at 1800 Atlantic being particular contemptuous of the passerby by taking a fascist command of the view.

To the right, and what most naturally sucks you down along it, is North Roosevelt Boulevard, the continuation of Route 1, and of course your heart will sink when you see the sprawl of Searstown, once a perfectly nice salt marsh, over which sea gulls soar, still puzzled, overhead. This is the strip of discount liquors, discount cars, discount pizzas, and Terminex Pest Control; this is the bawl of consumerism and doubtful services. Try to dismiss it from your mind. Kennedy Drive intersects the island shortly. To the right, by the Magic Carpet Miniature Golf Course with its elephantine conch shell hazard, the road goes to Sigsbee Park, which is Navy housing.

Another large shopping mall, Key Plaza, as well as the *really* enormous Marketplace, lie ahead. The longer you stay in Key West, the stranger and more unrealistic these big malls appear. Beyond the City Pier and the charter boats of Garrison Bight, merge into the left lane if you wish to drop straight down Truman and into the downtown. To the right Palm Avenue moves

The southernmost house, at the foot of Duval Street

around the Bight (bight meaning a bend, after all), skirting the
Navy yards off Trumbo Point to eventually turn into Eaton.
This is, perhaps, the quickest route to the Pier House and Mallory Square if you don't want to cruise Duval, but of course, you
must introduce yourself to Key West by cruising Duval. So take
Truman past Bayview Park and the tennis courts, past the big,
lemon-yellow B & F Cleaners which can shrink the unshrinka-
ble, past the Overseas Fruit Market, and the Margaret Truman
Launderette, and the old and inexpensive motels, the El Ran-
cho, Key Lime Village, and the Red Rooster to the big DOWN-
TOWN sign that means DUVAL.

Yet if you were to pass this temptation nonetheless, in the
interest of getting to the rock-bottom end of Florida, and continue one block more to Whitehead, two alternative conclusions
to your journey would still remain. A few blocks to the right is
the Monroe County Courthouse with its big kapok tree and its
sign End Of The Rainbow End Of The Route, a sign that could
be perceived as being somewhat ominous. Yet you would not
think you were at the end of anything here, even Route 1, for
Whitehead continues down to the Civil War Monument (a memorial to Union soldiers) and Mallory Square (named for a
native son who became the Confederate Secretary of the Navy)
and stops, ambivalently, there.

However, were you to travel to the other end of Whitehead,
you would be at the real foot of the street, the **Southernmost
Point,** which is marked by a large, odd buoy planted firmly in
cement. With the water beyond, you will now certainly feel
yourself to be at the end of something even though a painted
curb says America Begins Here.

KEY WEST

WALLACE STEVENS wrote *her mind had bound me round* —and he was speaking of Key West. This peculiar and unlikely town does have a mind quite of her own with attitudes and habits which can either charm or exasperate, seduce or dismay the new acquaintance. The traveler seldom wants to see what he sees, he wants to see something else. And in many respects, Key West, which is so singular in its architecture and attitude, its posturing and fancifulness, its zany eclecticisim, its seedy tropicality, is a town come upon unseen, unexpected, the something else almost felt. It is an urbane, isolated, freewheeling, lighthearted, gossipy, and eccentric town. There is a sense of adventure here, of excess and individuality. It's odd. Actually odd. It is rather a dirty town and has very little dignity, but it has style. Its architecture is a charming, intriguing mélange of fine houses and shacks, painted primly white or weathered right down to the silvery bone, a mix of gingerbread grandeur and mañana collapse with an abundance of verandas and porticos, columns and pilasters and balconies. Comparison and exception are everywhere. The town can look somewhat like old New England, but with a decidedly un-puritanical cast. Jonathan Edwards would never have slept here. The Navy is a presence, certainly, owning a good quarter of the town as well as two thirds of the waterfront and all of Boca Chica, but it is not a highly visible one from land. From the air and water the extent of its holdings is clearly seen—the piers and berths, the housing, the ammunition dumps, the runways, the radar towers. In the early 1980's when the military was, to a considerable extent, pulling out of Key West, the former mayor water-skied to Cuba in an attempt to get the Navy to stay in full force by demonstrating how close that island was to our shores. The mayor water-skied to Cuba. It took him six hours and ten minutes. Key West, being Key West, didn't even think it a particularly strange thing to do.

Homosexuals, who probably command another quarter of the town in terms of real estate and influence, are more visible, providing a sleek and somewhat mordant glaze to the town. Tennessee Williams came to Key West in the 1940's, attracted by the sailors who all seemed "to be walking to the tune of Managua, Nicaragua," and was influential in introducing the town to artistic gays. Now, many of the shops, guest houses, and dance halls are owned by gays, and much of the town's restoration is attributable to them.

Key West is tolerant, very tolerant. What passes for the society column in the local paper, the *Citizen,* abounds in news of gay couples and events, and a wooden pier that elbowed out into the Atlantic and was a popular lounging spot for years before it collapsed (now recrudescent) was known breezily as "Dick Dock." Gays provide much of the gloss, sophistication, and outrageousness of Key West, as well as the money which keeps the town bubbling along.

Key West is certainly tolerant and tropical. Island. Cuban. Black. In the morning one hears roosters crowing, although the sense is not particularly bucolic. Some are fighting cocks bred for the gambling pit. The birds pecking in dusty runs beneath towering breadfruit trees are a good example of the decadence and innocence that is Key West. As is the sight of a charred and blackened lot where once a fine old building stood—a lot that might remain charred and empty for years, accepting with the seasons, the bougainvillea petals that fall upon the smashed bottles there.

One knows where Key West lies in a geographic sense. Forty-five miles north of the Tropic of Cancer. Closer to Cuba at 90 miles than it is to Miami at almost 150. Due south of Cleveland, Ohio. (Cleveland, Ohio!) A glittering, balmy, perhaps not terribly legitimate rock beneath vast sea skies. Key West's economy over the years has been based on a curious and volatile array of occupations—wrecking, shrimping, fishing, and smuggling. In the 1970's, certainly most of the money that came into Key West was drug money, but things have quieted down somewhat in that regard. Now the money comes from real estate. And things are changing fast.

Key West is now a tourist town, one million people visit it

each year, but it is still a town of contrast and contradiction, threat and carelessness and charm. The bars should be sampled, of course, and the reef investigated. The gold should be seen and the forts and the galleries. One should dance or stand on one of the balconies that line Duval and watch the prowl of the street. The beaches should be duly attended and a tan obtained. The yellowtail stuffed with crabmeat should be eaten, and conch fritters and, since you must, Key lime pie. Café con leche or the intense little energizing espresso must be bought from the window of a Cuban grocery. The flowers and trees should be puzzled over and appreciated, and their lovely names said aloud. Jacaranda. Bougainvillea. Poinciana. Frangipani. One should catch a fish. Or if one likes to see the fish others have caught, one should go to Garrison Bight at the end of the afternoon when the party boats come in. One should be in the water, and travel over and on the water as much as possible. And, when one is on land, one must assuredly walk. Stroll, linger, wander. For Key West is a walking town, and a bicycling one too. Architectural surprises are around every corner, and other interesting sights less classifiable.

THE STREETS

In Key West, "downtown" isn't in the middle of town at all, but up on the northwest corner of the island, on the harbor. All the keys veer west as they run south, and the streets of Key West, although straight, are laid out on an angle—just about on a diagonal to main compass points. The corners of intersections becoming, in fact, compass points.

Whitehead and White are the parallel boundaries of Old Town. Whitehead is where Hemingway's hoary ghost hovers in the house where he often experienced "the black lonelies." Then there is Duval, followed by Simonton, a big street which once could have been counted on to hold the post office, but no more, the new post office, landmark, and comfort to the postcard laden, being built on Whitehead. The next streets, Elizabeth, William, Margaret, Grinnel, Francis, and White, can easily be recalled if you put them in the order of three friends—nice old souls who rock and converse with each other across the porches of their white, Conch houses—Elizabeth William, Margaret Grinnel, and Francis White. Actually, Francis has a middle name, Ashe, and a lovely street it is, to have as a middle name.

Basically, now, you have memorized the streets paralleling Duval. Walking the other way, up Duval from the Pier House to the Atlantic, remembering the streets will be a bit more vexing. You begin at Front, nicely enough. Then there is Greene, a street named after Pardon Greene, an early settler who left his wife and children back in Connecticut rather than subject them to the rigors of the tropics, but this will probably be of little help to you in remembering that Greene is between Front and Caroline. Caroline used to be marked by the Caroline Lowe house on the corner which, unfortunately, is no longer there. Two sequential letters of the alphabet follow next, E and F. Eaton and Fleming. Eaton has the Episcopal Church right on the corner, and Fleming has Fast Buck Freddie's on the corner. Up Fleming a bit and on the left is Fausto's Famous Food Palace, the town's premier grocery store. Fleming is easy, the only thing you have to remember about it is that it's one way. Southard, marked by the large clock, is the next street and that is one way in the other direction, terminating at the entrance to Fort Taylor. Following Southard are Angela, then Petronia and Olivia (again alternating one way streets) and Truman. Think SAPOT. It might be best to pause here, for there is a confusing bevy of young ladies' names ahead: Julia, Virginia, Amelia, Catherine, and Louisa. In the mind of the newcomer, they seem simply United. Which is the next street, just before the last long one, South, which runs down, appropriately enough, to the Southernmost Point. (Numbers run upward from the harbor to the Atlantic and from the Navy Base and Fort Taylor northeastward across town.)

CHANGES AND CONFUSIONS

The land of Key West behaves most peculiarly. It cannot quite be counted upon to be *terra firma,* for its firma keeps getting changed, rearranged, created, confiscated. What used to be on the water doesn't even have a view of it any more. What used to be water is now land, or concrete. What used to be separated by water is now joined firmly to land, like Fort Taylor which had, in fact, almost disappeared *beneath* the land. Pine trees had grown on top of it, and the martial mausoleum had to be excavated, appearing bit by bit.

Weather moved things around a lot. After the hurricane of 1846, the graveyard was moved inland. So was the lighthouse, now one of the most landlocked in America. The military moved things around a great deal, reshaping, building, and abandoning, and playing a big role in changing the shape, direction and accessibility of Key West. On the eve of the Civil War, the Army cut a road through the wild part of the island so that troops could be marched directly from the barracks on one end to the fort on the other, this road being first called Rocky Road, then Division, most recently Truman.

During World War II, the Navy created additional land and islands for munition dumps and housing, including Sigsbee Park, Fleming Key, and Tank and Christmas Islands. For years, the reason one couldn't get to Fort Taylor, a state park and a National Historic Landmark since 1973, was because of Naval security for the Caribbean Command enveloping the land around it.

One half of the land area of Key West didn't exist 150 years ago when William Whitehead, brother of one of the four original owners of the island first surveyed the town. He laid out lots in tiny 46 × 90-foot pieces and the houses, built mostly by ships' carpenters, were constructed without any particular regard for their relationship to one another, and alleys and paths angled off the main streets and entered the lots at irregular intervals. Whitehead platted everything, including the bottom of a two-acre pond which existed in what was then the middle of the city. The pond was nameless, though described as a "miserable, stagnant lagoon" and was filled in by the rearranging hurricane of 1846. Land in Key West has blown in, blown away, and simply, or not so simply, been made.

Henry Flagler created 134 acres of land on what is called Trumbo Point, Trumbo being the name of the Overseas Railroad project's head engineer. After the bridges of Long, the Seven-Mile and Bahia Honda, the construction of the railroad approached Key West with no available dry land for the depot. When Flagler was informed of this oversight, he said, "Then make some."

All this is partly why Key West, a busy speck in an abyss of sky and distances, seems so confusing.

But the town is small. If you're invited for dinner and you become hopelessly lost, you'll still only arrive fifteen minutes late. That is, unless your hosts have moved their house. For that is another problem. Key West moves things. The Bahama houses were moved, plank by plank, all the way from Green Turtle Cay in the Bahamas. The enterprising David Wolkowsky lifted the nineteenth-century Porter steamship office off its foundations on the old Key West to Havana ferry dock and moved it three hundred feet out into the water, building first a restaurant and then the entire Pier House complex around it. The gun turret from the *Maine* was moved, all the way from Havana Harbor to an elementary school on Southard, only to be moved once more to grace the new post office on Whitehead. The Conch home that now houses the restaurant Bagatelle on Duval was moved from its site on Fleming when the library expanded—the library, the first in south Florida, having moved from its birthplace farther up on Duval where the Red Barn Theater is today. The Oldest House was moved. And E. H. Gato was a big mover. He built a mansion on Truman in an area which is now Bayview Park, then moved it to Virginia Street on rollers. The trip took two weeks and employed one mule and a windlass. His son, E. H. Gato Jr., built a rambling Victorian house at the end of Duval where it intersects with South Street, but found that he didn't like the way the sun struck one of his favorite porches, so he turned the enormous structure around on his yard.

The only place that seems determined to remain exactly on

the spot where it began is St. Paul's Episcopal Church at 401
Duval Street. Built here in 1838, it was blown down in the 1846
hurricane. Promptly rebuilt, it burned in the great fire of 1886,
a fire which destroyed two thirds of the town. Promptly rebuilt
again, it was toppled by the hurricane of 1909. It took the parish-
ioners a little longer to get organized this time and they did not
begin rebuilding until 1914. The white concrete structure you
see today has stayed put now for over sixty-five years. When you
find the right rock, you stay on it.

MYSTERY AND HISTORY

There is a mystery about Key West, and it is not just behind the
name the Spanish gave it in the 1500's—*Cayo Hueso*—Island of
Bones. It's true the bones are a puzzle. For whose were the
bones, and why were they here? No one knows if the island was
actually littered with bones. If it was, they probably belonged
to the Caloosa Indians who used the place either as a burial
ground or were massacred here by some other tribe, possibly the
Seminoles, although how that somewhat placid group were able
to extirpate the ferocious Caloosas has never been explained. In
the 1700's, the English felicitously altered the sound of Hueso
to the name of West. But the murky etymology of the name is
not the mystery. The mystery is in Key West's very self. Why
does it look the way it does? And why is it still here? In 1934,
the state suggested that the city, which was bankrupt, be abandoned and that the people be relocated to the mainland. It has
endured hurricane, fire, and neglect. It is the oldest city in south
Florida, an area known to suffer greatly from the heavy, obliter-
ative hand of speculation, development, and redevelopment,
and yet the old part of town, the town platted out by William
Whitehead in 1829 and built throughout the nineteenth century, remains startlingly, strikingly intact.

In 1822, the year that the island of Key West was sold by a
Spaniard, Juan Salas, to a Mobile businessman, John Simonton,
for $2000, the only beings that frequented the place were mos-
quitoes and pirates—pirates at the time being a bigger problem

in the area than malaria, heat, and lack of fresh water. In the
same year, Lieutenant Matthew Perry sailed down to raise the
American flag over the country's new possession and confirm
that it had one of the largest, finest, deep-water anchorages in
the country. The flag was raised in the vicinity of what is now
Mallory Square, the event attended by a few sweating sailors
and some black and Cuban fishermen. Several months after the
raising of the flag, the energetic Naval Commodore David Porter arrived with the ships of his West India Squadron to set up
headquarters in Key West and suppress the pirates who had
been scooting around the Caribbean and the Gulf in their
shallow-draft boats for years, murdering, plundering, and engaging in their sleazy piratical rites. Porter's depredations
caused the town more grief than those of the pirates, for he
considered Key West a military post and appropriated the settlers' livestock, buildings, and supplies. He wanted to lay out
the streets in a starlike pattern radiating from central plazas
which could be controlled by artillery in the event of civil un-
rest. He even tried to change the name of Key West (as had
Perry who wanted to call it Thompson's Island after the then
Secretary of the Navy) constantly referring to it as Allentown.

After establishing himself here, however, Porter found that
his ships, which were mostly deep-draft frigates, could not pursue the pirates over the reefs and into the winding mangrove
creeks where they hid, so he acquired several small light-draft
schooners and built five flat-bottomed 20-oared barges which he
called the *Mosquito, Gallinipper, Midge, Gnat,* and *Sandfly.* He
also acquired a steam ferry boat that had been retired from the
New York–Hoboken service named the *Seagull.* With the ferry
towing the agile bug squadron up and down the Keys, Porter
was soon successful in the pursuit and extermination of pirates.
He had driven them from the Keys by 1830 and continued to
pursue them to Cuba and Puerto Rico. Court-martialed by
America after Spain protested his intrusion into Spanish territory—Spain being in the habit of protecting pirates as long as
Spanish ships were allowed safe passage—Commodore Porter
indignantly resigned, joining first the Mexican Navy, then the
Turkish one. Porter never cared for Key West and urged the
government not to establish a permanent station here. After

the pirates were eliminated and he was court-martialed, the West India-Anti-Pirate Squadron was transferred to Pensacola.

With the pirates gone, the only fears the captain of a vessel had were hurricanes and running aground on the reefs, a likelihood that Key West profited from, for they made the salvaging of wrecked ships a regulated industry. Between 1832, the year John James Audubon dropped by, and 1855, the population of the island had risen from 500 to 2700, most of them New Englanders or English Bahamians, almost all involved in wrecking. Millions of dollars worth of salvage cases involving ships wrecked on the reefs were being adjudicated in Key West courts by the city's own Judge William Marvin who literally wrote the book on salvage laws, *A Treatise Upon the Law of Wreck and Salvage,* the standard authority in the admiralty courts of both England and the United States. (The judge's other work was on the internal evidences of the authenticity of the Four Gospels.) It was an educated and colorful group on this tiny island far from mainland America, this place that the poet Richard Eberhart calls "umbilically extravagant." The men wore silk top hats, the ladies served suppers on fine china, on occasion, gold plates. All the wealth was wrecking wealth. Indeed, much of the exotic furnishings that filled the houses, and the formal clothes the people wore, came directly from the foundered ships.

Ava Parks, in her book *The Forgotten Frontier,* wrote about the Key West of the time:

> There was nothing else like it; a city crowded on a small island in the middle of nowhere . . . this was it—civilization began and ended here.

By the end of the 1850's, however, the first of the reef lighthouses (pgs. 77–79) was being constructed, bringing the beginning of the end to the profitability of wrecking, and in 1859 the look of the town was changed when the first of Key West's two great fires occurred.

There was no fire-fighting equipment in town. There had been a small, hand-pump engine, used mostly for parades, which, failing to be effective against a small fire in 1843, was carried to the wharf by irate citizens and thrown into the water. The fire of 1859 began in a warehouse on Front Street and Duval and gutted two square blocks before it was stopped when a man named Henry Mulrennon got a keg of gunpowder from Fort Taylor and blew up his own house on Greene Street. The town was rebuilt quickly and many people felt that the fire had been a benefit rather than a liability because the new structures were more "elegant." Key West's newspaper of the day, *The Key of The Gulf,* said the new buildings were "not only an ornamental embellishment but gave an air of permanency and durability to the town."

Wealth no longer came from wrecking but from a new discovery, sponging. Cubans were also emigrating in great numbers from their country's ten year war with Spain, and cigar manufacturers were establishing large factories here and employing thousands of men. The town was a great mélange and somewhat baffling to casual visitors, one of whom wrote in the 1880's:

> It is densely settled, and about as un-American as possible, bearing a strong resemblance to a West Indian town. The houses are of wood, plainly built, and, with few exceptions painted white. The houses are of all sizes, jumbled up in the oddest way ... The interior of each block is filled up with one-story shanties ...

On April 1, 1886, the second and great fire engulfed Key West. It started in the Cuban patriotic club and school, the San Carlos, on Duval Street. (The building of today is the third San Carlos to be built on that site.) The town's single fire engine was in New York for repairs (it's *still* hard to find a good mechanic in Key West) and the fire quickly spread, burning the same area as before along the waterfront as well as turning inland, destroying Fleming Street from Whitehead to Bahama. Once more, an attempt was made to stop the fire by blowing up houses with kegs of gunpowder from the fort, but this time the blaze raged on and the three sailors who lit the fuse were "blown to atoms." The fire burned for twelve hours, consuming fifty acres of the town. Again, Key West was rebuilt quickly, carpenters working day and night, building homes on the outskirts but bringing them into the burned out areas once they were cleared. The peculiar thing, of course, is that after both fires, the town was rebuilt in wood, with the wealthier citizens building even grander homes than they had occupied before. There were some commercial, military or public buildings made of stone and well-laid brick and a few homes made of cast or "rusticated" stone, a concrete block formed in a mold—a fad of the mainland which came quickly in and out of fashion. (Several of these houses, large and side by side, can be found on South Street, near the Southernmost Point.) But Key West was a wooden town and when the town abruptly stopped growing early in the twentieth century, wooden it remained. Silence entered the picture—a deep and sleepy silence. Nothing happened. The Florida land boom boomed, but was unheard in Key West. The railroad came and the railroad went and Key West slumbered behind its vines and flowers. The trees grew and blew in the heat-thickened wind, and termites sculpted their own interior columns and castles out of porches undisturbed.

COLLAPSE AND RESURRECTION, COLLAPSE AND RESTORATION

From being the richest city per capita in America in the 1880's, Key West by the 1930's had become the poorest. The sponge industry had declined; the cigar makers had moved to Tampa; the railroad and shipping trade with Havana had diminished; and the Navy and the Coast Guard had pulled out. Henry Flagler's train chugged across the waters "carrying nothing, nowhere, for nobody." Things were so bad that the city's Economic League recommended that only bread baked in Key West be allowed to be sold here and only local orchestras be allowed to play.

On July 5, 1934, with no economic base other than fish, five million dollars in debt, and with 80 percent of its 12,000 citizens on welfare, Key West relinquished all its powers of government to the state. The governor, David Sholtz, was aghast. He immediately turned the problem over to the New Deal's Federal Relief Administrator in Florida, Julius Stone. Stone arrived in

Key West and saw the abandoned cigar factories and Navy barracks, the collapsed piers and dilapidated houses. He saw the privys, the cisterns, and the trash, and learned that most of the people were living on fish and coconuts. He also learned that Key West was the only city in America never to have frost. He decided that the only way to save her was to turn her into a resort town, a "Bermuda" as it were. Key West's salvation was to be The Tourist.

Stone was a debonair fellow and a flashy administrator, using FERA funds to subsidize air service and to underwrite the rehabilitation of houses and the reopening of hotels. He organized the Volunteer Work Force to spruce up the town and in six months, four thousand people had donated a million and a half hours, planting trees, building a thousand park benches, painting murals, and shoring up houses. The beaches were cleaned of seaweed and a "smart cabana colony made available." A Maids' Training School was established, with the few remaining grande dames of Key West tutoring young girls in the cleaning and serving arts. There was also a school for fishing guides. Out of work musicians were recruited into the Hospitality Band which met every arriving ship and train. The submarine base, abandoned by the Navy, was turned into a private yacht basin. (A nice and nasty description of the yachty set is in Hemingway's novel *To Have and Have Not.*)

Key West needed a lot of cleaning up. There was trash everywhere, tons of trash. There is always someone who likes to figure out the quantity of one thing in terms of the quantity of another, and trash is no exception. A writer of the time drew this picture:

> Or, if someone had constructed small bungalows, say, 42 feet × 20 with a 9 foot ceiling, the garbage and trash would have filled 176 such bungalows. Figuring eight lots to each side of a city block, such procedure would have necessitated five solid city blocks of bungalows!

There was a lot of trash and it was hauled off and put somewhere, if not in five blocks of newly built bungalows.

Classes in handicrafts were organized and people set to work making hats, pocketbooks, and belts out of coconut fronds, and ash trays and buttons out of shells. A guidebook was published touting the attractions which included the Southernmost House, the Martello Towers, and the Turtle Kraals, as well as "Raul Vasquez's tame fish." The fish were in a pond at the rear of his night club on Roosevelt, and one could stroke them as one "would a cat." Also mentioned was the home of a retired school-teacher, Miss Dunn:

> The house, with Miss Dunn still residing within, stands as a monument to the appreciation of her students.

(Actually, Miss Dunn's house at 420 Simonton Street, may be the oldest house in Key West. If it was built around 1823, as is suspected, it would be older than the "Oldest House" on Duval.)

Fifty-three attractions were mentioned, many of them, including various tropical parks and the magnificent Convent of Mary Immaculate, are now gone. There were also listings of fishing guides, churches, and mixed drinks.

Julius Stone even specified how long a visitor should be prepared to stay:

> To appreciate Key West with its indigenous architecture, its lanes and byways, its friendly people and general picturesque-ness, the visitor must spend at least a few days in the city; a cursory tour of an hour or two serves no good purpose. Unless a visitor is prepared to spend at least three full days here, the Key West Administration would rather he did not come.

Stone's experiment in massive volunteerisim, which turned a bankrupt and shabby city into a vacation mecca, was wildly successful. Tourists poured in and the demand for accommodations was so great that residents moved out of their houses and lived elsewhere in order that winter visitors might have the more desirable locations, a practice, certainly, that exists today. But only six months after the best tourist season Key West had ever had, the Labor Day hurricane of 1935 hit the Middle Keys and blew the railroad away. And tourism was forgotten for many years.

As for Julius Stone, the man who introduced Bermuda shorts to the Keys (Conchs maintained it was his underwear), in 1940 he returned to live in the city he had saved, involving himself in investment, banking, and law. In the next twenty years, as leading citizen, he had managed to represent and bilk just about everyone in town. In 1960, the master of the shady deal fled, practically as a fugitive, settling first in Cuba, later in Jamaica, and dying in 1967 in Australia.

It took World War II to bring people and prosperity back. In those randy war years, Key West became known as the "Singapore of the West." The Navy swept up the town in a dizzying, flustering embrace, but after the war abandoned her once again, and Key West looked more dilapidated than ever. It had entered its own time zone once again—the old houses in Old Town jostling together in eccentric neglect, the roots of banyans erupting through sidewalks, the docks rotting, the streets deserted and silent.

In the late 1950's, things began to change. Action arrived in the guise of destruction. Demolition began to follow dereliction. Fine old buildings were razed and an unseemly demand for vacant lots for parking arose. The handsome Jefferson Hotel on Duval Street with its cupolas and wide verandas, built in 1886, burned and was demolished in 1958 to create the drive-up window facilities for the Southeast Bank.

In 1958, the Geiger House on the corner of Greene and Whitehead was slated to be demolished so a gas station could be put there. It was this possibility of loss, more than any other, that finally roused Key West. Jessie Porter Newton, a fifth generation Conch, invited some wealthy and influential people into her garden, and the Old Island Restoration Foundation was formed. Their first act was to purchase (with the help of millionaire Mitchell Wolfson) the Geiger House and restore and transform it into the Audubon House. Miss Jessie was instrumental in saving and moving dozens of houses but even her energy and the increasing effectiveness of the OIRF as a lobbying and preservationist group could not prevent fire and bulldozers from leveling some of Key West's most beautiful structures. The huge Curry and Sons Ship's Chandlery, a twin-towered landmark for

more than sevent-five years, taking up an entire block on Simonton and Front Streets, burned in 1963 and the beautiful
Convent of Mary Immaculate on Truman Avenue was destroyed despite wails of protest in 1966. The convent is probably
the most-mourned lost building in Key West, and Conchs, many
of whom were educated here, still speak of its demolition with
bitterness. It was made of coral rock and took years to build,
first completed in 1886, then enlarged to twice its size in 1906.
It was a rounded, graceful, airy structure surrounded by rose
gardens and palms. The wounded from the battleship *Maine*
were brought here and it served as a Navy hospital throughout
the Spanish-American War before being turned back into a
school. There was a large museum inside the convent, filled
with relics of the *Maine* and a number of oddities including a
little wooden chest covered with seashells that Dr. Samuel
Mudd had made when he was imprisoned in Fort Jefferson on
the Dry Tortugas. It seemed that no one wanted the convent
torn down except the Catholic Bishop of Miami who was determined to put up more modern concrete-block classrooms. Many
fragments of the convent—fanlights, gingerbread trim, shutters—can be found in various homes in Key West today, and
over the convent grounds, beside St. Mary Star of the Sea
Church, the after-image of the lovely structure seems to hover
in the empty air.

Each year, during February and March, the OIRF sponsors
house and garden tours as part of "Old Island Days" celebra-
tions. The houses are shown in groups of five or six and there
are three separate tour dates. Tickets cost $10. There have been
four categories of houses established—Old Historic, Uniquely
Located, Famous Occupants, and Island Living. This covers a lot
of territory so don't expect to see merely "classic" homes—the
selections have a fine Key West eccentricity. The OIRF-
sponsored **Hospitality House** (294–9501) in Mallory Square can
give you current brochures and information on the house and
garden tours and other seasonal events. The Hospitality House
is the former ticket office for the Mallory Steamship Company
which used to ferry passengers to Cuba.

TOURIST TOWN

Mallory Square is difficult, perhaps impossible, to experience with style. It certainly is no place to pretend you're not a tourist. Hundreds of gallons of ice cream and piña coladas are consumed here daily and the streets are jammed with curio shops and bad

---

SPONGES

A sponge is a living marine animal of uniform structure, though varying greatly in appearance, that grows in a plant-like fashion and is remarkable for its power of absorbing water. Keys' spongers would go out in skiffs, spot the creatures in the shallows through a glass-bottom bucket, pull them up with a long-handled three-pronged hook, then beat the bejesus out of them with a paddle. A phosphorous-smelling liquid called "gurry" would ooze out of them until it didn't, then the sponges (now the skeletons of the animal) were rinsed and trimmed.

A lady named Violet Turner recalled her daddy, sponging: "To identify these horrible looking black creatures isn't that simple," Violet noted. "They are sleeping in the beds at the bottom of the sea. An amateur would assume they were merely seaweed. It is so fascinating to see how the spongers would lower their long poles with a hook on the end to the bottom of the bed and extract the creature with many eyes. After the dinghy is filled, the men head back to the mama boat to kill their catch. They are alive and must die to become useful and beautiful."

Sponging and cigar-making were Key West's primary industries in the last half of the nineteenth century. The city provided 90 percent of all the sponges sold in the United States. There was a great demand for sponges. Everyone used them. There were hundreds of boats employing thousands of men harvesting millions of sponges for a great deal of money. When Greek divers came down from Tarpon Springs to work deeper waters in their suits and helmets in the early 1900's, walking over sponge beds in their heavy boots, the locals blamed them for the fact that there were fewer and fewer sponges to be had. There were battles between the two groups, boat-burning and hose-slashing and the like. In 1953 a movie was made, *Beneath the Twelve Mile Reef.* Robert Wagner and Gilbert Roland were two of the Greeks. Terry Moore and Richard Boone were two of the Conchs. Robert Wagner and, of course, Terry Moore fell in love, an event which did not increase the number of little sponges one whit.

The Greeks eventually returned to Tarpon Springs, but the sponge supply remained depleted and in the 1930's a blight (some said caused by the dredging involved in the construction of Flagler's Railroad) and the introduction of artificial sponges virtually wiped out sponging as an industry.

Some of the last to buy them in any quantity were the Japanese. A sponger said in 1935 that he suspected there was going to be a war soon because of all the activity on the Elizabeth Street dock.

"The price sponges bring in Key West right now is fantastic. . . . They surely must be planning a war before too long. That's always when we get our best prices, when a war is being planned. Especially sheepswool and glove sponge. They use a lot of those in hospitals. In a hospital they are used only for cleaning wounds, no lint to shed! They are much more sanitary and more absorbent than any other material. On the battlefield they are used for sponging and cleaning weapons. Nothing can stand that rough treatment as well as sponges. There are so many foreigners in Key West buying sponges . . . gotta be a war coming."

Today, an occasional tourist buys an occasional sponge, probably one of three species—*the sheepswool* for bathing, *the yellow* for washing up the car, *the grass* for decoration. A sheepskin sponge about the size of a grapefruit costs $13.

restaurants. There is also a seemingly inexhaustible supply of young and smiling time-share panhandlers for **The Galleon,** a huge Miami mirage that's not going to go away, at the end of Front Street. (Its pilings are the cleanest in town, for they're crayola-shaped to keep the pelicans away.) At the newly *re-* refurbished Mallory Square Dock, enormous white cruise ships —the *Bermuda Star,* the *Galileo,* the *Vera Cruz,* and the

Boheme— take turns in waiting out the day. They loom above the town, making everything appear Lilliputian, including the already toylike Conch Train.

The square is named for Stephen Mallory, a prominent Key West citizen who in 1861 was appointed Secretary of the Confederate Navy, a job it is true, grander in illusion than in fact. The little Civil War monument is dedicated in turn to the Union. In Key West, the soldiers who died during the war died from yellow fever. There are some dignified old buildings here which seem to stand back a bit, bemused at all the bustle. The large brick **Customs House** was built in 1891 and served as the federal courthouse during the Keys' wrecking years. It will probably be restored as a yacht club. The buff-plastered brick building beside it was built even earlier, in 1856, and was originally used to store coal. It is the sole surviving building from the earliest naval base in Key West. It is referred to as **Coast Guard Headquarters** for its last tenants but the building also served as headquarters for the Lighthouse District when that now defunct organization administered the reef system of man-tended lights. The niche above the arch on the buttressed pier facade is filled with the bas-relief decoration of a lighthouse. Another impressive structure here, built in the same year as the Customs House, and of the same seemingly untropical brick, is the **First National Bank Building.** Built by Cuban cigar manufacturers, the decorative yellow design on red and the ornate balcony is in the style of Havana architecture.

Trinket traps fill the Mallory Market area and there are also a number of dummies standing about, not dolts, but rather statues of old sea captains and bearded fishermen holding aloft sponges or shells. Sponges abound, big drab heaps of sponges. The big ones are splendid to plant ferns in.

Shopping, Warships, Time, the Conch Republic, and the Conch Train

Key West has become the T-shirt capital of the world; it is believed to have some forty-five T-shirt shops. You can buy other things here, of course. Shopping swings between low tack and high fashion. Pritam Singh, the owner of the **Truman Annex,** has plans for a number of classy shops on his grounds, and the old Coca-Cola bottling plant on Simonton and Front streets has been transformed into the **Bottling Court**—more fancy shops. The new word is "upscale." Upscale, upscale, upscale. We'll probably come to miss those tatty T-shirt shops. In the Mallory Square-Front Street area take a listen of the simple and melodious brass wind chimes at the **Shell Warehouse**, a rugged building of coral rock, part of what was once Tift's Ice House, the oldest commercial building in Key West. **Shades** at 306 Front is definitely the place for sunglasses with a hundred different styles and colors available, whereas **Sweet Mischief** (335 Duval) is where to go for the niftiest bikini. **The Cigar Factory** in Pirate's Alley is a microscopic touristic representation of a Key West industry that in 1890 employed more than six thousand workers and produced a hundred million hand-rolled cigars yearly. Two men now roll Honduran tobacco in the dim light. A box of "El Presidente" will set you back $50, but you can have "El Hemingway" for less. Just beyond the Pier House on Front is the **Pier House Market** which has a sophisticated offering of cheeses, coffees, and wines and has a deli with sandwiches to go. **Key West Hand Prints** at 201 Simonton is a silk-screening institution. The colors are mixed up in old Navy soup kettles. If you enjoy watching paint dry, you'll like seeing the printers working behind glass at 60-yard long tables. There are a few chairs around in which exhausted men sit while their wives and granddaughters browse through the delicately colored skirts and sundresses. Lots of tea towel specials here. (A place for bolder hand-painted fabrics is **The Sign of Sandford** at 328 Simonton Street. Sandford designs fabrics for the decorating trade but everything in the window is for sale, including the bright and witty hand-painted canvas beach chairs.) **Key West Aloe** at 524 Front is also a Key West institution, even though the aloe, that soothing succulent, is imported from Haiti. The sights and smells in here are a bit overwhelming—so many perfumes vying for dominance—so much "White Ginger," "Black Coral," "Frangipani," and "Sexy Afternoon"—so many immaculately complexioned girls with long bright nails sweeping about in white lab coats. When one regains the street once more, the homely smells of seaweed, engine oil, and frying fish seem refreshing. There's a tiny public beach and boat ramp squeezed between the **Pier House** holdings and the high-Bermuda design of the new **Hyatt** at the end of Simonton. There used to be nothing down here but gasoline storage tanks and the old and decidedly midscale **A&B Lobster House.** (No one's known to have gone to the A&B for years, but it determinedly anchors down this end of the island, just as the dim and dowdy **Logun's** anchors down the other end.) Things have changed, it's clear. The **Galleon** now takes up a lot of space, its dockage fees perhaps the highest in all Florida. Even sunning has become more expensive. Some locals and long-term visitors buy a Beach Club membership card at the Pier House. The club has a $350 initiation charge and yearly dues of $125 and the card enables you to enjoy the beach and pool and to charge drinks and food. You are also given a nice fluffy beach towel daily, towels in Paradise not being cheap.

While lounging about the Pier House, it is likely that you will see one of the town's more intimidating sights—a Navy hydrofoil. Several of these warships are stationed at Trumbo Point

A Navy hydrofoil

and they prowl back and forth, to and from maneuvers in the Gulf where they make their acrobatic turns and reversals and barrel about at classified speeds. Hydrofoils are agile and fast war vessels, each equipped with eight computerized surface-to-surface missiles and an assortment of rapid-fire machine guns. Because, thankfully, they have nothing to shoot these weapons at, they cruise the waters off Key West and intercept drug boats, making the town no longer the primo port of call for drug smugglers that it once was. As a psychological weapon against a coke-laden cigarette boat, a hydrofoil is without peer. When the foils of these "flying ships" are deployed, they generate lift that raises the ship a few feet above the surface of the water, allowing it to move unhampered by the waves. A Navy commander said, "The Navy built this ship and now they're trying to find jobs it can do." So the hydrofoils roam the waters. And when, in their stately, sinister fashion, they pass by in the channel, they are arresting enough to cause people to stop sipping on their strawberry daiquiris for a time. People pause, they are silent, they look. They then return to their shockingly red drinks, perhaps resuming their discussion concerning the pretty glass. The strawberry daiquiri at the Pier House comes in a pretty glass only on the upper decks. Around the pool and on the decks adjacent to the beach, the strawberry daiquiri comes in a plastic glass. Which diminishes its enjoyment, somewhat.

At 512 Greene Street, a little behind Sloppy Joe's on Duval, is the abandoned, brick **Old City Hall**. (The new City Hall where the stormy City Commission meetings take place every Tuesday night is at 525 Angela Street.) Built just at the turn of the century, it replaced a wooden City Hall that had burned in the fire of 1886. Only ten years before, that structure had been dedicated at the centennial Fourth of July celebration for which W. C. Maloney, a prominent citizen of the town, had prepared a speech. The speech, entitled "A Sketch of the History of Key West," which he later published, would have been three hours long. Midway in his presentation, however, a bar caught fire from one of the celebratory rockets that were being shot off and Maloney's audience ran off to see the blaze, never to return.

The Old City Hall has four large clock faces in its tower. Few people glance at them, though, thoughts of time being eschewed here.

The Conch Republic

The Conch Republic was born on April 20, 1982, in reaction to roadblocks set up by the border patrol near Florida City. The federal government maintained they were screening for drugs and illegal aliens, and everyone leaving the Keys was stopped and questioned. After insult came annoyance at the long delays, then protests in the form of lawsuits and letters to the governor. Then came inspiration, the idea of secession, followed immediately by plans for a party. On April 23, at high noon in Mallory Square, there were secession ceremonies. A Key West flag was invented and raised; the establishment of a new republic was marked with speeches; a loaf of stale Cuban bread was tossed in the air as a token shot declaring war against the United States, and then the Conch Republic quickly surrendered in order to be eligible for foreign aid from the state of Florida. There were T-shirts of course, and flags and border passes and passports. And there was a party which lasted a week. "Conch Republic Days" have now become an annual event each April with parades, dances, powerboat races, and a very peculiar *bed* race in which teams of five people decorate beds which must consist of four wheels, a mattress, and themselves, and race down Duval Street with four team members pushing the bed and one riding on it. Prizes, of course, are awarded to the winner, as well as for the most creative bed.

The Conch Train

The Conch Train is a pretty curious number. Imagine a little amusement park train with open cars and a fringed top, pulled by a Jeep camouflaged to look like a locomotive, rattling through the streets of a living town (not a theme park, not a wildlife safari, but a *real* town), the driver babbling about trees,

The Conch Train

houses, gingerbread, cisterns, hydrofoils, presidents, and emeralds. The train goes past bars, and little old men rocking on porches, and ladies watering palms in the graveyard, and mustached cruisers wearing shorts and thigh-high black lace-up boots, the driver babbling all the while. You don't have to imagine this, of course, because the improbable thing exists and has since 1958, faithfully serving tourists from 9 A.M. to 4 P.M. daily.

The train was Bill and Olive Kroll's idea. They were running the aquarium, the first tourist "attraction" in town and just about the only one in the 1940's. Built in the 1930's with Federal Emergency Relief Funds, it was abandoned during World War II while the Navy used it as a pistol range. The Krolls took pictures of the way it was and put it back together again, stocking it with the funny looking fish that the local fishermen would bring them. People would pay a quarter, stare at the fish and ask the Krolls what else they could do to wile away the afternoon. Where do we eat? What else is there to look at around here? They had a lot of questions. What is that weird tree with those *things* dangling from it? Where does Harry Truman get those shirts? What's that big pile of bricks out by the beach? Why isn't the lighthouse on the water? Such a tiny town and so many questions! Bill Kroll realized that there was a thirst for information, *accurate* information if possible, that the town's cab drivers were often loath to provide. (Note: For a pink taxi, call 296-6666. Maxi-taxi, a van, is 294-2222.) He decided to get into the sight-seeing business, patterning his vehicle on something he had seen once in, of all places, Helena, Montana. The Conch Train, hauled by its little propane-powered Jeeps, proved to be far more profitable than Henry Flagler's venture. The Krolls have sold the train, but the spiel remains pretty constant after all these years. Pirates are mentioned, and cigars, and sponges, and Ponce de León. The new owner owns all the taxis too, and the Trolley. The Trolley is warmer in cold weather and drier in wet and is somewhat more nimble than the train (it can pick up passengers at certain motels and it drops them off at certain attractions) but the itinerary and route are similar. But it is not the train. It is definitely not the weird little train.

You needn't feel embarrassed riding the Conch Train. A strange cloak of invisibility is dropped over your self as you board. Once in a while a tourist will take a picture of you, a tourist on the Conch Train, but mostly no one pays the slightest attention to this contraption whirring down the streets, the driver repeating outlandish jokes without the slightest trace of shame.

> . . . on your right is the only free hotel in Key West, the county jail . . . and on your left is a famous old bar which used to be the city morgue. You'll still find old stiffs hanging out there . . .

On one modest little street that must be working out some unfortunate karma, the driver talks about crotons. Unfortunately, there is a clump of crotons growing on this street. Now, crotons grow all over Key West, indeed all over Florida, but this is the street where all the Conch Train drivers in the world, a dozen times daily, mention the croton and its medicinal properties. Its purgative qualities actually. Its use in a tiny chocolate bar called Ex-Lax. ". . . don't laugh, folks, you didn't laugh when you needed it. . . ." You will hear these exact words, believe me.

Sixty subjects are covered in the course of the tour, including a listing of all the ways in which "Conch" is used—the high school athletic teams are called Conchs, the drill team Conchettes, a Conch Cruiser is a dilapidated Key West car bought for less than $500 . . . and so on. The passengers listen, earnestly invisible. *See,* the driver states, *Ernest Hemingway's home and feel the personality of the man radiate around you.* It's hard to know how much radiating gets through. What you see as a passenger on the train are people milling in the Hemingway gardens, taking pictures, milling. After passing the airport and the houseboats nosed up to the sidewalk on South Roosevelt Boulevard, the train takes a boring jog down Flagler through the development of new homes there. There is not much to talk about here. The driver is reduced to talking about fill. He talks quite a bit about fill and how much of the island is built upon fill, and what fill is. The driver never stops talking, actually. You will deboard almost refreshed, invisibility being quite relaxing. **Conch Tour Trains** leave from two depots—Mallory Square and Roosevelt Avenue at U.S. #1. 1 1/2 hours. Frequent departures daily 9–4. Adults $11.

Sunset

In the Keys, the best place to ponder the descending globe of gas, our sun, is just about any place other than Mallory Square where actually only a small wedge of horizon is visible. Audubon beheld a few sunsets in the Keys and couldn't get over them. "A blaze of relfugent glory streams through the portals of the west," he wrote, "and the masses of vapor assume the semblance of mountains of molten gold." The sun, as we know, appears to grow larger as it sinks in the west. This is one of the many illusions which nature presents, perhaps, as a children's astronomy book suggests, "to sharpen our wits in deciding between sights that are real and those that only seem to be." At Mallory Square, the sunset definitely plays second fiddle to the unreal people and events that accompany it. In order to get your attention, a young man will lie on a bed of nails, place a concrete block over his groin, and have someone shatter the block with a sledgehammer. You can buy a freshly woven palm hat and see some white cockatoos. You can't pet an iguana anymore because the Iguana Man died and the iguanas don't come down to see sunset by themselves. You can buy a chocolate chip cookie.

You can watch a rather wide-eyed cat jump through a flaming
hoop. You can watch fire-eaters and jugglers, some of them
quite talentless. Everything is giddy and determinedly carefree.
And everyone is there . . . breakdancers and frightful bikers
. . . little kids and deeply tanned weirdos . . . old ladies in their
Lily dresses and guests from the Casa in their tennis whites
. . . college students in their Bahama Mama buzz . . .

The hippies began this sunset viewing in the 1960's when they
congregated here to pound drums and smoke dope. Now the
camera is king. If you don't have a camera you will probably be
elbowed away from various sights by those who do. The pier
itself has been refitted for part of the new cruiseport facility.
The mayor had to promise sunset devotees that whatever gar-
gantuan ship will be docked there will have left each day before
the sun goes down. The crowds mob this congested spot. Street
entertainers quarrel with parking lot attendants. Merchants
quarrel with street vendors. The City Commission wanting sunset "to be maintained," has set up a committee to explore the
possibility of an alternative site for sunset activities. The sunset
has become something of a problem.

Key West Aquarium

Your Favorite Seafoods Alive! The oldest attraction in Key
West, it was once open to the sky with individual coral tanks for
the fishes. An admission ticket is good for several days so you
can wander in more than once if you're at terribly loose ends.
Kids come back often. It's one of the few things available for
them in Key West—the town not exactly being Toys "R" Us.
There are some very wiggy fishes in here. The big-eyed, flaccid
porcupine fish, for example, which has no fish enemy. If anything tries to swallow it, it just puffs up and the predator gags
to death. The Atlantic guitar fish, the sawfish, the peculiar reef
squid, all representing life as we certainly do not know it. The
butterfly fish, with splotches of color near the tail, resembling
eyes, draws would-be attackers to the wrong end of itself. The
coral-crunching colorful parrotfish with its big bright lips
wedges itself between rocks and secretes a gelatinous cocoon of

mucus around its body when it goes to sleep at night. Fish, if not exactly leading rich, emotional lives, have developed some very peculiar characteristics. The old shallow coral pools are used as well as glass-wall tanks and a deep outside pen where there are turtles and tarpon. The tarpon have been here for years but are small, not growing because there's no room for them to grow. At one point there was a good-sized permit, which some selfless angler had donated, in the enclosure. Outside, there's the usual array of cats and pelicans.

There are half-hour tours four times a day, much of the talk eliciting enthusiastic "yarggghs" and "yuks" from the kids. There's a touch tank, and the feeding of lemon, blacktip, and bonnethead sharks. You can pet a barracuda, and pick up a sea cucumber and watch it squirt—the Conchs don't call them "sea pissers" for nothing. You might be able to identify some of the fish you've seen on the reef in here, but the multitude of wild water life in the Keys is vast and enigmatic, and the number of species in here represents only a small percentage of the variety out there. People often come in and try to explain what it was they saw, not realizing how strange it actually was, or how difficult to describe. Open 10 A.M.–7 P.M. Adults $5.

Truman Annex

Just off Mallory Square, behind the iron gates on Greene Street, is **Truman Annex**, forty-three acres which became highly controversial when the Navy deemed it surplus property and put it up for sale. The Navy had been annexing the land piece by piece for over a century and it had been off-limits to the town for almost fifty years.

The oldest building in the annex is the **U.S. Marine Hospital** built in 1844. It was designed by Robert Mills who was the architect for the Washington Monument. The high, steep steps which distinguish it seem ill-suited for a hospital entry, but the building originally stood directly on the water and patients were brought by boat to the rear.

Another structure which once had a water view is the Naval Commandant's Quarters, more commonly known as **The Little**

White House. Built in 1890, it is recognizable by its symmetrical double facade and its encircling porches enclosed by wooden louvers. President Harry Truman first came here in 1946 and returned ten times for vacations during his administration, arriving at the Boca Chica air station on the presidential plane *Sacred Cow*. Truman enjoyed walking around town buying coffee with autographed dollar bills, eating the best coconut cake in town which was made especially for him by a Miss Etta Patterson, and playing poker. His habits also included swimming in the waters off the front porch (no one in The Little White House was allowed to flush during these ablutions) and being downstairs in the kitchen every morning at seven for a shot of bourbon, followed by a glass of orange juice, a practice which, it was said, "always astonished" the Filipinos. The Old Island Restoration Foundation has recently restored The Little White House and it is now open as a museum. Admission $5.

In September 1986 the Navy conducted an auction of the land and all its buildings. Many came ready to bid, including a group of Eskimos, but it was purchased by a 36-year-old, rich Sikh from Maine named Pritam Singh for $17.25 million. Singh seems a democratic sort, although he frequently, unnervingly, refers to his "covenant" with the people of Key West. He wears a turban and has a sparse beard even though he hasn't shaved it since he was seventeen. He razed a number of buildings that had been running down for years with Key West panache but rehabilitated the ones most important from a military or historical perspective. His plan was a mix of condos, residences and shops, all mixed in with amazing trees (two of the most fabulous banyans in Key West live in the Annex), white-picket fences, walkways and parks, everything architecturally correct and lavishly landscaped. He promises not a chicken in every pot but a hibiscus tree in every yard. Other plans included an 80-slip marina (flanked on one side by the town's cruiseship dock and on the other by the Navy's port, recently expanded and deepened to accommodate warships—pleasure and war having apparently been judged compatible); the transformation of the Romanesque Revival Customs House, the most imposing structure on Mallory Square, into a yacht club; and the development of Tank Island, the 27-acre spoil island created by the Navy to hold its fuel tanks. Singh's plans were for a hotel to pop up here —a Ritz-Carlton hotel no less—all turreted white clapboardy gingerbread Victorian with a pitched roof and French door. Mullions and millions. His plans were for aviaries and croquet courts and instant jungles too. He worried that the "sleaze factor in Key West" would keep this all from happening. But it wasn't the sleaze factor that has so far prevented all this fancy development of Tank—it's the end of the boom 80's. The only thing that's changed with Tank is its name. Singh renamed it "Sunset" Island.

The Treasure Salvors

The large raised stone building near the Greene Street gate to the Annex is an old Naval storage building, home of **Mel Fisher's Treasure Exhibit**. Fisher is a successful computer-age salvor whose most spectacular discoveries were the gold-and-silver laden Spanish galleons, the *Nuestra Senora de Atocha* and the *Santa Margarita* which sank in a hurricane in 1622.

The Spanish referred to all the Florida Keys as Matecumbe, and for some time Fisher and his Treasure Salvors searched the waters off Matecumbe for the *Atocha*. Wrecks which had previously been discovered were in an area between Key Largo and Long Key and most had been salvaged by the Spanish themselves who had mapped their locations. The correct sites of the *Atocha* and *Margarita* wrecks, 100 miles south of the area in which they had been searching, was discovered by a historian going through seventeenth-century Spanish documents in the archives in Seville. The manifests of the ships indicated that they had been loaded with over forty-seven tons of gold and silver from the mines of Potosí, Lima, Mexico City, and Bogotá. The galleons had gone down within miles of each other, the *Atocha* on a shallow reef in fifty-five feet of water, the *Margarita* on a wide shoal, an area referred to as the Quicksands. Fisher discovered some of the wealth of the *Atocha* as early as the 1970's—gold and silver bars, gold chains up to 8 1/2 feet long, coins, crucifixes, and navigational devices, the most important being the ship's astrolabe, a precursor to the sextant.

As of early 1985, however, only a small portion of the *Atocha*'s treasure had been found. The wreck had scattered, most of its cargo lying beneath twenty feet of sand and shell. Most of what had been retrieved was contraband gold, smuggled on board and not listed on the manifest at all. Still to be found too was a suspected, but unlisted, seventy pounds of raw emeralds. Almost daily, the Treasure Salvors were out searching for the "Big Pile" with their divers, ships, and planes, plotting and mapping, scanning inch by inch the ocean bottom with magnetometers, sub-bottom profilers and side-scan sonar, and moving sand with their "mailboxes," a device of Fisher's which forces the wash from a boat's propeller down through an elbow-shaped tube aimed directly into the sand.

On Memorial Day, 1985, thirteen gold bars, sixteen emeralds mounted in gold, and piles of pieces of eight were discovered, but it was not until July 20, when divers found a telltale wall of ballast stones about five feet high and began bringing up hundreds of silver bars, that it was known that the "Big Pile," the mother lode, the largest shipwreck treasure in the world, had at last been found.

The yield is enormous—large, loaf-shaped silver bars (forty-seven tons of silver alone have been recovered), gold bars, and chests of coins—and is all being cleaned by an electrolytic reduction process, and catalogued on the upper floors of the Treasure Exhibit with typical Key West insouciance by a large staff. More exciting even than the gold is the recent emerald bonanza, thousands of which have now been found. The divers put their first discoveries in a Mr. Peanut quart jar. As for the site itself, forty miles southwest of Key West, it is protected from possible piracy by a great deal of potential muscle. Mel Fisher says, "We have instant direct scrambled communications and on a moment's notice can have Navy dive bombers, hydrofoils, radar blimps, Coast Guard helicopters, marine patrol boats, and lots of other security on the spot."

All this is heady, even giddy, stuff, but the typical visitor to the Treasure Exhibit does not, in fact, see a great deal of the

Atocha discovery. It is a huge building and one might think one would be wandering around for hours viewing tons of artifacts, but the exhibit is small, all taking place in a single, curving, dark room. There is some gold and silver prettily displayed on sand and velvet and some impressive globs of silver coins fused in the shape of the mahogany boxes they had been carried in. Each chest contained 2500 coins. There is also a gleaming exhibit of silver bars. The most interesting items are a gold bar which one can heft by worming one's hand through a small hole —a solid gold "anti-assassin" cup with handles in the shape of dolphins and space in the pedestal to hold a bezoar stone, which was meant to absorb and be an antidote to arsenic—and an 8 1/2-foot gold chain brought up by diver-photographer Don Kincaid. Kincaid was new on the job as Treasure Salvor when he discovered the heavy chain bright as the day it was in 1622 when the *Atocha* went down. He thought that the other divers had planted it there to tease him. Gold remains impervious to time and seawater, but silver will corrode—thin silver coins becoming big as biscuits from calciferous buildup. As part of the exhibit there is also a long-winded National Geographic film concerning the Treasure Salvors which plays all day with a wheezing soundtrack, and a gift shop where you can buy shipwreck coins, and T-shirts with Mel Fisher's trademark cry *Today's The Day* imprinted on them.

Mel Fisher's Treasure Exhibit, 200 Greene Street. 10–6. Admission $5. Children under seven, $1.

The Audubon House

Across the street at 205 Whitehead is the **Audubon House**. Audubon was ubiquitous, seemingly sleeping in as many places as George Washington. But the fact is, Audubon did not sleep here, in the Geiger Home on Whitehead Street, nor did he even step inside the door. According to a sketch made by William Adee Whitehead in 1838, no two-story house existed on the site. Audubon spent only a brief time here in 1832 and probably spent most of his time on the vessel, *Marion*. There were but five hundred people living in Key West then and only eighty-one buildings of any note. Captain John Geiger is not even mentioned by Audubon in his journals even though he had been a pilot for Commodore Porter and he was supposed to be such a wit that his sayings were referred to as "Geigerisms."

The Audubon House *was*, however, built by Captain John Geiger sometime in the 1830's and possibly moved to this site. Geiger was a wrecker who furnished his home with treasures salvaged from foundered ships. He introduced the Geiger tree *(Cordia sebestena)* to Key West from the West Indies. He must have been interested in this tree since it possessed the same name as he did (no one knows who the *real* Geiger was). He planted it in his front yard where the much pruned specimen with its pretty orange blossoms is extravagantly noted today. The captain had many children, and his descendants lived in the house until 1956, the last one being a drunken hermit named Willy Smith.

Audubon's host and helpmate in Key West was one Benjamin Strobel, a doctor, newspaper editor, and amateur ornithologist. It was Strobel who procured the Geiger twig that Audubon used in his painting of the White-Crowned pigeon. In his newspaper, Strobel enthusiastically wrote of Audubon:

> It is impossible to associate with him without catching some portion of his spirit; he is surrounded with an atmosphere which infects all who come within it, with a mania for bird killing and bird stuffing.

Audubon indeed had a mania. Though his name has become synonymous with wildlife preservation, he was in no way at any time concerned with conservation. He killed tirelessly for sport and amusement as well as for his art, and he considered it to be a very poor day's hunting in Florida if he shot less than a hundred birds. From St. Augustine he wrote:

> We have drawn seventeen different species since our arrival in Florida, but the species are now exhausted and therefore I will push off . . .

Audubon shot thousands of birds and never in his mind made the connection between the wholesale slaughter he so earnestly

engaged in and their decreasing number, although in his forties
he did begin complaining about the scarcity of mammals and
birds for his studies. "Where can I go now," he grumbled, "and
visit nature undisturbed?"

It is ironic that the Audubon Society has taken as their standard the name of a man who had no interest in the survival of
the birds he so painstakingly drew and that the Audubon
House, which is worthy because it began the preservation and
restoration movement in Key West, was a home which Audubon never visited.

The two birds which are connected to Key West in *Birds of
America* are both pigeons, although the Key West pigeon which
he named for the town was actually a dove. The detailed back-
ground painting of Key West that is behind the Great White
Heron, Audubon's prize find on his trip to the Keys, was done
separately by George Lehman, a Swiss landscape painter who
accompanied Audubon on his southern trip aboard the *Marion*.
Three of the birds done on the trip were sketched in the Dry
Tortugas—the Noddy Tern, the Sooty Tern, and the Brown
Booby.

In all, 1065 birds appeared on 435 plates in Audubon's master-
work, the Double-Elephant Folio (so called because of the size
of the paper, 40 × 30, double the size of an ordinary folio sheet)
of *Birds of America*. The engraving, printing, and coloring of
the plates took eleven years and was done in England by Robert
Havell and his son. Around 175 complete sets were published
and the Audubon House had one on display for a while but
someone stole it. It was later recovered but is now being exhib-
ited at an ostensibly more secure location in Miami.

What you do see in the Audubon House are delicate ceramic
pieces of warblers, flycatchers, and wrens by the English artist
Dorothy Dowdy, who was commissioned by Royal Wooster in
London after World War II to produce collection sets to be sold
to help relieve England's war debts; a dozen framed bird prints;
and antiques "typical of the period." Upstairs, on a "self-guided
tour," you trip a recording device as you enter the bedroom and
a voice comes booming out from beneath the mattress, talking
about shaving mirrors, Queen Anne footstools, and "m'Lady's
hipbath." A film describing the Elephant Folio is shown on a

small screen in one room. A small, very pale, and very dusty stuffed roseate spoonbill perches disconsolately on a desk just inside the door of another. Its presence here is carefully explained. It was not tracked down and shot by a bird fancier but "found in Key Largo, tangled in wires and choked to death." There is also a photograph of Audubon's shovel-jawed wife Lucy, who once wrote, "I have a rival in every bird." **Audubon House and Gardens.** Corner Whitehead and Greene. Daily 9 A.M.–noon and 1 P.M.–5 P.M. Adults $4.50. The gardens are very lovely. There are even places to sit.

Caroline Street

Caroline begins in official pomp at the wrought-iron presidential gates on Whitehead Street, moves regally past shaded, stately homes for several blocks, turns abruptly into homely marine practicality, and dead-ends at the City Electric stacks. Its variability is pure Key West for here is a history of mansions and rough bars, turtle slaughterhouses and pretty little lanes.

Just opposite the gates is the old **Airways Building,** the former home of Aero-Marine Airways which flew passengers and mail to Cuba in the early 1920's. Each flight would carry a passenger pigeon to be released in case of trouble over the open water. As part of the operation, the trained birds were kept in cotes in the **Pigeon House.** Aero-Marine went out of business in 1924, to be replaced by Pan Am, the first international airline recognized by the Post Office. It made its first flight from Key West in 1928. The restaurant in this great old building serves perhaps the worst food in town. Even the drinks are beginning to taste a little peculiar here.

There are some fine old houses in this first block, built by nineteenth-century businessmen, wreckers, and judges. The stately house at 410 was built by a British barroom owner, George Carey, in the 1850's. He boasted that his ancestors could write evenly on paper without lines, but only when drunk. The second block of Caroline is perhaps the prettiest in town with eight splendid wooden houses and one, at 529, made of brick,

complete with tin roof and turret, built by a Turkish sponger in
1906.

The **Milton Curry Mansion** at 511 is a miniaturized version
of a Newport cottage with all expected excessive embellishments. Milton built this home in 1905 as a wedding present to
himself and his new bride. He was the son of William Curry who
had come to Key West from the Bahamas as a child in 1837. It
was said that the elder Curry's "capacity for making safe and
lucrative investments amounted to genius." He became owner
of the largest ship's chandlery in town and when he died in 1896,
he was considered the wealthiest man in Florida. More than
seventy carriages accompanied his body to the graveyard, although the solid gold dinner service he had purchased from
Tiffany and Company in New York over the years stayed at
home. The mansion is now open to the public. Behind it is a
recently built, wickered-up inn.

At 522 is the most graceful example of Queen Anne architecture in Key West, the **George Patterson House**. It was built
immediately after the annihilating fire of 1886, as were many
of the grandest homes in town including the **Richard Kemp
House** at 601. This beautiful home has an elegant simplicity of
style and proportion and represents the "Conch" style at its
very best, employing shipbuilding techniques as well as Classic
Revival and island architectural design. The house was built by
John Sawyer (who also built the twin-towered Armory on White
Street) for the Kemp family who had become wealthy in the
sponging business, after William Kemp introduced Key West
sponges to the New York market. Great care and detail was
given by the builder to the outside appearance of the house.
Inside, old odd lumber was frequently used, for wood was dear
in Key West and little of it was wasted. Many of the beams had
been salvaged from other structures and show old square holes,
caused by a previous use of pegs rather than nails. Today the
Kemp House, which is built of pine, is called the **Cypress
House**, a gay guest establishment which sometimes flies flags
from the balcony.

The following block of Caroline offers a lovely array of Classic
Revival homes before the street opens up into the more utilitar-

ian, humble, and often raucous structures that, past and present, have served the fishing and shrimping docks. Look into the marine hardware store at 818—a great supply store with everything for the boater. Across the street is **Land's End Village**, over which the sky is spindly with shrimpboat rigging. The party boat *Conch Pearl* is berthed here and the Tortugas "fishing machine" *Yankee Capts*. The Key West Rowing Club rents sculls and a variety of pure and simple watercraft. **Seasports Dive Center** goes out to the reef twice a day. Here too is the popular **Half-Shell Raw Bar** and the old **Turtle Kraals**, a former butcher shop and cannery, now a restaurant where you can "drink your way around the world" with a staggering selection of imported beers. The Kraals is a cozy place and nice to go on a cold day for it has a pot-bellied stove. (**Capt. Tony's** is another place jammed when the temperature drops, for it has a fireplace.) The Kraals has an aviary, and some fish tanks and maintains a clouded pen where a few green turtles, those fabulous travelers, drift aimlessly enclosed. Down a short pier is the old slaughterhouse, now a "museum" devoted to the artifacts of what is often referred to as the "colorful" industry of turtling, although the only color which comes to mind is red. Here are axes, grinders, photographs, and a painting of an old turtle schooner, the *A. Maitland Adams*.

Green turtles, a species virtually extinct, were hauled back to Key West from the coast of Nicaragua until the late 1960's when tourists would still gather eagerly at the docks with their cameras to see them being butchered. The butcher would sometimes have a bit of fun with his "neat trick" of slitting the turtle's throat so that the blood would spring twenty feet toward the insatiable observers' eyes.

A WALK UP DUVAL STREET

One mile long and certainly no Zona Rosa, Duval stretches from the glass-bottom boat *Fireball* docked on the Gulf to a little beach beside the Southernmost House on the Atlantic. Perhaps the most interesting strip in Florida, Duval trembles, even tot-

TURTLES

The life of the green turtle in the vast oceans is mysterious, but not mysterious enough to insure its survival. Its behavior on land is better known and has steadily doomed it. The turtle's fate is to come ashore to lay her eggs—a hundred of them at a time, several times a year—in a deep sand nest which she covers up with her flippers before returning to the sea. She always nests on the same beach and her female hatchlings, those that survive, will come back to the beach where they were born when it is their time to lay eggs. Male turtles never return to land. The nests are dug up by raccoons, dogs, and men. If the nest is not discovered by the second day, the eggs are usually safe for the following sixty days when the nest erupts, the little turtles emerge en masse and make their rush to the sea, a dash which is often cut short by hordes of feeding birds. Hatchlings instinctively head for the brightest spot they see and for millions of years, this was the reflection of moon and stars on the water. Now, however, street and house lights often attract them to death on highways and lawns. If the water is reached the first wave releases in the baby turtle its sea knowledge—it is the water that teaches the turtle how to swim—and it is then only a matter of luck how many survive the onslaught of predatory fish.

The green turtle is considered to be the world's most valuable reptile and it is a form of life that has almost been extinguished. The United States banned the import of all sea turtle products—meat and shell and calipee—in 1979. The calipee is the gelatinous cartilage cut from the bones of the bottom shell and is used to flavor soup. Huge nesting turtles are often killed on the coasts of the Caymans, the Caribbean Islands, and Costa Rica for the sake of a few ounces of calipee alone—the rest of the turtle left for buzzards.

Hunted and harassed and exploited, protection of sea turtles has probably come too late. In remote areas they are still killed regularly and all the eggs in a nest taken. In built-up areas, tenderhearted condo dwellers guard the nests of turtles who stubbornly return to beaches now bright with the lights of development. They protect the eggs, even taking them back to their balconies where they try to hatch them in cardboard boxes. If the turtles hatch, they feed them raw

A shrimp boat

hamburger for a while before releasing them into the sea. It isn't known whether this sort of assistance raises or lowers the incredible odds against their survival. The fact is no one knows where young turtles go. They are seen only after some years have passed and they are old enough to mate, the female then making her perilous journey ashore.

A Key West newspaper of the 1890's, *The Daily Equator Democrat,* wrote:

Thousands of these monster turtles weighing from 100 to 1200 pounds are taken in these waters. They are shipped to the larger cities in the U.S. and command a high price. The turtle business is growing rapidly on the coast and seems to be, like the fish business, inexhaustible.

SHRIMPING

Nocturnal shrimp were discovered in the waters off Key West in the 1970's and now shrimping is the new hot industry of the town which is the winter headquarters of Gulf and Atlantic coast shrimpers. About 400 boats search the waters from November through July, dragging 65-foot-long, cone-shaped nets behind them. The business has become very competitive and the shrimp, of course, are not as plentiful as they once were.

In 1980, during the Mariel Boat Lift, initially called The Freedom Flotilla, then Operation Alien Assist, ultimately A Disaster, shrimpers abandoned their nets and went to Cuba to bring back refugees, sometimes at $2000 a head. "Hauling Cubans paid a lot better than shrimping," one captain said. Boats left Garrison Bight by the hundreds and returned with thousands of people, depositing them on the pier at Truman Annex from which they were sent by bus to an old railroad shed converted into a hangar on Trumbo Point from which they were airlifted to Homestead and Miami. President Jimmy Carter, after first declaring "an open arms, open heart policy," changed his mind when it appeared that a considerable number of emigrés were deranged, or were thieves and murderers, the latter being marked by tattoos on the inside of their lips. When he declared a halt to the flotilla, Key West fishermen ignored him, preferring to continue their lucrative missions of mercy. Forced by the Cuban authorities at Mariel Harbor to take on increasingly unsavory individuals, the shrimpers returned home and had their boats seized by the U.S. government. Boats rather than people started piling up at Truman Annex. At one point, 80 percent of the commercial fishing boats of Key West were red-tagged and impounded on the docks. The seizure was later declared unconstitutional, 100,000 Cubans were absorbed into the city of Miami, and Key West's shrimp boats returned to their former occupation. At the Blessing of the Fleet ceremony recently, only seven local shrimp boats showed up. The rest were out shrimping.

ters, between sleaze and restoration. Duval has it all—emeralds and chicken wings, dance clubs and missing elks, lewd underwear and failed fountains. It's got chic shops and forbidding hotels, twinkling galleries, and bars. It hums at night and in the sun. In the rain it appears less than electrifying. Old-timers feel they've lost the real Duval which was darker, danker, noisier, had even more bars and certainly fewer postcards. The Duval Crawl is a must. It's done in a car at any time, slowly, very slowly. Be cool now.

The street was named before Florida even became a state, for William Pope duVal, the first governor of the territory. It was a dirt road until the 1920's when it was paved with brick. People bought milk from vendors who milked their cows and goats at the door. Much of Duval burned down, was rebuilt, and burned down again. In the 1950's it was wild, in the 1960's dirty, in the centennial year of 1976, after rejecting a plan which would turn it into a canal with Venetian gondolas poling people around to the shops, it was not exactly rehabilitated—and certainly not restored—but made more reputable. False fronts appeared. Brick planters. Balloons and cookie and croissant shops were invited in—particularly in the 600 and 700 blocks. Beyond this, well into the 80's, was terra incognita to the tourist. It was a mixture of cans, cats, old convertibles, a few Cuban groceries and many empty lots as derelict buildings burned down with regularity. Other than La-Te-Da and the cavernous old-time Valladares newsstand, which carries more magazines than could possibly be published each year, it seemed the big empty. But now retail has moved in and there are malls and squares and shops, shops, shops. Cigar makers' cottages now sell lingerie, soft pretzels and kayak trips, and the dour Holmes Auto Body building is an art gallery. "I'm upscale and uptown," the proprietor of Oink's Originals, a new shop on Duval Square, said. (Oink's Originals sells what looks an awful lot like T-shirts.) "I wanted to be away from the T-shirt shops." (See also "Where to Eat," pp. 210–217, "Galleries and Antiques," pp. 169–70, and "Bars, pp. 217–21.)

The 200 block is the bar block. Always carnival time here: **Durty Harry's, Rick's Cafe, Bull and Whistle**—they all rock and roll. The **Whistle** and **Rick's** have skinny upstairs porches

and do well for hollering and howling. **Sloppy Joe's** hammers
down the corner at Greene. "I'm going over to Sloppy's," you
hear from the most elderly and exhausted tourist as well as the
most energetic short-shorted youth. Everyone makes the pil-
grimage to Sloppy's—"Hemingway's favorite bar." Parachutes
billow from the ceiling. Pictures of the writer beam or brood
from every cranny. The waitresses clang a cowbell every time
the Conch Train goes by (as does the funkier **Green Parrot**.)
Two Germans recently rushed into Sloppy's, then rushed off to
the library on Fleming to copy all the photographs of the interior available. They were going to open a Key West Sloppy Joe's
in Munich. What they were going to do about the Conch Train
is a puzzle. **Rumrunners** has innumerable bars squirreled
away in a shambly building. There's a psychic next door for
those who are aware they're lost.

(For jazz, go to **Captain Hornblowers** at 300 Front or **Two
Friends** where there's also Dixieland. Catch the Junkanoos,
who play black Bahamian calypso music, whenever and wherever you can.)

On the corner of Caroline, opposite the Bull and Whistle is the
Fogerty House built by yet another son of William Curry, Key
West's first millionaire. The walrus-mustached President William Taft was once entertained here as well as Henry Flagler
during the festivities accompanying the arrival of the first train
into town. The Fogarty House has been reclining in its decline
for years, ever since a group of French sailors on shore leave
used the fountain as a pissoir. The restaurant here need not be
investigated.

In the 300 block, the **Joseph Porter House** on the corner of
Caroline reflects the best of Conch formidable design—taking
the architectural flavor of the Bahamas as well as New England
and New Orleans. It is now apartments, and houses two small
specialty shops which are worthy of approach if only for the
opportunity of being able to linger for a moment on the wide
cool veranda. Up and across the street is the **Red Barn
Theatre**. Tiny (85 seats) and terrific with skillful professional
performances. Call 296–9911 for information on their seasonal
offerings. At 322, next to the melancholy **Southern Cross Hotel**
is The Oldest House.

The Oldest House

As mentioned, this may not be the oldest house but it is the one researched, restored, and made accessible and it is old enough, certainly, having been built only a few short years after John Simonton bought Key West in 1822 and found "no living person" about. The house was built by Richard Cussons, a grocer, and probably moved here from Whitehead Street. It sits on unusually tall three-foot piers to protect it from the storm tides which used to flow unimpeded up Duval and it has low ceilings and shuttered windows. The early scuttles on the roof were later replaced by dormers, and these are the house's most peculiar characteristic, for they are wildly dissimilar in size, the sort of dormers fairy tale bears might fancy.

The house is pleasantly askew and homely. Another house was added to the original structure early on, probably around the time Francis Watlington bought it in the 1840's. Watlington was a wrecker who raised seven daughters here. During the Civil War, when he was in his sixties, he went off to fight for the Confederacy, but returned to Key West and is one of the few early settlers buried in the graveyard.

The house is now a museum and is open every day but Wednesday. The "Rules of Wrecking" are on display and there is a dollhouse upstairs furnished as eclectically as the house itself. On the grounds there is a cookhouse, the only outside kitchen remaining in Key West.

Anchoring the corner of the 400 block is **St. Paul's Church** with its towers from which hurricane-cracked bells peal daily. The big empty **La Concha Hotel** held down the other side of the street for years, motorcycles parked in its lobby and revelers reveling in the seedy bar at the top. It now has a new life as a Holiday Inn. The two-story waterfall they promised for the lobby never materialized and the pool is only 3 1/2 feet deep, but the new **La Concha** is pretty and pink and tropical *de rigueur* art deco, and the view from The Top in the now-fancy bar is the same great view. You can't be much closer to the heart of Duval

Street than this. Rooms run between $100 and $200 a night.
(296-2991).

Here, Fleming is the cross street of the 500 block, up which
is **Fausto's** (a grocery store that takes Visa, and has the coldest
air-conditioning in town) and the nice pink library. Commanding the corner is sleek, slick **Fast Buck Freddie's** where in the
shimmering, heady recesses people are heard to cry out, "I have
to buy something from here!" Fast Buck's has great clothes,
toys, jewelry, kitchen equipment, and flashy souvenirs. Nobody
misses Fast Buck's. See if they still have the battery-run, super-
realistic writhing rat in a trap that was the sensation of a
Christmas past. "People *love* them," a salesman said. "Those
things just *fly* out of here."

The San Carlos (516 Duval)

The original San Carlos was built in 1884 and named for Carlos
Manuel de Cespedes, a Cuban plantation owner who in 1868
cried Cuba Libre! from the balcony of his estate. He wasn't
talking rum and Coke; the cry sparked the Ten Years' War
against Spanish rule, a war which the patriots ultimately lost.
(Cespedes' son, Carlos, became the mayor of Key West in 1876.)
Cubans who fled to Key West founded this political and social
club, financing it with the abundant profits of cigar-making.
The fire of 1886, which destroyed most of the town, originated
in the San Carlos. It was rebuilt three years later and became,
as well as a political club, a cultural center and opera house.
Anna Pavlova and the Russian Ballet danced here in 1915. In
1919, it was virtually destroyed by a hurricane and in 1924, the
present structure, its interior lined with beautiful tiles, was
built with money donated by the president of Cuba. It was later
converted to a movie theater but since 1962 has stood empty. In
1982, $10,000 was spent on restoring the facade, most of the
money being used for an injection process which literally glued
the building back together. Plans were to make it into a theater
for dramas and musicals, but this was met with such protest by
the Cuban community that the idea was dropped. New inten-

Fausto's Food Palace

tions are for the San Carlos to be a tourist attraction where the history of Key West and Cuba will be dramatized in film, lectures, and exhibits. The second floor will be used as a school for Cuban children and as a Cuban-American Studies Center. (In 1991, mired in typical Key West controversy, the San Carlos remains unused.)

The Strand (527 Duval)

A movie house built in the 1930's, its "boomtown" front is elaborately decorated with lions, Roman legionnaires, and bowls of fruit. When a fire destroyed the roof, the building was used for a while as a boxing ring beneath the stars. The sherbet-colored circusy facade was painstakingly restored recently and inside, for a time, the interior became a state-of-the-art video, dance, and music complex with ever-changing shows—rock, reggae, blues, mud wrestling, male strippers for the ladies, etc. Food was also served here—most particularly sandwiches named for local politicians. For example, there was the "Bum Farto," in honor of a former Key West fire chief. All this was just too good

to last, of course. The money ran out, and The Strand, for the
moment, is shut.

Somewhere around here, there is a shop which has, as part of
its window display, a man's bathing suit with an elephant trunk
sticking out of it. This has been there *for years.*

The 600 block is the area snatched from the skids in 1976.
Merchants and politicians had the year 1910 in mind here, but
they wanted the block to appear as it "should" have appeared,
not the way it actually did appear. The result was this street of
appearances, sticky with fudge and ice-cream nooks, only a
pawn shop clinging to the brassy taste of yesterday. The co-op
art gallery, **Guild Hall**, is here, near to where the old Picture
Show *used* to be. The theater sold beer right along with the
popcorn and showed a variety of old, flaky and message flicks
as well as the very funny homage to Key West, *The Key West
Picture Show.* You can still catch it at the Paradise Store at 1
Whitehead Street.

Key West transportation

The Copa

A movie theater built in 1917, it had been showing *Deep Throat* for a decade before it was transformed into this glossy gay cruise bar. Flickering lights and longings and heavy-duty dancing on the big dance floor flanked by bars below. Upstairs is male erotica. Out back is the "Cowboy" bar of pool table and electronic games, then the fresher, yet still considerably tumid air of the "Patio" bar, above which, for fern admirers, hangs the largest stag horn in town. The Copa has fascinating entertainment but it varies. You'd better check. You don't want to go down there on Wednesday thinking it's "Doris Day Night" and be disappointed when it turns out to be "Wet Jockey Short Night" instead.

The 700 block once had the distinction of having the dustiest and most forlorn collection of seashells in town at the Key West Conch Shell, but someone discovered Windex, then found they didn't want to sell seashells at all. There's something for everyone on this street. You can even go into the **Greenpeace Store** (**Yo Sake** lies in weird conjunction across the street) and assuage your eco-guilt by buying lots of statement stuff. The shops and restaurants of upper Duval have all been wrested from what was once a Cuban enclave, but the restorationists met failure in their attempt to transform the area Ernest Hemingway used to call Jungle Town into *Bahama Village*. A colorful wrought-iron archway was erected not long ago and adorned with a flamingo, a marlin, a demi-sun, and conch shells. *Forward,* the swirling iron spelled out—*Forward Together Upward Onward*—but through the splendid passageway moves—nothing. In fact, the adornments are periodically found missing from the gateway. Off Duval, Petronia Street hovers encapsulated in a very ungentrified bubble. And there's the recent reopening of the cool and easy **801 Bar**, purportedly catering to a more gay clientele these days.

More galleries and good food (including the garlicky bollos and Cuban mix at the Laundromat around the corner on Olivia) lie ahead and it is at the intersection of Truman where you become conscious of the ocean, beckoning from several blocks away. If you're interested more in doing laps in an Olympic-size pool, turn right, where the 1200 block begins, down Catherine. The **Community Swimming Pool** is at the intersection of Catherine and Thomas. The pool is clean and alfresco. In the dressing rooms below, however, there is the sad little sign —Showering in the Nude is Unwise. At 719 Catherine, to the left of Duval, is another sign, this one in Spanish, on the curious little stucco house of Octavio Castillo, which says Don't Believe in Anyone.

Farther up on Duval, past the newly erected and mostly empty shops of Duval Square, where tiny Amelia Street intersects, are two curiosities, one, a most sinister ice-cream parlor, and the other a tarot-card reading shop. The ice-cream parlor has black, steel-shuttered windows and opens at a late hour, at which time dancing within also apparently occurs. The fortune-telling den festoons its windows with puzzling and arresting placards such as Lies, Liars And The Believers In Lies All Share The Same Grave. Both of these visions may have vanished by now, right along with the automobile graveyard next to La-Te-Da where spectacular smash-ups from all over the Keys once accumulated. New visions are the Miami-style furniture at **Fletcher** (1024, lots of fossil accessories); the oriental rugs at **Kudu** (1208) and the zippy jewelry and custom-made, exotic, erotic masks at the mysterious **Iris**. For simpler tastes, there is the irresponsibly delicious ice cream at **Flamingo Crossing** (1105) where you can spoon until midnight.

Duval is a street one should see through from start to finish, unlike Whitehead which is hot and tedious. A street that runs straight to the sea is a fine street, and **South Beach**, the little beach that fits so easily on a postcard is the seaweedy termination to Duval. The pink and green Queen Anne mansion beside it at 1400 is the J. Viking Harris House, built before the turn of the century by a judge. For a time it was the nightclub, Casa Cayo Hueso, and is now a private home again. This is **The Southernmost House**.

The Southernmost Point

This is not at the end of Duval at all but over on Whitehead, at its intersection with South Street. You would logically think the low pink house, lushly compounded and sticking out into the Atlantic beside it would be the Southernmost House instead of the turreted, tottering creation on Duval. And it is! But it's not really because it's not the *original* Southernmost House. The same kind of spirited controversy that swirls around the problem of the Great White and the Great Blue Heron (is the White just a color phase of the Blue? or is the White a distinct species? if the White *is* just a color phase of the Blue why do they hate one another so much, unlike other herons which get along quite amicably?) muddies the waters around the *real* Southernmost House.

However, we do have, without question, in the continental United States, which allows us to exclude Hawaii, the Southernmost Point and this is marked with a black, red, and yellow object of many tons constructed to resemble a nun buoy. The Director of Monuments in Key West, Billy Pinder, designed this. People kept stealing the sign that said Southernmost Point In The USA, so the town decided to install something souvenir-mad tourists couldn't carry off. It is painted in ribbons of bright colors so that it will show up well in photographs. Billy Pinder invited President Reagan to the dedication ceremonies for the buoy in 1983, suggesting that if the president came, the town would rename South Street President Ronald Reagan Street. The president did not grace the proceedings, however, and South Street remains South Street. The lady who lives in the house diagonally across from this peculiar and very permanent object that marks the Southernmost Point was so upset by its shape, color, and enormity that she hung her American flag upside down during the ceremony.

Tables are set up here each morning laden with shells. There are, too, lamps made of shells—complete with plastic flamingo and palm tree, ready to brighten your life with a tiny red Christmas tree light—and an assortment of dried and pickled things from the deep—"Honey! Look at this little shark or something

The southernmost point in the continental United States

in the formaldehyde!" Sponges and shell necklaces hang from the chain-link fence separating the street from Navy property. The conch shells are very rosy, very pretty, but it's supposed to be bad luck to put them in your home, or so the Conchs say. It would be the only revenge the conch could have, in any case. On stormy days, waves crash against the sea wall and surge into the street, soaking the Conch trains as they make their turns past.

BEACHES AND SALT PONDS

Key West's beaches are not her crowning glory. They are mostly man-made, marly, and bumpy and covered with seaweed, and the waters offshore are shallow. The longest, skinniest beach on the island is **Smathers**, which begins just west of the airport on A-1A (South Roosevelt Boulevard). It's lined with cars, taco trucks and raft and Windsurfer rentals, and parasailors (no age limit, no dress code, and no skill required!) take off from a float on the southern end. All this considerable activity is bleakly gazed down upon by the nervous inhabitants of condominiums.

On the other side of the beach and the highway are the remnants of salt ponds which were once scattered over 340 acres. Evaporation of seawater to make salt, an important preservative before the advent of ice, was an intermittent business here until 1868. Airport construction and condo development have reduced the ponds and the flow of water, but there are still a number of feeding birds to be found back here, particularly early in the morning. The ponds themselves contain extensive grass beds and are filled with blue crabs, shrimp, minnows, and killifish all being lunched upon by herons, egrets, and migratory ducks. A portion of the land is the **Riggs Wildlife Refuge** and behind a locked green gate is a small observation deck. You can struggle around the gate by wading through the mangroves, but call the Audubon House at 294-2116 and they will give you the combination to the lock. You'll be surprised at the serenity to be found here so close to the commerce of traffic and planes.

Just beyond Smathers on Atlantic Boulevard is an area now rudely jammed with condos but once known as Rest or Picnic Trees Beach. Despite its placid names, it has long been a troubled and disturbed area. Early on it was a dump, then the butchering pens for cattle were located here (livestock was also kept in the abandoned West Martello Tower). The pens were torn down in the cleanup of the 1930's and for years it was a spot, not for sunbathing but for digging. People would hunt for old bottles here, the aficionados of that art fashioning bomb-sized craters with their shovels and picks. Intersecting with Atlantic is White Street which terminates in the **White Street Pier**, a popular slab of a thing where people fish and hang out. Very busy at sunrise. The second largest beach in town is **Higgs Memorial** right alongside. Families with small children come here because of the playground, and there are picnic tables and a sandwich shop. Large flocks of skimmers and sea gulls (Were you aware that sea gulls have a high divorce rate? Twenty-five percent of couples split after the first year!) stake out one part of the beach near the West Martello Tower during windy winter months, while gays have reclaimed the rebuilt and oft-described "well extended" Reynolds Street pier nearby.

There are also two tiny patches of landfill where the undaunted seeker of waterfront can go. At the end of Vernon Street, just beside the restaurant **Louie's Back Yard,** there's a bit of public land—which usually goes topless—with a nice coconut palm and forty feet or so of rocky shoreline. At the end of the sternly unimaginative **Casa Marina** complex on Seminole Street, there's a slice of concrete and a slice of sand where dogs with jaunty bandanas around their necks like to congregate. Snorkeling around the remnants of an old pier is fun here, and a little farther out, just to the east and west of markers that mark a channel through some scattered coral heads, are some nice patch reefs.

The better bodies hang out at Smathers but the best beach in town and really the best place to see the sunset is at **Fort Taylor** (pgs. 178–181). The entrance to the fort is through the Southard Street entrance to Truman Annex. The beach is open from 8 A.M. to sunset and has picnic tables and grills. The fee is $2.50 per car, $1 less if you're a Florida resident. Bring sneakers because the beach is rough coral. It's difficult getting into the water gracefully at Fort Taylor. People teeter, hobble, crawl. . . . Once in, the tendency is to stay in for a considerable time, putting off the teetering, hobbling and crawling-out as long as possible.

GALLERIES AND ANTIQUES

The Haitian Art Company (corner Francis and Southard). Several rooms jammed with Haitian primitives. Voodoo bottles, spirit flags, gloriously painted boxes. Very reasonable. Open 10–6.

The Sea Store (614 Greene). A nice little store. Bottles and old coins. A variety of Keys hardwoods which could possibly be made into something handsomely custom-made for you. The owners are gregarious and knowledgeable too about poking around the Keys.

Perkins & Son is a salty store at 901 Fleming. Great shorts and shirts as well as brasswork, ships' clocks, models, charts and a nice selection of books about the sea.

Lucky Street, Gingerbread Square and **Great Southern** galleries are all in the 900 block of Duval. **Lucky Street** is the most exuberant. Pottery, jewelry, painting, books, Arcosanti wind chimes, great receptions. **Great Southern** has the prettiest garden and the widest offering of artist supplies if not the most arresting art, although recently one wall sported three framed constructions showing 1) alligators planning a bank heist, 2) the flubbed heist, 3) the alligators in jail watched over by flamingo guards. This took *thought.* **Gingerbread Square** is the longest-running gallery in Key West. It frequently shows the soft other-worldly acrylics of an artist whose work has been described as "idealized realism" or "attainable fantasy." Attainable fantasy . . . it's such a 90's concept.

Just off Duval in the 500 block of Fleming by the **Key West Island Bookstore** are a cluster of interesting shops. **The Collectional Institute** has nifty 40's, 50's and Deco treasures. This is the place to go for your panther lamp. There are tropical birds at **The Bird's Nest,** and Fred and Ginger dance on at **Memory Shop West** which specializes in movie stills. **Antiques 'n Things** has jewelry, old wicker and postcards, all matter of things moving in and out. **Sam's Treasure Chest** is junky and jammed, some of the treasures having resided there for years.

NEWSPAPERS

The *Key West Citizen* is Monroe County's only daily newspaper, although it does not appear on Saturday. It is a thin paper, sometimes astonishingly thin, and poker-faced in its accountings. It is known as the mullet-wrapper and depicted itself thusly in papier-mâché during one Fantasy Fest parade. A now-departed editor investigated, with two reporters, rumors of occult disturbances at the Little White House. They spent the night in the house where Harry once slept, equipped with high speed film, a tape recorder, a German shepherd, and notepads. The trio experienced two ghosts. One was a lady named Rose. The other was a slight man with blue eyes named Tom. Tom wore a brimmed felt hat, a cardigan sweater, had thin bony fingers, an eye for the ladies and owned a green parrot. It is not

CAVEAT AUDITOR

Esquire said that propaganda these days is being exalted as a misunderstood art form. Propaganda is in. Anyone can play. Everyone's an environmentalist, too, a naturalist, defending his or her right to be part of nature. Recently, in the *Forbes* magazine *FYI*, there was an article about bird hunting in Kenya (you feel this is somewhat beyond the scope of this book, I bet). The author began, "I like to move among the wild things of which I am a part, and to collect some to recycle through my own body." This is spinmanship of the highest order. Here is a chap, wild and natural, who spends $8,000 to take his 20-gauge to Africa in order to recycle some guinea fowl after dinner. If we believed that this is what recycling really was about, we'd be surprised to learn that our human wastes are destroying and degrading waters everywhere. The reef is becoming increasingly stressed by sewage that flows quickly through the porous rock of the Keys and into the ocean, as well as by agricultural runoff from the mainland that gets dumped into Florida Bay from the Everglades. But we're not surprised, not really, although we long to be assured that things are super, better than ever. Some of the new "guides" seem to have rushed right out of the Chamber of Commerce offices. One man in the Lower Keys who conducts canoe trips into the back country preaches that the Keys are being inundated by "do-gooders" whose only concerns are litter and jet skis and who do not realize that man really has no "control" over the complex and cyclic systems of wild waters. Of course man has control. His messy hand falls upon everything. Half of the historic Everglades is now farms, groves and cities, and this marvelous ecosystem isn't working anymore. Over the last fifty years, 90 percent of the "glades" wading-bird population has been lost. To read the roll of its endangered species is heartbreaking. This same "guide" claims that the birds in the back country are much better off today than they were ten years ago when drug runners were machine-gunning them. "That's what you'd see if you went back there then—thousands of birds machine-gunned by adventurers." Well, you can listen to this stuff. You can listen to another tour "expert" who says, "The Key deer isn't endangered—it can swim." You'll be listening to a lot of stuff. But the fact is that our "nitrogen-rich" waste (it sounds almost helpful, doesn't it?) is smothering parts of the reef. The fact is that litter, besides being ugly, kills things. The fact isthat some birds' food is being literally chased off the flats by caroming motorboats and jet skis and that these birds, being such territorial creatures, are starving to death. The fact is that the Keys and the delicate waters that surround them are complex, and it is our obligation to understand them the best we can and treat them with the highest sympathy and regard. The bill is coming. It's not like a bill from **Louie's** for the lovely dolphin, the lovely wines, the lovely brownie with bourbon ice cream and caramel sauce at the lovely table. It's the bill for all our environmental misunderstandings past. The big bill.

known what the German shepherd thought, but the reporters' observances were duly reported in the *Citizen*. The pictures of babies, newlyweds, and high-school sports are nice, and, of course, the drug trials of prominent local citizens, including police officers and real estate ladies, are followed with great interest, but the most fascinating section of the *Citizen* is by far the police blotter on page two. It is here where Key West sings her strange song. It is here where much is exposed, but little explained—the complaints to the police of break-ins where pots of black beans vanish and wet clothes are rearranged. The thefts of car bras and meatball subs. The reports of voodoo roosters and murdered palm trees. The headline of choice on Page Two is "Thieves, Wackos Keep Police Busy." Or, "Minor Burglaries Galore."

Solares Hill is a monthly free paper begun in the 1970's. It was named in those heady days for the "highest" point on the island, a bit of land sixteen feet above sea level at the intersection of Elizabeth Street and Windsor Lane. (The lowest point in Key West, at least for the undercarriages of cars, is at South and Simonton.) *Solares Hill* is a paper with style and conviction, a community paper of the very best sort with articles on local concerns, politics, and personalities. As well there are helpful supplements for the visitor such as a walking and biking guide

to Old Town. The paper is published around the end of each
month and can be picked up at almost any store or guest house.

WRITERS

It is known that writers hang out in Key West, and after the
brisk, rather flamboyant tour of the Hemingway house, one is
probably curious to catch a glimpse of the other homes where
novelists, playwrights, and poets ply their grisly, solitary trade.
The Hemingway house is, of course, big business. The other
houses can only be reflected upon from outside. Why people are
fascinated with the shells these souls inhabit is curious. Perhaps they're actually not that fascinated, but have been encour-
aged to believe they are.

Key West writers have done well. Eight of them have won the
Pulitzer Prize—Ernest Hemingway, Elizabeth Bishop, John
Hersey, Joseph Lash, James Merrill, Richard Wilbur, Tennes-
see Williams, and Allison Lurie. Writers like Key West—there
may be more writers in town now than bars—but many of them
are faithless creatures and they come and they go. One of them,
Hart Crane, often mentioned as a Key West writer, was in fact
never here at all. The nearest he came was the Isle of Pines in
Cuba, although a grouping of his poems was entitled *Key West
Sheaf.* Tom McGuane, Phillip Caputo, Thomas Sanchez—all
are intimately associated with this strange rock, Mile Zero.
Their houses of Pepto-Bismo pink and lime-green and proper
white could be duly noted and located but this guide, believing
that all living writers have enough problems, most of which are
still with them, prefers to address only those who have passed
on in a permanent sense. More specifically the former homes of
two of Key West's fixed and illustrious dead—Elizabeth Bishop
and Tennessee Williams.

Bahama anole lizard under a periwinkle

Elizabeth Bishop and Tennessee Williams

The **Bishop House** is at 624 White Street, not far from the pale yellow, twin-towered National Guard Armory, now a Senior Citizens' Center, at 600 White. It is a fine, simple weathered structure, almost hidden behind palms and plantings. Bishop lived here between 1938 and 1942 and many of the poems in her first collection *Poems: North and South,* winner of the Pulitzer in 1946, were written here and are about Florida, the state which she considered to have "the prettiest name," a "careless, corrupt state, the poorest postcard of itself."

Elizabeth Bishop was a poet of stunning gifts who had a painterlike fascination with appearances in themselves. Key West and New England were the early compass points of her work, although after leaving here, she lived for eighteen years in Brazil. Two of her wonderful prose pieces concern Key West: *Mercedes Hospital* and *Gregorio Valdes.*

Gregorio Valdes was a Cuban sign-painter whom she met

after purchasing one of his paintings out of a barber shop on Duval. The painting was of a neat row of royal palm trees and was in the window of the shop, covered with dust and termite wings.

Bishop wanted him to paint a picture of her green-and-white White Street house but she wanted him to add more flowers and a parrot. She also wanted him to include a monkey that lived next door and a traveler's-tree. She liked the appearance of the traveler's-tree which she described as looking like the "fan-filamented antennae of a certain gigantic moth." There being only one such palmlike tree in town at the time, Valdes sketched it separately, then worked from an enlarged photograph of the house Bishop gave him. She was delighted with the final result. "He put in flowers in profusion and the parrot on a perch on the verandah and painted the monkey, larger than life-size, climbing the trunk of the palm tree." But Gregorio Valdes was apologetic because the living tree he had copied had seven branches on one side and six on the other, but in the painting he had given both sides seven to make it more symmetrical.

The **Tennessee Williams House** at 1431 Duncan Street on the corner of Leon is noted for the large, highly *a*symmetrical traveler's-tree in the front yard. A writer of genius in his early years and considered by many to be the greatest living playwright since O'Neill, Williams continued to write prolifically even though his later plays were poorly received, one critic referring to them as "mere mystic mazes of lyrical mumbo-jumbo concerning human despair." This little house with its tomato-colored shutters is almost a miniature house, reminiscent perhaps of one of the small torrid symbols of *The Glass Menagerie*. On the lot he added a white gazebo, in honor, he said, of his friend, Jane Bowles; a pool; and a studio where he produced some of his best-known work, including *Night of the Iguana* and *The Rose Tattoo*. *The Rose Tattoo*, with Burt Lancaster and Anna Magnani was filmed in Key West, at this house and on the Casa Marina grounds, in 1956. Williams loved his studio, pointing out its "complete bath-shower and female sockets for electric grills."

Williams was happy in Key West. In the pictures taken of him here, he is always smiling, happy with his pet bulldogs, his writing (in which the town never figures), and his friends. He entertained his beloved, mad, sister Rose here. She occupied her time by watering the trees in his garden with glassfuls of water from the kitchen sink. The master of duality took up painting here, as did Elizabeth Bishop. He said it was relaxing and didn't wear him out like writing did.

There was an incident in the late 1970's where Williams and a friend, Dotson Rader, were roughed up late one night as they walked drunk and singing up Duval Street. They were singing the old gospel hymn "In the Garden":

> Ohhhh He walks with me
> And He talks with me
> And He tells me I am his own
> And the joy we share as we tarry there
> No other has ever known

. . . the lyrics achieving certain implications never dreamed of by their creator. Some young toughs pushed the men down and kicked them and although the incident was highly publicized and caused considerable concern among Key West gays, Tennessee dismissed the misadventure. "Well, I suffered no injury," he said. "Fortunately, an ice-cream shop was being shut right behind us and a man picked up the phone, called the police, and said, 'Some men are attacking Mr. Williams on the street.' "

Three weeks prior to the incident, the caretaker of his house on Duncan Street had been shot and killed. While going through his effects, the police found that he had pilfered many of the original copies of Williams's manuscripts. "Well," Tennessee said dryly, "I guess he thought he was going to die after I did."

Tennessee Williams, whose own wish was to be buried at sea between Key West and Cuba, "dropped overboard in a clean white sack," died in 1983 in New York City and is buried in the city he loathed, St. Louis.

The Historic Preservation Board of Key West hopes to acquire the house where he lived and worked on and off for thirty years, and turn it into a visiting playwright's residence and museum.

The Council for Florida Libraries has been hosting a **Literary Tour and Seminar** in Key West in January for the last several years, one of the more informative of local festivals. Although in the past they have depended upon the tried and true famous —Williams and Hemingway—they do plan to deal with a variety of works and personalities. The seminar should not be confused with **Hemingway Days** which take place in the doldrums of July and consist of drinking mostly, plus a costume party where people dress up like Hemingway characters, the winner one year being a fluttering Portuguese Man-of-War from *The Old Man and The Sea*.

The town's fine bookstore is the **Key West Island Bookstore** on Fleming, just off Duval. The library up a ways at 700 Fleming is a terrific place for a rainy day or any other. If you're a resident of Monroe County you can take books out for nothing. A visitor's card is $15 a year. There's an excellent Florida reference room, and on the first Saturday of each month, there's a

---

TRUMAN CAPOTE IN KEY WEST

Truman Capote was in a bar in Key West with Tennessee Williams and a woman came over to the table where they were sitting and asked Capote to autograph her navel with an eyebrow pencil. She handed him the pencil and pulled up her T-shirt. "Just write it like you would the numerals around a clock," she said. So Capote wrote his name around her navel. T-R-U-M-A-N-C-A-P-O-T-E. She returned to her table, but her husband got up, seemingly quite enraged. He came over to Capote, eyebrow pencil in hand and, as Capote relates, hauled out his "equipment" and howled, "Since you're autographing everything, how'd you like to autograph *this*?" Truman paused and said, "Well, I don't know if I can autograph it, but perhaps I could initial it."

book sale behind the library. All hardcovers cost 25¢. During the winter there are weekly coffees and talks, some of them *most* intriguing. How could one resist, for example, early on a Monday morning the desire to hear one Poochie Myers discuss "The Serpent-Handling Religions of West Virginia."

Hemingway and His House

In 1851, Asa Tift, a "brainy, cultured, suave gentleman" from Groton, Connecticut, a merchant and builder of Confederate ships, built a limestone mansion from native coral rock at 907 Whitehead. With its mansard roof and iron-flanged pillars, of vaguely Second-Empire or Spanish Colonial design, the **Hemingway House** is unlike any other house in town.

Ernest Hemingway and his wife Pauline bought the house in 1931 for $8,000, a monetary gift from Pauline's wealthy Uncle Gus. The house was in a gross state of ill repair with a grassless yard dotted with a few scraggly trees. It was a "miserable wreck" according to Pauline who also referred to it as a "damned haunted house" after a piece of plaster fell from the ceiling and lodged in her eye. Nonetheless, just before Christmas, the Hemingways, with their two small sons, nurses, and cooks, moved into rooms still jammed with carpenters, plumbers, plasterers, and crates of furniture shipped from France. Hemingway worked here winters in a small room over what had once been a carriage house until his divorce from Pauline in 1940. At that time he crated all his belongings—papers, books, guns, and hunting trophies—and stored them in a back room at Sloppy Joe's. (When Mary Hemingway, his last wife, went into the room in 1962 and opened the boxes untouched for decades, she found original manuscripts blackened with mildew and eaten by rats, uncashed royalty checks, and rotted animal skins.) He then went off to Cuba for a new, if brief, marriage with Martha Gelhorn and a new house, the Finca Vigía or "Lookout Farm," nine miles outside of Havana. It was at the Finca where the ghastly collection of inbred cats roamed and not in Key West, where the pet population, which numbered several peacocks, included only two cats, one of which the children once dyed a dark green, producing unknown consequences. Hemingway, however, did have over fifty cats in Cuba and once boasted of shooting a peasant's dog who had molested one of them. He had intentionally gut-shot the animal so that it would take three days to die.

Ernest Hemingway, as every schoolchild knows, fished, drank, and wrote in Key West. He wrote *Death in the Afternoon, The Green Hills of Africa,* and *To Have and Have Not,* as well as a play, *The Fifth Column,* and a considerable number of short stories, including "The Short Happy Life of Francis Macomber" and "The Snows of Kilimanjaro."

A Farewell to Arms was completed in 1929 in a house he and Pauline had rented at 1100 South Street, the same house where his mother had sent a chocolate cake and the Smith and Wesson revolver his father had used to commit suicide.

"Christ, this is a fine country!" Hemingway wrote a friend, enthusiastic about Key West. Between trips to Arkansas, to shoot grouse, pheasant, ducks, and geese; Wyoming, to shoot bear, elk, mountain rams, and eagles; and Africa, to shoot elephant, lion, rhino, buffalo, and kudu, Hemingway fished the Gulf Stream. As the biographer Carlos Baker remarks, in somewhat of an understatement, he "enjoyed life immensely without being sensitive to it." Once, when the poet Archibald MacLeish visited him and they went kingfishing, they found the fish weren't running so Hemingway "took to shooting terns, taking one with one barrel and the grieving mate with the other." Besides shotguns, he also carried on board a harpoon and a machine gun for sharks and the stray pod of whales.

Hemingway liked marlin fishing best, for marlin were "fast as light, strong as bucks, with mouths like iron." Tuna, perhaps, were not so exciting, even though they could take just as long to catch. It took him seven hours to land one 11 1/2 foot, 540-pound tuna, and after getting drunk, he strung it up and used it as a punching bag. (Hemingway had also once used the poet Wallace Stevens as a punching bag in Key West. He blackened his eyes and fractured his jaw after the older man had apparently remarked that Hemingway's writing was not his "cup of tea.")

During his first years in Key West, Hemingway had chartered

the boats of Bra Saunders, Charles Thompson, and Sloppy Joe Russell. In 1934, at the height of the Depression, and in the same year that the town had declared bankruptcy, Hemingway bought his own boat—a 40-foot black cruiser with mahogany trim built to his specifications in a New York shipyard. "A really sturdy boat," he described her, "sweet in any kind of sea, and she has a very low-cut stern with a large wooden roller to bring big fish over." He called her the *Pilar,* one of his early names for Pauline, as well as the name of a Catholic bullfight shrine in Zaragoza, Spain. He docked her at the Navy station, in the submarine pen where he and his friends, the "Mob," liked to swim. She rode out the 1935 hurricane there.

Hemingway did a lot of fishing on the *Pilar.* In 1942, he employed her in a daffy manner as a submarine hunter in the Caribbean, having convinced the Navy to equip her as a Q-boat with a supply of bazookas, grenades, and short-fuse bombs. The *Pilar* was seized by the Castro government in 1960, a year before Hemingway's death, and is now rotting on the lawn in front of the Finca in Cuba.

Hemingway thought his house on Whitehead Street resem-

The oldest house in Key West, on Duval Street

THE TOUR

You will enter the grounds. The plantings are nice. It is lush. Figs, elephant ears, a magnificent date palm. Then you will see the excessive inauthentic collection of cats, clumping around on their malformed toes—cats eating, cats brawling, cats having more cats in little cages. You will take the tour. It will cost you $5 (children $1) and it will take thirty minutes. Four people give tours ten times a day. The most eccentric tour is given by a tiny man with a tiny belly in tiny, tight, shiny black pants. You will be in a mob and he will call you "beanies," he will call you "little sparklers," he will tell you to keep it "flowing and glowing" as you follow him tripping through the rooms. He is a movie buff and you will hear about Loretta Young and Rock Hudson and Lauren Bacall. There's a chair in the bedroom which he will point out because Franchot Tone sat in it in the production of *The Fifth Column*. Franchot Tone was married to Joan Crawford at the time. The bedroom abounds in strange little chairs, uncomfortable chairs, key-hole chairs, even a midwife's chair. Later, of course, you are shown *The* chair, the cigar maker's chair Hemingway wrote in. The books of the house are all enclosed behind wire mesh, although there is a good selection of his works in paper for sale in the drawing room. "I had no idea he wrote so much," you'll hear. Glance inside the pages. Other than this, his life's work, Hemingway is dead as a doornail in this place.

bled "Joan Miro's 'The Farm' as it might have been painted by Utrillo." If that does not exactly crystallize the vision for you, imagine it being, in the 1930's, the finest house in town, a mansion with tall French windows, staffed with servants on an acre of land and possessing the only basement, bathroom, and swimming pool on the island. The pool is sixty feet long and was dug by pick and shovel for $20,000, an amount, which the guides like to point out, would be equivalent to spending around $225,000 today. Hemingway lived very well here. In 1936, he was putting the finishing touches on his Key West book, *To Have and Have Not,* a novel that showed the poverty-stricken plight of islanders during the Depression, as well as showing Hemingway's considerable disdain for fellow writers, literary hangers-on, Gulf Stream yachtsmen, and tourists. *To Have and Have Not* is actually an unsuccessful attempt to fashion a novel by taking three previously published stories about a fisherman and smuggler named Henry Morgan (based on Sloppy Joe Russell) and attaching them to subplots of love triangles and capitalistic boorishness. But it's Hemingway's Key West book and it captures the jarring rhythms of a town on the skids.

Hemingway became Key West's most famous citizen. In 1937, Toby Bruce, a driver, friend, and general handyman for the Hemingways, built a privacy wall around the property from bricks salvaged from Duval Street, dug up when the town laid down their first sewer system. By 1940, Hemingway was gone. "Those who live by the sword, die by the sword," he said rather uninspiredly, explaining Pauline's replacement by Martha. After all, Pauline had replaced Hadley. And Mary was to supplant Martha. Pauline, who had provided him with the wealth he so enjoyed and despised, died suddenly in Los Angeles in 1951. When asked by Tennessee Williams, who had met her in Key West, how she had died, Hemingway replied, "She died like everybody else and after that she was dead."

FORTS, TOWERS, AND MUSEUMS
The Lighthouse Military Museum

Close across from the Hemingway house, the museum is housed in the lighthouse keeper's cottage. This used to be more interesting, but unfortunately in 1988 a great deal of well--intentioned housekeeping took place and the rooms lost their messy, intriguingly atticy quality. The grounds were once cluttered with various torpedoes, depth charges and gun mounts, even a Blue Angel stunt jet, all innocently moldering. All of this has been carted off now, and the oddest object of all—a miniature Japanese submarine from World War II—is soon to go. This captured sub (small windows cut in the hull and two man-

nequins in Japanese uniforms placed inside) toured the country
during those war years collecting money to raise the ships sunk
at Pearl Harbor. It will be returned there to be part of the
Arizona Memorial. The museum still includes many artifacts
from the *Maine,* including life preservers and a capstan to
which the nuns of the Convent of Mary Immaculate added a
spire. The new emphasis is on lighthouse history and memora-
bilia. The impressive original Fresnel lens from the Sombrero
Key light is on display and more interpretative exhibits are
planned.

You can climb eighty-eight steps to the top of the lighthouse
and get a good gull's eye view of Key West. When it was built
in 1847, it was fifty-eight feet tall but it had to be raised over the
years so that the light could be seen over growing trees and the
new buildings of an expanding town. The tower stopped growing at seventy-eight feet and the light was extinguished in 1969.

The lighthouse at Key West

Fort Taylor

The Fort is scarcely visible from the exterior, either from the land or from water. It is not imposing until one is inside.

Begun in 1845 as part of an ambitious coastal fortifications system and named five years later for President Zachary Taylor, it was originally built 1,200 feet from shore (sand and fill eventually connected it to Key West) and had two tiers plus a top platform for cannon just behind the parapet. The fort is built in the shape of a trapezoid and rests on a foundation of Keys' limestone and New England granite. Millions of bricks, shipped down from Pensacola, were used in the twenty-one-year project, set by slaves and German and Irish masons. (Ironically, the slave population of Key West increased fivefold when Union authorities imported them to work on military fortifications during the Civil War.) Construction was plagued by strikes, shortages of material, the antipathy of European craftsmen toward Negro laborers, and hurricanes. Most importantly, there were the vicious periodic attacks of yellow fever, blamed on "miasma" in the air. Indeed, the only time the fort's cannons were fired was in an attempt to dispel this "miasma." A swamp, close to the workmen's quarters and teeming with mosquitoes was not suspected.

On the night that Florida seceded from the Union, January 13, 1861, a small group of Union soldiers marched to the fort, and with the assistance of a Lieutenant Edward Hunt, in charge of the fort's construction, secured it for the Union, delivering an immediate blow to the Confederacy. Less than fifty Union men held a crucial fortification in what was the largest town in Florida. Sentiment in town was mostly Southern, but there was no attempt to take the fort by rebel sympathizers, although many of the young men of Key West sailed away immediately to join the Confederate Army. Several months later, with the arrival of additional troops, the Union blockade of the Confederacy began, and captured blockade runners, their ships, and cargoes, were brought into the harbor and anchored beneath the massive guns of Fort Taylor, guns which now numbered almost two hundred. An average of thirty-two ships were stationed here during the war years, and at one time there were three hundred vessels of various description held captive.

Key West was the only city south of the Mason-Dixon line to remain in the hands of the Union during the Civil War, but Washington officials did not consider it that important militarily. Frantic requests for supplies and reinforcements were largely ignored. Many Union commanders considered it a fetid place of disease and desired neither their ships nor their men to come near Key West. In 1862, of the 448 men garrisoned at Fort Taylor, 331 contracted yellow fever and 71 died.

The fort was still in the process of being constructed in 1866 when it was declared obsolete. The innovation of rifled cannon which projected a spinning cannonball that dug into masonry rather than bounced off it, made huge brick fortresses useless. Only a few soldiers remained stationed here and it became a favorite spot for the townspeople to picnic. A local druggist, J. Otto, made a written request to the authorities for picnicking privileges using his letterhead:

Apothecaries' Hall
Pharmaceutists and Embalmers
Bodies Disinterred
Hermetically Sealed
and Forwarded to Friends.

In 1867, the president of the defeated Confederacy, Jefferson Davis, visited Key West for a day on his way to Cuba where he hoped to regain his health. He did not picnic at the fort, but while here he was given a sapodilla to sample. He broke it neatly in half, took a small bite, and put the halves back together again. When asked if he liked the fruit, he said politely, "I cannot say that I care for it particularly, but I fancy some people are very fond of it."

In 1898, for the Spanish-American War, the Fort was reactivated. It was also modernized by cutting it back a level and equipping it with newer weapons. This new emplacement of guns was called *Osceola Battery*. The refuse from the demolition was packed into the casemates with all the obsolete Columbiad and Rodman cannons, cannonballs and gun carriages, and the whole thing covered with cement and sand. Over the years, through World Wars I and II and the Cuban crisis, other weapons, radar, missiles, and antiaircraft guns were mounted and removed, but the treasury of Civil War artifacts, including the Parrott rifle, the type of cannon that had reduced Savannah's Fort Pulaski to rubble, remained untouched. (The Parrott can be identified by the wrought-iron jacket shrunk around the breech and the grooves inside the muzzle.)

By the mid 1960's, Fort Taylor was abandoned, forgotten and buried beneath dredge material and weeds. Then in 1968, the Navy (the Army had turned the fort over to the Navy in 1947) directed their base architect and historian, Howard England, to investigate the site, although they did not want to spend any money for excavation. It is to Howard England that the "discovery" of Fort Taylor should be attributed. With borrowed equipment and volunteer help from townspeople and Navy personnel, including perhaps most enthusiastically, men from the brig, Fort Taylor emerged. After months and years of hand shoveling, the beautiful vaulted brickwork of the gun rooms was exposed and cannon unearthed. Also discovered was America's first water desalinization plant—*Dr. Normandy's Patent Marine Aerated Fresh Water Apparatus*—which had once produced 7,000 gallons of fresh water daily from the sea. The military artifacts you will see have been recovered from only two of the fort's twenty-four casemates and represent only a fraction of the buried arsenal which is the largest collection of Civil War cannons in the United States.

The fort and fifty acres of surrounding land is now under the management of the Florida Park Service. It has an interesting little museum and the best swimming in Key West. Don't miss Fort Taylor. Truman Annex at Southard Street. Telephone: 292-6713.

East Martello Museum and Art Gallery

A charming museum and a great place to acquaint yourself with Key West history.

The Martello Tower was an ancient Corsican means of defense, a cylindrical structure, often described as an "upside down flowerpot." Key West's two untraditional towers were constructed during the Civil War to assist Fort Taylor in repelling a coastal landing force. Begun in 1862, work on them ceased two years later. The towers, like the rest of the Keys' huge brick fortifications, were never completed. Cannon were never installed here. Before the Art and Historical Society took over the East Tower in 1950, there was not even a roof.

The museum has exhibits depicting sponging, turtling, pirating, and whatnot, as well as a Cuban life raft, found floating empty ten miles south of Key West in 1969, made of bamboo, wire and tractor inner tubes and bearing a feed sack sail. There is also a "Key West Writers" room, the books of the venerated fixed behind glass.

The gallery has rotating shows of contemporary and local art as well as an interesting permanent collection where "the welded found materials" of Stanley Papio of Key Largo and the wood carvings of Old Key West by Mario Sanchez can be found.

Papio was a junk dealer and welder, despised for years by his neighbors on Route 1. After being arrested six times for violating local ordinances concerning orderliness and neatness, a friend suggested he claim the junkyard as an "Art Museum" and charge 25¢ to see the peculiar and parodic conjunctions made between bedsprings, toilet fixtures, and Buick chrome. Papio is the Keys' John Chamberlain and his works are witty, crude, and very charming. When he died suddenly in 1982, Key Largo, home of the movie lie and Port Bougainvillea, still had no interest in the collection and Martello was eventually able to purchase the pieces.

The Cuban primitive, Mario Sanchez, was born in Key West in 1908 in what was known as "Gato's Village," an area bounded by Truman Avenue and Whitehead, South and Simonton Streets. This is where the flourishing cigar industry was located —one of the larger rebuilt factories still exists today as the Navy Commissary—and the heart of the Cuban community. It is this lively and departed village that Sanchez recreates in his meticulous, colorful carvings. What is nice about his work is that he, like a kind angel, restores lost things. The Convent of Mary Immaculate was demolished, but Sanchez recreates it, complete with its stupendous plantings. To the sightseer at the corner of Amelia and Duval, the Cuban Club is nothing but a simulation (more shops!)—just a bit of hygienic faux, but Sanchez paints it as it was when it was the soul of the neighborhood, beside the long-gone El Anón Ice Cream Parlor.

Sanchez draws his scenes first on grocery bags then transfers it to wood with carbon paper. His tools are chisels, a mallet, a piece of broken glass, and a razor blade. Sometimes he uses coffee grounds, coral rock or kitty-litter to make streets. He likes horses, parades, funerals, pregnant ladies, chickens, and clouds. In the amazing clouds of Key West, he carves things too —doves, blossoms, trumpets, and even the themes of Mr. Hemingway. In one of the explanatory notes to his carvings in this carefully presented exhibit, Sanchez says, "I have featured two of his best known works in the clouds: *For Whom The Bell Tolls* and *Death In The Afternoon.*" And there they are.

Mario Sanchez spends the winter in Tampa, Florida. Any other time he can be seen working outside his brother's home, in his "Studio Under The Trees" on Catherine Street. **East Martello Tower,** its museum, gallery, and garden is right in front of the airport on South Roosevelt Boulevard. Open daily 9:30 to 5:30. Adults $2.50, ages 7–15 50¢.

West Martello Tower

The West Tower, on Higgs Beach, between the picnic grounds and the White Street Fishing Pier, is the home of the Key West Garden Club. It is far more low-slung and battered than the East Tower because bored soldiers stationed at Fort Taylor used it for target practice, and since it was closer to town, people pilfered many of the bricks for their walls and gardens.

Within the garden center at West Martello are plant-identification books, seed pod exhibits, and a tattered arrangement of stuffed birds. There is also a checklist of plants, ninety-two of which are marked in the rambling, ruined confines of the tower's grounds. Below the mounded fortification on the beach-ward side are topless sunbathers, and above you, according to the season, is flowering or fruiting this and that.

A GONE GARDEN AND TWO GROWING ONES

The beautiful **Peggy Mills Garden** which was once open to the public at 700 Simonton Street, is now privately owned and locked tight. One can only glimpse the treasures within—the huge earthenware jars called *tinajones* from Cuba, the curving brick walls, the orchids and lilies, the tall old palms —from outside a narrow wrought-iron gate. The plants grew so vigorously inside Miss Peggy's that people said if you parked your car outside on the bougainvillea cuttings, you'd get a flat tire. The most intensely planted acreage in Key West was recently "improved" with a tennis court and swimming pool, and is for sale again.

The **Botanical Gardens on Stock Island** was the pride and joy of horticultural ladies of the 30's. An intriguing spot with a varied number of trees in a natural hammock setting, it was allowed to decline, its rare and indigenous species pushed out by brazilian pepper and neglect. Difficult to find —it is behind the golf course, sandwiched between the Easter Seal Society, the dog pound, and the jail annex—and a tangled shadow of its former self, it is now being cleared and replanted. Once again, the oddities of monkey's dinner bell, egg fruit, horseradish, and soapberry trees might grow here.

The **Indigenous Park** at the end of White Street near the pier is only a little over three acres but it seems much larger as you wander and linger among these palms and trees—the real natives here. Everything is identified but, relaxingly, not explained.

The West Tower is free and erratically open. Each year, in March, there is an orchid show, and on the last Sunday of April there is a large, lush, and frantic plant sale. Open Tuesday through Thursday and Saturday and Sunday, 10 A.M.–noon and 2–4 P.M.

OLD TOWN
Conch Houses

Most of the beautiful old homes and intriguing lanes and alleys of the town can be found in the blocks between Caroline and Angela (which borders the graveyard) and Duval and Francis, and many of these buildings are well documented. The *Pelican Path,* a free descriptive folder published by the Old Island Restoration Foundation, is available from the Hospitality House in Mallory Square. The route is marked with directional yellow signs and the buildings sport neatly numbered plaques. (So much of the Keys seems recently numbered. Even the birds of the air are sometimes seen bearing pancake-size discs on their wings, numbered, by those great numberers, the field researchers, who roam armed with nets and tranquilizing darts.) The Historic Key West Preservation Board has published a striking collection of black and white photographs by Sharon Wells and Lawson Little entitled *Portraits: Wooden Houses of Key West.* The oversized paperback costs $10.

"Conch" architecture is the indigenous look of Key West. It is what's here. One of the prettiest houses in town, passionately regarded as "Conch" is the violet-hued **Artist House** (a guest house) at 534 Eaton Street, which can only be described as Key West-West Indian-Colonial-Victorian in design. Conch too is the dignified rawboned **Albury House** at 730 Southard as is the modest **Eyebrow House** at 1025 Fleming, its attic windows tucked beneath the shelter of the roof; a most efficient breeze capturing and air-circulating architectural eccentricity and one not found elsewhere in Florida. With this exception, however, the Conch style is not one unique to the country—it is a coalescence of styles, a high density of nineteenth- and turn-of-the-century classically built wooden houses that gives the town such an appealing and distinctive appearance.

The practicalities made necessary by a remote, hot, and wet location were combined with mainland fashion and local wealth. Many of the houses have thermally efficient roofs of galvanized steel, embossed with a pattern, and virtually all have porches. In the case of the larger houses, the porches often curve around three sides of the house with the pattern being repeated on the second story. Top-hung shutters are prevalent as a blind to the sun, and ventilating scuttles (simply a hole on the roof, with a lid) are outlets for hot air. Frequently, houses large and small are built not on foundations, but on piers, which may explain why Key Westers so enthusiastically undertake the task of moving them around. Piers are slabs of coral rock which elevate the house, protecting it against rot, flooding, and even hurricane winds.

Paint was not employed until the cleanup of the 1930's. Houses were left to weather and silver in the sun. Plaster was never used. Inside, the wood of preference, pitch-rich pine from Pensacola and Dade County, was used on floors, ceilings, and walls, often hand-planed and fitted without nails. Dade County pine has become extinct, Dade County being Miami now, but the wood lives on in Key West houses, beautiful wood, personalized by each home's resident termite population. Chimneys are rare, except on those Queen Anne mansions whose all-embracing style insisted upon them, but there are a number of cupolas to be seen, resembling the widow walks of New England coastal towns. Here, however, they should be referred to as wrecker's walks, for they were not employed so much by desperate ladies awaiting the return of their men from the sea, but by anyone with an eye out for ships which would hopefully run aground on the reef, providing the household with a variety of new possessions. Another vessel, eagerly awaited by all in the 1800's was the ice boat, delivering its precious and disappearing cargo all the way from Maine ponds. Ice was also often used as ballast in ships traveling from the North. Good examples of wreckers' walks can be seen on two houses built before the 1886 fire, the Albury house at 730 Southard and the John Lowe house at 620 Southard. The **Lowe House** is built of heart of pine and Honduran mahogany with all mortise and tendon joints secured with wooden pegs so that the house would give in strong winds. An early historian noted that Lowe was rich because he never embarked in a "bubble enterprise." He owned a sponging fleet and enlarged his home as he grew more prosperous. Sponges were responsible for much of the wealth and many of the fine homes of Key West, as were foundered ships, turtles, and cigars.

An ice palace, indeed, having been built in 1885 by George Curry, the president of the ice company, is the large classical home at 620 Eaton Street—a temple of columns, porticos, and entablatures, all tropically garnished with louvered porches and Canary Island date palms.

Eaton Street presents many beauties, the lovely triplets at 401-405-409, and the equally impressive clutch at 511-517 and 523. The octagonal tin-towered **Richard Peacon House** at 712 Eaton is somewhat notoriously known for the price it once commanded. It was originally built by a banker and grocer in the 1890's and bought by the late designer Angelo Donghia in the 1970's. Key West realtors went into deliriums when it was later bought by Calvin Klein for close to a million dollars, approximately $700,000 more than everyone admitted the house was worth. Klein said it was "probably crazy" but he "wanted it badly." The house at 724 is a handsome example of a Bahamian house with Victorian influences. Adorned with flourishing columnar trim and cranberry glass, it is owned by the county sheriff.

Two of the most remarked upon homes in Key West were brought here from somewhere else. The **Bahama Houses**, one at 730 Eaton, the other directly behind it at 408 William, were made in the Bahamas, dismantled, brought over by ship and reconstructed in 1847, after the hurricane of 1846 had destroyed much of Key West. Wood was scarce, so two brothers-in-law, Joseph Bartlum and Richard Roberts, returned to their home in Green Turtle Cay and sailed these structures, made simply of random-width, hand-beveled pine boards, back. The twin-gabled roof, with the valley in between to collect rainwater for the cistern, and the large shuttered windows are of typical Bahamian design. The low ceilings inside indicate the age of the houses, for the cooling benefits of high-ceilinged rooms were only recognized by later Key West builders. Bartlum was a shipbuilder who built the only clipper ship ever made in Key West, the *Steven Mallory*. The ship was launched in 1856 and bore a life-size figurehead of the cherubic Mallory upon her prow. The Roberts House on William has been very little altered over the years. Crowded at right angles to the street, its double porches run the length of the house on two sides and are built under the roof. Both houses are rather unassuming, intriguing primarily because of the journey they once took.

Gingerbread, Courtyards, and Shotguns

Key Westers love their gingerbread. The town embraced this fanciful fashion of the mid-1800's and people today are still gleefully remodeling by slapping up baluster patterns of pineapples, fleurs-de-lis, and urns. Most of the elaborately turned railings of Old Town were not made locally, but were brought here as stock items for the building trade, although there were several local craftsmen who did scroll-cut work from flat boards. One of these was John Carroll who set up his turning lathe near the lighthouse in the 1880's and produced brackets, cornices, and trim according to the customer's whim. Another was Francisco Camellon, a black Cuban, whose lathe was turned by a blindfolded horse. His shop was on Simonton Street under a big Spanish lime tree.

There are more than sixty different baluster patterns to be found in Key West, the most popular being Grecian urns, dia-

Examples of gingerbread trimming

monds, hearts, ship wheels and—after the railroad reached Key
West in 1912—viaduct arches. Lovely examples of scroll-cut ship
wheels can be found at the **Cuban Consul House** on the corner
of Eaton and Grinnel. The same gingerbread stringcourse
adorns the house at 615 Fleming.

One of the most intriguing examples of personalized gingerbread and a design that was used for professional advertising is
found on the old Conch house at 1117 Duval. The saloon keeper
who once lived here had this pattern of whiskey and wine bottles and the hearts and diamonds of playing cards sent from
Cuba and installed as balusters.

Two of the most elaborate gingerbread dwellings in town are
the grey Victorian **George Roberts House** at 313 William
Street (its beauty assisted in the late spring and summer by the
blooming of a towering poinciana tree) and the **Benjamin
Baker House** at 615 Elizabeth Street. Baker was the owner of
a lumberyard, a contractor, and an undertaker and he built this
house for his daughter in 1885 as a wedding present. His workmen, freed from the rigors of nailing together coffins, spared no
flourish here—the trim is all scroll-cut. The house was so well
built that when a tornado moved it seven feet off its foundation
in 1972, not a single wall or window cracked.

The **William Kerr House** at 410 Simonton Street has gingerbread embellishments of a more Gothic sort. The style of this
little house is unclassifiable, put together by a carpenter-archi-
tect who had designed many of the striking buildings of Key
West in the last twenty years of the nineteenth century. Born
in Massachusetts Kerr became one of the town's most versatile
and original builders, responsible for the design of the convent,
as well as the Customs House and the Old Stone Church at 600
Eaton Street. The house is heavily ornamented inside with
hand-painted landscapes over the doors and in indented panels
in the ceilings.

A building of erratic history, so common in Key West, is the
structure at 314 Simonton, the old **Trev-Mor** apartments. Built
with bricks taken from the ruins of Fort Taylor, the first Ford
dealership in Key West was located here in 1919. There were
apartments upstairs and it was here where Hemingway and his
wife Pauline, fresh from Paris, stayed for several weeks while

The Patterson house

they awaited the delivery of a new car. It remained a rooming house and hotel until the 1970's when it was completely gutted by fire. The new owners kept the core empty and it is now a one-bedroom private home with a vast inner atrium. The old cistern is in the middle of things and is used as a swimming pool. A number of water craft continue their lives most peculiarly behind these walls. An Ecuadorian canoe is used as a planter, a glass-topped Haitian dory serves as a coffeetable, and a wet bar and dumbwaiter have been created from a lifeboat off the yacht of one no less than Adolf Hitler.

The old **Mercedes Hospital** or **Casa Gato** at 1209 Virginia Street, just around the corner from the Gulfstream Market on White, is out of the way, but noteworthy. It too has a courtyard, of an initially more intended sort, and a history even more eccentric and variable.

Eduard Gato was a wealthy Cuban cigar manufacturer who had come to Key West in 1868 at the start of Cuba's Ten Year War with Spain. The town was jammed with wealthy Cuban cigar manufacturers building factories, banks, and mansions, and hiring and housing thousands of their fellow emigrés to work as strippers, trimmers, rollers, pickers, and packers. Gato

built his mansion, embellished with balconies and cupolas, and
enclosed a patio, in the Spanish style, but it appears a little odd
because it was built out of wood, covered with clapboard and
decorated with a bit of gingerbread. It is a high square building
with long Gothic windows and large, dark, tall-ceilinged rooms
(eight to a floor) that look out onto the somewhat stern courtyard. It was said that after Gato got his Spanish courtyard he
was puzzled as to what to do with it, so he stabled his horses
there for several years.

Gato and his family did not live here long. He returned to
Cuba after the Spanish-American War of 1898 (the war in which
Teddy Roosevelt disappointed Key Westers by having his Rough
Riders sally forth from Tampa) and gave the house to the town
to be used as a hospital. The hospital was named for his wife,
Mercedes, but it was locally called *Casa del Pobre*—the house
of the poor. It remained a poorhouse until the 1940's. Elizabeth
Bishop, once paying a call, described a patient as possessing an
"apocryphal appearance," her bright, milky blue eyes seeming
"like the flames of a gas burner when they have just been
turned off and are about to sink back into the black pipes." The

Sand Key Light

Mercedes Hospital had a reputation of harboring gloomy ghosts and there are still some old Cubans in town who refuse to walk on the Casa Gato side of the street.

When its days as a poorhouse had passed, it became an arena for cockfights and a storage area for newspapers collected during World War II paper-drives. It was "a monster nobody wanted" until the 1970's when it was restored as apartments. Musical events take place here now during Old Island Days. String quartets play, and champagne is served in the courtyard.

Many cigar barons like Gato built houses for their workers, creating instant neighborhoods around their factories. Most of the factories are gone but many of the little company houses remain. These narrow houses were simplicity itself, consisting of three rooms, one behind the other, the front and rear doors in alignment with the door connecting the rooms, and were called *shotgun* houses, perhaps because of the narrow and uninterrupted passage the space allowed. Most were no more than twelve by thirty feet in floor area, had galvanized steel roofs and little porches. Tired of termites, many shotgun owners later replaced the wooden pillars and porches with concrete ones. Tidy, cherished examples of shotguns can be found between 822 and 834 Olivia where the street parallels the graveyard.

THE GRAVEYARD

"I'd rather eat monkey manure than die in Key West," Ernest Hemingway said. He said this one summer day, sweating in the sulfurous, warm, and brownish waters of his swimming pool, years before he chose to die in Idaho. But people not as fortunate, one would assume, have died in Key West, and it is here where they remain, smack in the middle of things on the lip of Old Town. This is referred to euphemistically as "The Cemetery" in yet another attempt to gingerbread Key West. But what it is is the Graveyard. The graveyard was established here in 1847, although some of the graves date before that. The original burying ground was closer to the lighthouse but was moved

The graveyard

here when many of the graves were disinterred in a hurricane. There are still funeral marching bands in town that will "play the dead home."

The graveyard is hot, white and built up, the graves all in above-ground vaults, both because of the water table and the toughness of coral rock, and it is virtually treeless, although some citizens are hard at work planting frangipani cuttings and mock oranges in available scraps of ground. "Palm Avenue," which intersects the graveyard, is now neatly lined with tiny Christmas palms. Other citizens, however, are just as determinedly cutting down large, bearded, Washingtonian palms, fearing that a high wind will bring them crashing down on what James Merrill describes as "whitewashed hope chests." Neither conchs nor Cubans care for trees as a rule, and in fact the graveyard is a fine, impressive place without them. There are flowering shrubs planted here and there and something is always in bloom. White egrets drift among the markers giving an Egyptian effect.

This is a wonderful place to see birds, particularly at the end of the day. This is the Nighthawk's territory, for instance. The large, mottled bird is known in Key West as the Mosquito Hawk although it is not a hawk at all, but belongs to the voracious insect eaters known as goatsuckers. A flying mouth, it darts and scoops at twilight here, saying *piskkk*.

A sausage tree, notorious for its preference to be pollenated by bats, stands at one of the entrances on Angela Street opposite the "bottle wall." Look upon it and be grateful that once again it appears to be fruitless. If R. C. Perky had been successful in raising bats on Sugarloaf, Key West would have been up to its rooftops in sausage trees with their weird seed pods swinging on long stems.

The graveyard is crisscrossed with paths that bear concrete road markers. For example, the brick Otto plot which contains the graves of three Yorkshire terriers—Sonny, Little Boy, and Little Derry Otto—as well as the one of a pet deer, Elfina, is located at the intersection of Second and Laurel. A varnished marker on the crypt of B. P. Roberts which complains *I Told You I Was Sick* is at the end of Seventh Street just before the fenced Jewish plot. There are angels, large and small, swans and lambs, open books, and amputated tree trunks. There is a full-sized cement sculpture of a man, done by his friend, utilizing the boots of the deceased. His name is Earle Saunders Johnson and he is smiling. *The Buck Stops Here* one gravestone says. *Here Lies Our Heart* says another. Wander and read epitaphs of loss—*We Miss You at Home*—longing and regret—*Yesterday Is Gone and Tomorrow Shall Never Be Mine*. Even gratitude—*God Was Good to Me*. There are pictures of some of the dead in small plastic frames. There are benches beside some of the graves and wrought-iron fences around others. There is a pretty plot which contains the graves of the victims of the *Maine* with a handsome statue of a sailor holding an oar. And there is a monument to *Los Martires,* Cubans who died during the Spanish-American War.

An infamous grave that is not marked is the one of Elena Hoyos Mesa, a Cuban girl who died of tuberculosis in the 1930's but who even more unfortunately was the object of affection of an elderly and lunatic X-ray technician named Karl von Cosel.

Before he met Elena, von Cosel's obsession was with airplanes. He was building an experimental craft that would land on either water or land. The plane had huge wheels made of wooden slats and covered with paper. After Elena died, von Cosel was seen visiting her tomb just off Francis more than frequently. He played records and sometimes cooked breakfast there. Eventually he carted the body off in the plane to his house where he loved, lived, and experimented on Elena for seven years until the grisly affair was discovered. Held together with wire and waxy compounds and wearing a wedding gown, the corpse had glass eyes, fabricated breasts, and, according to a doctor who testified at the trial, "a tube in the vaginal area wide enough to permit intercourse." Poor Elena was viewed by thousands of Key West Citizens at the Lopez Funeral Home before she was interred again.

The dead are always with us, some more than others.

The graveyard's gates are open from sunrise to sunset. Tours are available on the weekends for $5. They even have a breakfast tour on Memorial Day. Have a pastry and contemplate the ever-approaching nothing.

WHERE TO STAY

There are many quaint, elegant and/or decadent places to stay in Key West. There are guest houses and motels (chain and unchain) and condominiums as well as suites in time-share resorts that can be rented by the day and week. The Key West Visitor's Bureau puts out an accommodation directory with rates and a helpful visitor "type" category. You can get one by writing to Box 1147, Key West 33041 or calling (305) 294-2587.

If you're planning a longer stay you may be interested in renting a home by the month or for the season. Most of the real estate agencies have furnished houses for rent. Knight Realty, in the oldest school house, 336 Duval (294-5155) is one of the larger ones. Or try Old Town Realty, 605 Simonton (294-1012) or Island Properties, 400 Simonton (296-7766) or Key Lime Realty, 507 Whitehead (296-8516). Specializing in vacation rentals is Property Management of Key West, 517 Eaton Street (296-7744). They have about forty houses in and out of Old Town that they'll rent daily, weekly, or monthly. They provide maid service and have their own maintenance department and will try to match your vacation needs, even your desires, with present availability—just like a dating service.

Remember, prices here are probably already history. Undoubtedly, they have risen. And will rise.

Chains

The chains are on North Roosevelt Boulevard as you come into town. The prospect—a jumble of the familiar, plus a highly harrowing four-lane highway teeming with illogical and neurotic traffic—is not pleasing. It's awful. There is the water but it looks so *sad*. Beware of ads promising Gulf views in this area. It's not that they're exactly lying, it's merely that you might be disappointed. Here are **Holiday Inn, Howard Johnson, Quality Inn, TraveLodge**, and **Day's Inn**. Prices are usual for chains in resort areas—$80–$125 a night.

On South Roosevelt Boulevard (A-1A) the expected appears much nicer. Set back from the ocean by the airport in pleasantly landscaped grounds are the **Best Western** (296-3500), $135–$185 a night, and the **Key Wester** (296-5671). The Key Wester has tennis courts and a good resident pro. Prices are $105 and up.

South Street-Simonton Street Beach Area

There are a number of reasonable motels here, all within walking distance of town, including the popular, old-timer **The Santa Maria** (296-5678) now cramped and dwarfed by the pink four-story **Reach**, and the easygoing, moderate **Hibiscus** (296-6711) neither quite so easygoing nor so moderate since renovation. There are the swimming-pool-in-the-middle-of-the-parking-lot variety like **Southeast Ocean Inn** (294-6663) and **The Blue Marlin** (294-2585), and the swimming-pool-on-the-street variety such as **Southernmost** (296-6577) and **The Spanish Gardens** (294-1051). Southernmost now incorporates

Southwest so they have pools both within the parking lot *and* on the street. Rooms here run $110–$150 a night for a double in season, slightly more for an efficiency and drop $20 in price from June until December. **Atlantic Shores** (296-2491) is a big place, no beauty on the street side but with a handsome swimming pool decked out on the ocean and a 150-foot pier. Rooms around $125, $50 in summer. Sunday night there's a rambunctious "tea dance." (A tea dance in Key West is bare-chested bump-and-grind kissy boogie.) But the bar **Papillon** is considered to be a "wrinkle bar"—for older gents. The more subdued and better designed **South Beach Motel** (296-5611) is next door with pool, pier, and balconied rooms. Rates are $120 a night for a double, Christmas through April; in summer, $80. Upstairs rooms with a balcony overlooking the ocean are $135. This motel also runs the adjacent **La Mer** (294-6691), a home renovated as a small hotel with a beach, which should be more interesting than it is. The rooms have been decorated by someone who must formerly have done offices. A grim and musty air prevails. In season $140–$200.

In the vicinity but a world apart at 1125 Duval is **La Terraza De Marti** or **La-Te-Da**, famed for its tea dance on Sunday nights and its night club. We give good paradise! is the cry here —definitely not the place to bring the kids. One of the prettiest compounds in Key West, La-Te-Da nestles outrageously in the quiet Cuban neighborhood in a maze of decks, bars, restaurants, and treetop verandas. Some of the more elaborate rooms have whirlpool baths and stereos. There are no televisions. "I don't believe people come to Key West to watch television," owner Larry Formica says. Sleek bodies lounge around the pool, the tables are covered with pink cloths and pretty china, and the tendency is to order more and more champagne while you wait for your elaborate breakfast (9 A.M.–4 P.M.) served from an excellent and ambitious kitchen. (See Restaurants.) Rooms with shared baths run around $85. Studios and suites go up to $188 per night. (294-8435)

Deluxe

Henry Flagler planned a chain of luxury resort hotels, which he referred to as "Halls of Joy," along his Florida train route. **The Casa Marina** with its Spanish Renaissance design, tiled roof, arched windows, colonnades, and loggias, in a beautiful garden setting at the end of the road on the Atlantic was to be the ultimate. The Casa opened New Year's Eve 1922, eight years after Flagler's death. It was a popular spot for the rich and famous until 1943 when the government leased it for Navy housing during the war. It returned to hotel status in 1945, but was taken over by the Army in 1962 during the Cuban missile crisis. Sentries replaced doormen, missile battalion troops were quartered in the rooms, and the beach was strung with barbed wire. After the Army left it was declared out of commission as a hotel. Indeed, it was described as a "termite-ridden firetrap." For the next ten years, only the dance patio and the Birdcage lounge remained open and it was messy and popular until 1978 when the Marriott chain took it over, renovating it completely, tearing down the Birdcage and adding a new, ugly four-story wing. The elegance is all beach-side. They don't do pretty for the street. The old building is grand, its walls "battered in" for hurricane proofing, receding in thickness from 22 inches at the foundation to 12 inches at the roof. The black cypress lobby is impressive, the grounds immaculate. The Casa has an 1100-foot beach, tennis courts, and several bars and restaurants, including **Flagler's**. Thirty-dollar lamb chops here in a reserved, even solemn, setting. It seems very far from town. And it is. In fact, going downtown from the Casa feels like a foray into exotic, uncontrolled, and unsecured territory. The Casa is great-looking but can't quite shake—despite her pig roasts and steel drum music—her reputation as being a bit . . . boring. Suites range from $320 to $695 in season. Ocean-view rooms are $300. The least expensive room is $210, $155 in summer. Reynolds Street on the Atlantic. Toll Free: 800-228-9290 or direct: (305) 296-3535.

The Pier House 1 Duval Street (294-9541). Toll free: 800-327-8340. The Pier House is well-known and very popular. Reservations should be made in advance even during the off-season when the rooms may all be filled with powerboat racers or rafters or fantastic participants in the Fantasy Fest revels of Halloween. The hotel is subtly and handsomely laid out, the rooms tasteful, the grounds palmy. Low-key, efficient, and friendly. At the Caribbean Spa annex next door, there's an awesome health club. The standard room here in season is $215. A nicer room in the courtyard by the pool is $275 and one overlooking the harbor is $325. From April 15 to December 20, these are $150, $195 and $235 respectively. Suites run from $425 to $725 in season, but if elaborate suites are your desire, you might be more content across the street at

Ocean Key House Zero Duval Street (296-7701). Toll free: 800-328-9815. The Ocean Key House, when built, was notorious for counting bay bottom acreage in their density computations. Out of scale with an enormous parking garage at its base which one must pass through to attain either one's room or the pool, the exterior is heavy-handed. But the rooms are perhaps the most luxuriously furnished on the island, all decorated in soft, tropical shades, with large balconies and kitchens. The showers are motel basic; you're supposed to luxuriate in the immoderate Jacuzzi in the bedroom. Suites overlook the street, the Gulf and Mallory Square parking lot. You may come back from breakfast, open the door and have the sensation of a cruise ship having entered your living room. Very comfortable one-bedroom suites run from $185 to $355 in season, $60 to $100 less April to December. Two-bedroom suites, $385–$450.

The Reach Simonton Street on the ocean (296-5000). Toll-free: 800-822-4200. The Reach is somewhat brutish in design, even though it's pink. This is the south end of town's answer to the Pier House. The rooms are attractive, but small, and each has the amenities of a coffee maker (which the maid fills with fresh beans daily) and a refrigerator. There is a fine beach and pool, an excellent restaurant (see pgs. 211, 212), an extravagantly stocked deli and bakery, a library, a health club, and a romantic pier. Rooms $215–$325. A one-bedroom suite on the ocean is

$475; a two-bedroom suite, $675. In the off-season the less expensive accommodations are around $75 less.

Hyatt Key West 601 Front Street. Toll free: 800-228-9000. Part of the new chic-ing-up of Key West. They call it a boutique resort as it has only 120 rooms. The beach could be the world's smallest, but the rooms with balconies are sited well for sunset-watching. The lowest rate in season is $200 a night. A suite is $450. If Fate brings you to the Rock in August, say, a suite is yours for $250.

The Marquessa Hotel 600 Fleming Street (292-1919). This old boardinghouse was refurbished in 1988 and it's charming. Fifteen lovely big high-ceilinged rooms with generous baths. One suite has a private balcony overlooking the street and many of the rooms have pretty window seats that are right out of a Jesse Wilcox Smith painting. Charming, but costly. Rooms and suites $175–$275.

Moderates

Near the Casa and not far from the beach is the secluded **El Patio Motel** (800 Washington Street, 296-6531). This is a discovery—quiet, clean and pleasant with a garden patio and a terrific rooftop sun deck where you can sail your gaze over the tops of palms to the ocean. The rooms are large with little view of their own but with classic Cuban-tile floors and, often, kitchens. This is the best of the little motels in the area. Rooms are $82 in season, $40 otherwise. A two-room apartment is $106 a day, $620 a week. **The Sea Shell Motel** at 718 South Street is a light-hearted, unexacting youth hostel which takes no credit cards and is $38 a night. It has a dormitory where one can sleep for $18. During spring break, however, the rooms are $100 a night because ". . . the kids trash the rooms," (296-5719). With a pool and accepting credit cards and even pets is **The Key Lodge Motel** at 1004 Duval (296-9915) and the **El Rancho** 830 Truman (294-8700). The Key Lodge is $75 a night in season, $45 in summer and fall. El Rancho, away from the action but on busy Truman, is $85 a night in season, $50 at other times. Recently, a guest here called police to report that he couldn't find the cocaine he had hidden in his room and feared that it had been stolen. (At your basic little bar on Applerouth Lane, Nasty Nancy's, people often call the police too, but often to turn themselves in . . . "I'm a fugitive from Texas and I just can't take it anymore . . ." Maybe they just couldn't find a cheap room.)

Guest Houses

Guest houses abound in Key West and most of them are very pretty, private, and friendly places with lovely gardens and dramatic pools. Many do not accept children sixteen and under either because of the cozily affectionate milieu or because patrons want to enjoy their complimentary quiche breakfasts and Jacuzzis in peace. A pleasant place that will take families is **The Island City House**.

Island City House 411 William Street (294-5702). Smack in the middle of the historic district with all its regal houses, Island City was built in the 1880's and served as a guest house as early as 1912. Another building in this small compound is **The Arch House** which faces Eaton. Restored and renovated down to its last nail, each unit is an apartment with full kitchen. The rooms are rather dark but high-ceilinged and beautifully furnished. Bromeliads bloom profusely over an old cistern. Pleasant pool, rampant garden, breakfast bar. One-bedroom suites are $175. Two-bedroom $100 more. **Island City House** should not be confused with **Island House,** a men-only cruise complex on the corner of Fleming and White (294-6284) that has rooms, a pool, and a complete gym.

Two small classic guest houses are **Eaton Lodge** and **The Artist House.** Neither has a pool.

Eaton Lodge 511 Eaton Street (294-3800). This is an inn both elegant and orderly, the drawing room a fine place to catch up on the Trollope you brought down to read. A lovely garden, a

Jacuzzi, and a little patio where complimentary breakfast is served. $105–$230 in season. $75–$160 May to mid-December.

The Artist House 534 Eaton Street (296-3977). Built in 1890, each room in this sweet old house is uniquely decorated. The large room in front has a pretty winding staircase which leads to a sleeping loft in the tower. The side rooms have claw-foot bathtubs on an enclosed porch. In one of the suites you can even bubble bathe under a chandelier. The garden is tiny and unmysterious, although it does have a lion's head sluicing water into a Jacuzzi and an obscure stone saint by the fish pond. The Artist House is formal, filled with seventeenth-century antiques, and can be noisy, particularly the rooms on the street. **The Pilot House**, behind it at 414 Simonton Street (294-8719) is more casual with a number of larger, often connecting, rooms with kitchens. There is no pool. A bedroom in The Artist House is $125; $165–190 for a suite. Suites in The Pilot House are about the same, but the double suites are $275.

The Banyan 323 Whitehead Street (296-7786). This is a grouping of eight handsome houses offering suites with kitchens. Pools and plantings, a little leafy bar. Rates in season run $125–$185 a night, $95–$125 May 1 to December 15.

Two attractive, voguish, more freewheeling guest houses are Heron House and Merlinn.

Heron House 512 Simonton (294-9227). One of the prettiest and best-located guest houses in Key West. Seventeen high-ceilinged, beautifully furnished rooms are available. Great attention to detail and design. Handsome yet lightly tropical. Rooms $75–$135 in winter, $45–$95 June 1–Nov. 30. A lot of style for the money. Pool.

Merlinn 811 Simonton Street (296-3336). The rooms here are a bit peculiar, narrow and very high, rather monkish in aspect. The garden, sunning decks, and pool, however, are decidedly not. Merlinn is a real charmer, a bosky retreat from the street with a beautiful, high-ceilinged pine kitchen from which delicious breakfasts are served. There's also an aviary and a library with free drinks and hors d'oeuvres served at the important sunset hour. Cocktails, coffee cake and cockatoos . . . what sort of heart could desire more? . . . Rooms are $80 December through April. Larger rooms with kitchens, $110. The singular "Treehouse" with its private sundeck is $120.

If you'd like to have the illusion of staying with your neat hippie sister in 60's Key West, try **Key West Bed and Breakfast** at 415 William Street (294-3630). A 100-year-old house with great porch-top views of town and lots of fresh fruit for breakfast. Most of the rooms share a bath. Your cohosts are the golden retrievers Sam and Dave. $75-$100. High for retro.

In a class by itself is The Eden House, a long time, low-key favorite which has been around since 1924 when it operated as The Gibson Hotel.

The Eden House 1015 Fleming Street (296-6868). This is some ways from downtown, but in a great walking and biking neighborhood. A simple, 30's tropical inn with fans and iron beds, it's been recently modernized with phones and air conditioners.

Night-blooming cirrus at 413 William Street

Just as the sprucing up was completed, Hollywood arrived and wanted to re-funk the place for the movie *Criss Cross*. Many coats of paint were employed to make the place look unpainted, and its engaging, slightly seedy quality reinstated. After the filming, it was all turned around again. A great old place. It seems to have interesting tenants, feeling rather like the Gramercy Park of Key West guest houses. Rockers on the porch, nice pool, little restaurant (**Rich's**) in the rear. A conch house next door has been converted into fancier suites ($135–$225) but you can still get the old rooms with the balcony overlooking Fleming Street for $85, and rooms with the bath down the hall go for $75, $45 in the summer.

Of the gay guest houses—**Big Ruby**'s on Applerouth Lane has the distinction of being the oldest in the country—**The Brass Key** at 412 Francis (296-4719) is newly elegant, mature you might say, while the all-male **Lighthouse Court** at 902 Whitehead is edgier and younger—New York style so described. **Colours, Coconut Grove** and the all-male **Oasis** are all on Fleming. **Colours** (410 Fleming, 294-6977) is in a lustrously restored Victorian mansion and **Coconut Grove** at 817 Fleming (296-5107) is a sprawling, breezy white gingerbread inn with lots of balconies and porches. Rates here run between $75 and $180. "Socializing is a requisite" and around the pools and sun-traps "clothing optional."

Simonton Court (320 Simonton, 294-6386) is in an 1880 building which was originally a cigar factory. Down a little alley are a number of well-designed wooden cottages with kitchens, porches and private bedrooms as well as sleeping lofts. There are two dramatic pools here, one black, and one set within the crumbling brick foundations of an old house. The cottages, which accommodate four people, are $215 in season, $165 in summer and fall. No kids here though. This is an adults-only compound which caters, as the owners say, to visitors who appreciate a "varied" life-style. . . . showing, once again, that euphemisms make strange bedfellows.

WHERE TO EAT
Breakfast

Breakfast is extremely important to some people who firmly believe that a magical amount of day-long energy and luck is inherent in an eggy morning plate. These are the same people who need to be apprised practically at sunup of world news —the bombings and threats, the kidnappings and disasters, the shocking and the pathetic—and read the newspaper while they eat. An odd marriage, but one indulged in by many. There are others who desire coffee only, perhaps a bun. Still others who prefer brunch. Eggs Benedict, Corned Beef Hash, Steak, . . . practically anything really, as long as it can be accompanied by a Bloody Mary.

Hemingway, before going fishing, would ingest simply of a piece of Cuban bread, a glass of Vichy, and a glass of milk. But alas, Mrs. Rhoda's electric kitchen, where he indulged, is gone, as is, more recently, **Shorty's** on Duval, famous for their biscuits and strange French toast since 1942. Shorty's had the thinnest, palest waitresses in the Keys and the day the joint closed was the day Truman Annex developer Pritam Singh announced that Ritz-Carlton would build a hotel on "Sunset Island." Everyone felt this said it all—the Rock was ruined. But the Ritz hasn't materialized. And probably never will.

For those who believe in breakfast, here are some possibilities:

Dennis Pharmacy (Simonton and South Streets). Everyone who stays in the beach motels ends up here. Plainclothesmen can be overheard discussing cases. The intriguing thing about the Pharmacy is that although the waitress never acknowledges your order, you end up being served anyway. Don't even dream about trying to jolly these ladies up.

The Eatery (on the Atlantic end of Duval). A shambly place directly on the ocean. Opens 6 A.M. with a big $5 breakfast buffet served daily 8–11. Don't try to start the day with their Key lime pie, which is gruesome. There's a good feel to this place, but the food isn't very good.

Camille's (703 Duval). Going strong. Classical music, home-made muffins, powerful espresso and con leche. Built breakfasts (some so complicated you feel you need directions to eat them), fresh and imaginative specials. Locals love this cozy, crowded spot. Open 8–3.

Chit-Chat (821 Duval). A simple enough breakfast for 99¢ (not including coffee) served by rather flamboyant middle-aged males with astonishingly flat midriffs, which they expose.

Emma's (at **The Reach**, Simonton Street at the ocean, 296-5000). Named after a helpful commissioner during the resort's controversial construction. Gratitude does not go on forever, however, and it may not be called Emma's by the time you get there. Serves breakfast from 7–12. Imaginative cooking prettily prepared. Raging pecan buns. Frittatas and fruit ensembles. Sit outside in the snappy breeze with the sunshine everywhere.

Croissants de France (813 Duval). The Breton owner has ex-panded this tiny pastry shop where you once had to sit on the curb to eat your croissant into a pocket-sized café where you can now wait in line for a table. Somewhat elevated from the street with a European clientele. People exclaim over the extensive menu here in many languages. Transcendental crêpes and croissants.

Lunch

Lunch can be an occasion, a necessity, or just a habit. You can munch on Conch fritters, Philippine food or a dolphin sandwich with fries from street vendors, or you can spend all day, more or less, at the **Club Tropic** (700 Duval) open to—practically in —the street, although it does get off to rather a laggardly start for breakfast (8:30). Good Cuban sandwiches can be had at **5 Brothers Grocery** (corner Southard and Grinnel) and the

M&M Laundry walk-up at 1026 White. Best place to eat in the Mallory Square area is the gardeny **Rooftop Cafe**. Good burgers and wonderful Apalachiocola oysters can be had at **Pepe's Cafe** (806 Caroline), a place of varnished walls, booths and tiller-topped tables. An awesome ceiling fan rotates slowly, slowly overhead. There's a nice patio here, too, with bougainvillea vines thick as trees. It's popular for dinner too, though the wait is often endless, the rule appearing to be that *just* as you get seated, the place clears out. The **Half-Shell Raw Bar** across the way in Land's End Village is well known for shrimp and chowders served at picnic tables overlooking Key West Bight. Fresh fish fried with a light touch and large sweet shrimp are simply served at **Danny's Fish Market** (627 Duval) but you've got as much room in here as a sardine does in a tin. The irresolutely named **Emma's,** at The Reach, specializes in fresh, simply prepared fish. They have five different kinds of snapper, all delicious (only the fish knows how he's different; the waitresses often don't). The **Margaritaville Cafe** at 500 Duval is where to go for a cheeseburger and a bracing brace of margaritas to get your afternoon going. Jimmy Buffet himself is wont to drop into his place some nights for the music—which always gives the tourist a tingle. **Harry's Island Hideaway** (618 Duval), though somewhat barren as gardens go, is an old and easygoing favorite. They're open from 10–3 and after a siesta, for supper as well. Closed Wednesdays. **Bagatelle** is a pretty old house at 115 Duval and eating on the cool verandas gives you a real sense of being on holiday. Very nice for lunch but dinner finds the Bag in more disarray. They will possibly be careless with your meal, perhaps be annoyed by your very presence. Once, when a patron protested some fish he felt was "funny," the kitchen said, "The kitchen does not agree with you." And that was that. **The Pier House** is always fun. Good raw bar, conch fritters, conch salad, fruit plates, and the best margaritas around. They have two Key lime pies available, frozen or chilled. Choose neither, for they are not very good. However, you should feel easy here, as though eating lunch is *exactly* what you should be doing. Strangely, there are often pigeons about, not on the grass, of which there is none, but on the deck, on the railings, on empty tables, eying you with their pigeon eyes, as though all the world were their monument. The management has had to string wire around to interrupt their flight patterns.

Dinner

Dinner is a far more serious engagement. It costs so much more and one is usually expectant, or at the very least, hopeful. One might even be dressed up.

Key West restaurants are notoriously unreliable. *The* place to be one season will be empty as a weekday church the next. Proprietors have nervous breakdowns. Chefs are shot. People get bored. The kitchen help's minds wander to thoughts of affairs, windsurfing, or cocaine. Restaurants are as capricious as the weather, as quickly changeable as the tides. And yet the number of pretty and ambitious restaurants here are very impressive and should be investigated with enthusiasm. All the restaurants serve Key lime pie but they have all become somewhat wary of recommending it. Really good Key lime pie is elusive. The bars have begun serving Key lime shooters with enthusiasim. They taste exactly like what you've been looking for but they're more fun.

Some very grand cuisine and prices have struck Key West. **Cafe des Artistes** (1007 Simonton), **The Buttery** (1208 Simonton) and **Flagler's** at the Casa Marina all offer meals and wines not to be undertaken with a skinny wallet. Cafe des Artistes and The Buttery are both enclosed, dark well-mannered establishments indicating the seriousness of their rich fare—buttery steaks, creamed chickens, stuffed shrimp, fish in pastry puffs. (The fancy Buttery is close by the funky, famous **Full Moon** and to leave the streets of Key West and enter it is to feel like Captain Kirk might on opening the door to an alternate world —like Sarasota.)

The pretty restaurant in the corner of the Marquessa (600 Fleming) was called Mira when it began, and was so awesomely expensive that it unnerved even the rich. You could charter a boat for weeks for the cost of dinner. But then they simplified themselves somewhat, painted over most of the trompe l'oeil,

Mexican flame vine

changed their name to **Cafe Marquessa** and became one of the smartest restaurants in town. Delicious food, good-looking people, chic and relaxed. In a way it could be called "Resemblances" for everyone looks vaguely "known." Open 6–11 (292-1244).

Louie's Backyard (corner Vernon and Waddell off South Street; phone: 294-1061). In a lovely old house of the palest pink on the Atlantic is the best known restaurant in town and the one with the best views. Deck dining offers spectacular arboreal prospects particularly in summer when silent lightning leaps across the sky. Porches, stars, excellent service and food. Sophisticated, pricey and romantic though there's a feeling in town that people are becoming a little weary of Louie's "reputation." Even so, it remains every traveler's culinary destination. In the winter at the shuttle terminal in Miami, everybody on the telephone is calling here, desperate for a reservation. Pleading and begging. Lying! ("We'll be out by eight, we promise . . .")

La-Te-Da (1125 Duval; phone: 294-8435). A most elaborate menu, prettily served 7–10 nightly. People rave about the veal zurichoise, a dish so complex that the chef who invented it hates to make it. In fact, recently the chef seems to have fallen into melancholy and many of the dishes on the extensive menu are unavailable. La-Te-Da has had its ups and downs, you might as well know, but it still can be fun and you might luck into an exceptionally prepared meal. Sit outside rather than in the

cramped, interior rooms. Something is always happening
around the little pool. Goblets sometimes topple in as well as
carefree diners. Certain fortunate dogs do their laps. For Sunday brunch, served from 9–4, everyone appears, even ordinary
folk with sunburns on the backs of their legs. The real trade is
resting up for the five o'clock tea dance. Upstairs is the grand
piano and the black-and-white mirrored decor of The Crystal
Cafe, which bubbles away until 2. Food is served here until
midnight.

Palm Grille (1029 Southard, corner of Francis; phone 296-1744).
This is the old, beloved Las Palmas. Same rickety apricot-and-
blue building. Same charm. Nice new menu. Lots of restaurants
try to garden up their places with the ubiquitous high-white
lattice, but here it works—the uneven brick, the old shutters,
the big breadfruit tree, the quiet night, the great bluesy vocals
from the record machine. It's a shanty with style. The menu is
varied, inventive and reasonable. The fish is delicious—always
carefully prepared—and the desserts exceptional, but the
freshly baked rolls from the Cuban bakery, La Dichosa, are so
white . . . Isolated in their little basket they look like drowned
things. Smooth wines but no bar. Dinner Monday through Saturday 6–10:30.

Kyushu (921 Truman. Phone: 294-2995). For those who must
have their sushi. There is a Japanese garden as well as private
Tatami rooms where you sit on mats at low tables. There is a
bar and the steak teriyaki is excellent. A gratuity is added in
for larger groups and sometimes even four people is considered
a "larger" group. The sashimi is great but the gratuity is a bit
too subtle. Beware you don't end up doubling your tip here.

La Trattoria (524 Duval; phone: 296-1075). A stylish restaurant
with a sleek bar. Italian and French specialties. Opens at six.

Antonia's (615 Duval; phone: 294-6565). Pretty and popular,
Northern Italian. Small and sedate, with an extensive, expen-
sive menu. The half portions of their pasta dishes are generous.
Wine and beer. 6–11:30.

. . .

The Lighthouse Cafe (917 Duval; phone: 296-7837). Southern Italian. Here there is an outside patio area which feels, and not disarmingly so, like eating in somebody's carport. The service is sloppy, the food can sometimes be good. Open 6–11.

Kokomo (corner Simonton and Truman; phone: 296-4900) is an open-air restaurant right on gaseous Truman, but they've planted a lot of areca palms that are growing nicely, so it's more attractively alfresco than it first appears. Excellent blackboard specials. Good grilled fish, salads and conch fritters. Open 11 to 11. They share the kitchen with the far pricier Cafe des Artistes.

An inexpensive restaurant fancied by the locals is **PT's** (920 Caroline Street). Pool tables, a couple of big TV's, smokey and dim. "Authentic" you might say. The fare is ribs, pot roast, meat loaf, mashed potatoes and gravy. Nothing nouvelle about this cuisine. It's pretty good actually, although it all gets to taste like meat loaf. Open til 4 A.M.

The best Mexican restaurant is **El Loro Verde** at 404 Southard next to The Green Parrot. Its virtues are that it's inexpensive and has enciphered crayon work displayed on the walls that only initially seems to have been done by the third grade. Chimis and burros here as well as some Caribbean dishes like Jerk Chicken. Opens at 6 (296-7298).

There are several Cuban restaurants in town. **La Lechonera** (3100 Flagler, 296-7881) has what might be, perhaps, the best collection of pig photographs in the state on the wall, but the food tends to be fatty. **El Siboney** (900 Catherine Street, 296-4184) boasts less decor but is reliable. ("Well, that wasn't so bad, was it?" an out-of-towner said to her husband upon emerging one evening. "No, no," the man said. He looked a little startled. ". . . but it wasn't very good either." **El Miramar** (914 Kennedy Drive near the Little League Park, 294-2721) is good with steaks and specials. Or have the shredded pork, the *plantanos* (fried green bananas) the *casava* (delicious, tastes like cold cream) the *frijoles negro*. **The Five Star** (1100 Packer Street near Margaret, off Truman, 296-0650) is newly and nicely expanded from its sandwich shop days. Tiny room. Tasty food. All Cuban restaurants close early, usually at 9, and none have decent wine. But the servings are abundant, and the prices low.

For late night suppers, **PT's** is available, also **The Full Moon**, the **Crystal Cafe**, and the upstairs **Café** at Louie's. **Sloppy's** serves up their Sloppy food window-service style until 4.

BARS

Ah, the bars of Key West, some more famous than the finest homes! It's said that the three hurricanes that hit town in the early 1900's blew down all the churches but left the bars standing. They change hands, clientele and whole personalities, and some, like so many of the structures in Key West, are even moved from one block to the next, or are burned or razed. But few are ever forgotten.

The oldest bar is **Captain Tony**'s on Greene Street. Names of the famous are paint-printed on the bar stools. Martha Gellhorn's name should be on one of the stools, for she was sitting in this joint when Hemingway first saw her in December of 1936. She would become the reason for his breakup with his second wife, Pauline; his third wife (people said that together they looked like Beauty and the Beast); and the reason for his move from Key West to Cuba in 1939. The bar is quaint as the dickens (a plastic shark mouths a lady mannequin and there is junk and bric-a-brac and signs hanging everywhere) and grizzled Captain Tony himself is a cutie. He doesn't own the bar anymore. He sold it after owning it for thirty-one years. Now, he's the mayor of the town. You can buy a poster of the Captain with the adage, *All you need in life is a tremendous sex drive and a great ego—brains don't mean a shit*. The bar began as The Blind Pig. The Blind Pig begat Sloppy Joe's which begat The Duval Club which begat The Oldest Bar which begat the bar that bears Tony's name today. Captain Tony's, when it was Sloppy Joe's between 1933 and 1937, was Hemingway's favorite

bar. It was named for a popular hangout in Cuba and was owned
by Joe Russell, who Hemingway liked to call Josie Grunts.
Their friendship began when Russell cashed a Scribner's roy-
alty check for Hemingway, something the fine old bank down
the block refused to do. Russell was a rumrunner and charter-
boat captain, and before he bought the *Pilar,* Hemingway did
all his fishing aboard Russell's *Anita.*

But *before* Sloppy Joe's was legitimately at the Greene Street
location after the repeal of Prohibition, it was a speakeasy by
the Naval base. It was not one of the better bars in town. Prohibition meant absolutely nothing to Key West. There were great
drinking establishments everywhere—Pena's Garden of Roses,
The Tropical Club, Baby's Place, Raul's, and Delmonico's. And
there was the infamous Havana-Madrid Club located on Front
and Duval across from the bank only a short distance away from
Big Annie's whorehouse. It had a huge dance floor of white
Cuban tile and a rambling combination of indoor and outdoor
rooms where "music, dancing, gambling, and fistfights went on
twenty-four hours a day."

In 1937 the rent was raised a dollar a week at Sloppy Joe's on
Greene Street, so Russell bought the building across the street
on Duval—it had once been a restaurant—and in the middle of
one night he and "every drunk in town" moved the bar. And
here it remains, almost fifty-five years later, still Hemingway's
"favorite" bar, still pushing the *Papa Dobles* (2 1/2 jiggers of
white rum, juice of two limes and a grapefruit half) and now
offering a taco stand, a rock and roll band, and a T-shirt kiosk.
You can't miss Sloppy's—it would be like going to Freeport,
Maine and not being able to locate L.L. Bean.

In the 1940's, the highway down the Keys was remembered as
a mangrove tunnel with birds screeching and nesting within
overhanging branches that completely covered the road in
shade. But in Key West there were forty-eight bars on and near
Duval Street plus strip joints and tattoo parlors. Where a score
of gentle shops exist now, selling suntan lotions, fabrics, and
postcards, were the hard-core dives—the Midget Bar, The
Conch Gardens, the Wagon Wheel and four or five saloons
known commonly as the Bucket of Blood. "The town was filled
with beautiful men," an old girl remembers. "No one took any-

Capt. Tony's Saloon

thing seriously. Life was sweet, lighthearted and fun." There
was the Mardi Gras where a stripper named Dixie Lee per-
formed with a little white muff held demurely before her. Inside
the muff was a snarling chihuahua that would bite any sailor's
hand that ventured near. Delmonico's boasted the only trapeze
stripper in show business. Her name was Alma and she swung
just above the heads of the drinkers. The very popular Tradewinds Restaurant and Night Club at the corner of Duval and
Caroline occupied the historical Caroline Lowe house. Caroline
Lowe was the young wife of a Confederate blockade runner
during the Civil War. Martial law was in effect, yet every time
Union troops went marching down Duval, Caroline would wave
a Confederate flag from the cupola on the roof. The soldiers
could never find the flag, which she would hide in a newelpost.
The Tradewinds was torched by an arsonist in the mid-1950's
and later demolished.

Gone, gone, but not forgotten! Gone are the Cave Inn and the
25¢ double martinis at the Garden of Roses. Most recently vanished are The Monster, a hot gay disco on Front Street; The Big
Fleet on Caroline, where strippers danced for the shrimpers day
and night; and the Boca-Chica Lounge, the grisly, hard-core
Navy institution on Stock Island. But there remains a plenti-
tude of bars in Key West. Drinking here is almost an obligation,

and close to being an art. As in Ireland, it's not the thing to
drink at home.

The Bull and Whistle (224 Duval). Super-loud and rowdy. Open
to Duval's parade with another bar and balcony upstairs. Cover
charge for live rock and roll which can be heard for ten blocks.

The Green Parrot (400 Southard). A well-known old-time
funky bar. "See the lower keys on your hands and knees" is a
popular adage here and the philosophy of the place is that of the
famous bumpersticker, *shit happens*. Pool tables, darts, pinball.
Great murals on the walls, professional drinks. A Key West
classic.

Hog's Breath Saloon (400 Front Street). On the site of the
legendary Monster. A nice breeze blows through the Hog's
Breath (better than no breath at all). Sometimes they sell more
T-shirts than drinks here, and they sell a great many drinks.

The Full Moon (1202 Simonton). A great bar, even legendary.
Phillip Caputo's 569-pound marlin caught off the coast of Cuba
engulfs one wall. No nonsense drinks. See-through martinis.
The bar itself is sunken, the room dark, except for a wobbly
brilliant painting of a sunset, which is lit. Former owner Vic
Latham once closed the Moon one New Year's Eve because he
considered it "amateur night." Open until 4 A.M.

Schooner Wharf (down by Wolf and the Waterfront Market).
This looks seedy but it's theatrically seedy. You expected Key
West to be sort of like this and here it is. All types of hip here.
Dark, dark dance floor.

Casa Marina (Reynolds Street on the Atlantic). There is the
Calabash Lounge off the lobby and the Sun-Sun outside bar.
Pricey but incomparable views. As you wander about with your
Poinciana (champagne, cranberry, cassis) across the green-
sward to the dimpled shore, note the sign that earnestly alerts
guests to the great untoward—Marine Life Exists Beyond this
Point . . .

. . .

Rumrunners (200 block Duval). Has a garden bar, a piano bar, a rooftop bar and two other bars they haven't even bothered to name. Live music goes until midnight after which canned disco plays until four. Pizza and burgers are served until 3 A.M.

Club Tropic (700 Duval). Dancing. $2 cover. Happy hour goes on until midnight with well drinks for $1. Drag persons with great legs and a talent for lip-synching are the entertainment some late evenings.

Pier House (1 Duval). **The Chart Room** is dark and small and can be very crowded late at night. The word is that important people hang out here so the drinks are expensive. **Havana Docks** is up a story and over the water. Dancing and live music inside. Generous decks outside. Very popular, of course, for sunset watching. People like to come down here too and see the fish swimming under the lights at night.

Louie's. On the other side of the island at the corner of Vernon and Waddell, this is the quieter, classier place to be when the sun goes down. The outdoor bar on the Atlantic is called **The Afterdeck** and is simply splendid.

The Conch Flyer (at the airport). Used to be open 24 hours encouraging some of the most sinister types in Key West to drop by for a 5 A.M. nightcap. Now it's only open 21 hours a day. It's a shame. The bar is barely separated from the airstrip and it has a tropical Casablanca air. Have a beer and a chilli dog for breakfast and watch the little planes drop in and out of paradise.

The Esquire Lounge (3340 No. Roosevelt Boulevard). Tired and tough. Topless.

FISHING, DIVING, AND THE WATERS BEYOND

The personality of a fishing guide, in terms of *your* personality, is almost as important as his expertise in leading you to fish. To find your guide you have to inquire, observe, be willing to ask questions, and know what you want. In Key West, the charter boats (28 deep-sea boats, 7 light-tackle and 3 party) are at **Garrison Bight Marina** (294-3093). Do you really want to go out on a boat called the *No Mercy*? Well, you can. Other boats for charter are at **Oceanside** (294-4676) and **First Key West Marina** (296-8504) on Stock Island. Gulf Stream prices are $150 per person a day, and the boats take four to six fishermen. Light-tackle guides who go into the back country charge around $250 a day for two fishermen. If you cruise in your car past the Bight in the slow summer months, unhired captains or their mates often beckon to you like true hookers—making an imaginary cast, reeling an imaginary reel. Many captains do not have telephones so the thing to do in the season is to go to the Bight around four when the boats are returning and make your arrangements there. This is also a good place to buy your fresh fish or be given it. The Key West Fishing Tournament runs from April 15 to November 30 with lots of prizes for dead fish and even some awards for tagging and releasing live ones. Some sportsman enjoy using extra-light tackle—6- to 15-pound test line for the big ones, sailfish and marlin. Those billfish have a tournament all their own in October. *Tight lines and screaming reels to you!* the fishing interests like to say. The fact is there are a lot fewer fish than there used to be.

Captain Vicki Impallomeni on her 22-foot boat *Imp II* puts together wonderful day trips into the back country of the Great White Heron National Wildlife Refuge. These are private, personalized trips. You can fish for grouper and snapper, snorkel, beach picnic, and bird-watch. She's an animated and knowledgeable guide and the trips are a good deal of fun. Charters are $250 for four hours, $350 for a full 9–5 day. Telephone: 294-9731.

In the **Key West Bight Marina** at the end of William Street is the *Wolf*, a great-looking topsail schooner which offers afternoon and sunset sails ($35 and $25) and can be chartered for parties (296-9653). Here too is *Stars and Stripes,* a replica of Dennis Conner's champ catamaran. Masterfully skippered by Don Kincaid, *Stars and Stripes* glides out among the islands and you can have a memorable day exploring reefs and beaches from 10–4 for $65. (Call 294-7877.) They provide snorkeling equipment and refreshments, you bring your own lunch. Go to the **Waterfront**, everyone's favorite market close by at 201 William Street and create a picnic from their deli.

There are three sight-seeing boats that depart from downtown. The *Fireball* and *Coral Princess* are glass-bottom boats while the *Miss Key West* is more of an aquatic Conch Train. Hers is the shortest cruise at little over an hour. The *Fireball*'s trip to the reef is two hours long. Cost is $12, $6 for children. You'll often see nothing through the glass but undifferentiated turbulence. Just as often you'll get to pitch and yaw a lot.

To dive the reef contact **Reef Raiders** on Duval and Front (294-3635); **Seasports** at Land's End (294-6172); or the **Key West Pro Dive Shop** at 1605 N. Roosevelt Boulevard (296-3823). They all regularly dive the Sand Key Light, Eastern and Western Dry Rocks, and Cottrell Reef, which is on the Gulf side. Remember, coral is protected. Enjoy looking at it and leave it where it lives. **Sand Key** is heavily dived—it can even be crowded. **Eastern Dry Rocks** and **Rock Key**, about a mile east, are noted for their wrecks and pretty stones. **Western Dry Rocks** is about three miles from the light and has the clearest waters and the most caves. It also has lobsters and sharks. **Cottrell Reef** is best for beginning snorkelers.

For scuba divers, the dive shops make trips to various deep water wrecks as well as **The Outside Reef** or **Ten Fathom Ledge,** or they can be chartered for longer trips to **The Lakes,** (a series of shallow lagoons protected by islands and reefs) the **Marquesas** (the only atoll in the Atlantic, formed not by a volcano, but possibly by a prehistoric meteor) or the Tortugas, where you are getting into deep, wild water with large coral formations and big turtles and fish.

FORT JEFFERSON AND THE DRY TORTUGAS

Nothing will really prepare you for seeing this gigantic fort in the middle of vast waters, seventy miles from Key West. Most people fly here by seaplane. Boats can take anywhere from hours to days.

Fort Jefferson is doomed and has always been luckless. Planned by Thomas Jefferson to dominate the Gulf of Mexico with walls fifty feet high and eight feet thick and with facilities for 1,500 men and 450 cannon, construction on the largest of America's coastal forts was begun in 1846 on Garden Key, enclosing a lighthouse that had been built there in 1825. Ten years later, with fantastic supply and construction problems to overcome, its hexagonal walls had risen only a few feet above the surrounding waters. Ten years after that, with almost 16 million bricks having gone into its construction, it was found to be sinking, the weight of the walls squeezing the sand out from beneath the foundation. The 16-acre key on which it was built did not consist of solid coral, as was believed, but of sand shell and loose coral rock. True coral lay 80 feet below the surface.

Fort Jefferson, like its smaller, trapezoidal sister, Fort Taylor, never fired a shot at an enemy and was obsolete before it was finished. Like many monuments of far more ancient times, the fort was built by slaves and prisoners, overseen by craftsmen and guards. When the slaves were freed by the Emancipation Proclamation of 1863, the Army employed prison labor—the death sentences of Union deserters were often commuted to work on Fort Jefferson, the very name of which was supposed to cause hardened criminals to shudder. Prisoners were frequently forced to carry cannonballs around all day or were hung by their thumbs.

The fort's most famous prisoner was the phlegmatic Dr. Samuel Mudd, the doctor who set the broken leg of assassin John Wilkes Booth after the murder of President Lincoln. Convicted of conspiracy and sentenced to life, Dr. Mudd spent most of his time in the scorching heat making little chests and boxes of mahogany and crabwood and writing to his wife. He missed his

Pieces of eight (Spanish silver)

children and the Maryland winters, writing, "I sometimes fancy I can see the dear little creatures coming in with chattering teeth and little snotty noses, shivering with cold."

Shortly after his arrival in 1865, Mudd attempted to escape in a departing ship, was discovered and confined for a time to a desolate gun room, a dungeon which can be seen today. One of his duties was to clean old bricks. "I worked hard all day," he wrote, "and came very near finishing one brick."

In 1867 a yellow fever epidemic swept through the fort; 270 people suffered from it and 38 died, among whom were small children of the officers and the fort's physician. Although Mudd made no discoveries in treatment or prevention, he assiduously nursed the ill, and when cooler weather came and dispelled the disease, Army officers sent a petition to President Andrew Johnson requesting the doctor's release. However, Mudd was not pardoned until the last day of Johnson's presidency, February 8, 1869, and was not released from the fort until March 11. He had been imprisoned for three years, seven months and twelve days. A reporter from the *New York Herald* saw him at his Maryland farm and wrote, "In his sunken, lusterless eyes, pallid lips and cold, ashy, complexion, one can read the word 'Dry Tortugas' with a terrible significance."

Victims of disease and mishap were buried on a nearby key, a mortuary island bitterly called Hospital Key. The officers had fine quarters, perhaps the most comfortable and luxurious bar-

racks in the United States, with roofs of Vermont slate, stair-
ways of New England granite, stately verandas, and beautifully
furnished rooms, but none of this splendid display protected the
men from boredom, yellow fever, brackish water (the cisterns
cracked and seawater fouled the fresh), crushing heat, drought,
and hurricanes. The fort was abandoned in 1874, although it
was briefly reactivated by the Navy in 1898 as a coaling station.
The fort's bad luck was as virulent as ever. It was here where
the battleship *Maine* coaled up on her way to Cuba. It is now
believed that the explosion of the ship was caused, not by a
Spanish mine, but by the spontaneous ignition of the gunpowder stored in the magazine, gunpowder which could be carried
safely enough in wooden-hulled ships but exploded in the heat
of steel ships powered by coal.

Hurricanes and fires have destroyed the coaling docks, the
officers' quarters, and the soldiers' barracks. The vast parade
ground is empty now except for the palms and trees introduced
by the National Park Service, and the hot-shot ovens which
once heated cannonballs so they could more effectively destroy
their wooden targets. A Rodman cannon was capable of throw-
ing a 300-pound shell 3 miles. But there were never any targets
to destroy. And nothing attacked Fort Jefferson but Nature
herself, in the inexorable guise of wind, water, and time.

Many people in Key West speak of going to the Tortugas, but
few ever make the trip. Good weather is necessary, and money.
Key West Seaplane Service on Stock Island (294-6978) flies
year round and charges $120 a person for half a day. A full day
costs $195. Flights leave at 8 A.M. and 12. The trip takes about
a half hour which allows you 2 1/2 hours at the fort. Most people
think this is all the time they need on this desolate spot, but a
full day is much more enjoyable, giving you time to snorkel,
swim, picnic, and explore.

Bart's at the Key West Airport (294-0999) also flies to the
Tortugas. The cost is $120 (only $30 more for a full day) for half
a day with discounts for college students and the military.
Bart's at this time operates only during the season, December
through April.

Bring a picnic lunch, cold drinks, snorkeling equipment (although the ranger will provide it free if you're without), and binoculars.

The flight to the Tortugas is astonishing. The planes fly low over the clear and multihued water, and you will see wrecked ships gleaming in the depths of reefs. The Navy still uses some of these wrecks to pound in target practive. You'll see living sharks and rays and the bleached bones of whales. You'll also see the macabre scrawl of hundreds of motorboat prop scars crisscrossing the seagrass beds. And then, there are miles of glittering ocean wastes, dotted by the whites of waves cresting the shoals and by the gliding shadows of birds, and then the fort rises into view in all its dark improbability. A short distance away is the lighthouse of Loggerhead Key and close to the fort is Bush Key where a hundred thousand noddy and sooty terns arrive to nest each spring. The terns mate in the air at night, as angels must, and when they land on the key, egg laying begins immediately, each couple staking out a two-foot homestead in the sand. Bush Key is off limits to people from March through September, and all the nearby keys, with the exception (ironically enough) of Loggerhead are closed May through September during the time the sea turtles lay their eggs. The moat around the fort is filled with young turtles, ten inches long, part of a National Park Service project which collects hatchlings from the Atlantic coast and protects them for a year before release.

You have to really want to get to Fort Jefferson for it is far beyond Mile O. People who have lived in Key West for some time and still haven't gone to the Tortugas blame it on "Tropical Creep" of the suddenly "Seven Years Came and Went" variety. Others, here for a short time, are rushed to do many things and opt for easier (and cheaper) memories—a party fishing boat or a group dive.

The fort is civilized enough these days. It has a pier and a helicopter pad. It has a fifteen-minute slide program and, like all national monuments, informative signs on a self-guided walk. There are picnic tables and grills and even rest rooms. You are not going into the heart of darkness after all. There is a sandy beach and snorkeling is excellent, both around the moat walls and on the reefs of Loggerhead Key. Camping is available here for up to twenty days, but as the ranger says, you "must provide for your own existence." There is nothing here but the beach, the bricks, the water, and the sky, in which the magnificent frigate-birds soar. Their bones are hollow, their color black, their elegant hooked wings span seven and a half feet. They are thieves and dandies, stealing fish from other birds, never getting themselves wet. They ride the currents of the air and there you are below them, far from home, almost nowhere.

Index

Abel's Tackle Box, 39
Adventure Island, 66
African Queen, The, 9
Airways Building, 152
Albury House, 190
Alligator Lighthouse, 48
Alligator Reef Light, 47, 77
American Diving
    Headquarters, 11
American Shoal Light, 77,
    79
Antique Shops (Key West),
    169–70
Arsenic Bank, 28
Artist House, 190
Audubon, John James, 31,
    45–46, 127, 149–52
Audubon House, 149–52
Australian pine trees,
    96–97

Bacchus, 68
Bacchus by the Sea, 74
"back country," ix, 28–33
Bahama Houses, 192–93
Bahamas, 6
Bahia Honda Bridge, 84–85,
    98, 124
Bahia Honda Key, 83–85
Benjamin Baker House, 194
bars, in Key West, 217–21
Bart's, 226–27
Bat Tower, 109–10

beaches, on Key West,
    167–69
Benwood wreck, 15
Bermuda Star, 135–36
Big Coppitt, 112
Big Pine Channel, 97
Big Pine Fishing Lodge, 91
Big Pine Key, 92–97, 98, 99
Biscayne Bay, ix
Bishop, Elizabeth, 173,
    174–75, 176
Bishop House, 174
Blue Lagoon Resort, 20
Bobo, Cuco, 25
Boca Chica Key, 112
Bogart, Humphrey, 8–9
Boheme, 136
Bonefish Fly Tournament,
    39
Book Nook, 14
Botanical Gardens, 189
Bottle Key, 31
Bottling Court, 137
Bowles, Jane, 175
Breezy Palms, 42
Browne, Jefferson, 78
Buccaneer, 72
Bud Boats, 91
Buddy's Dive Shop, 48
Bud 'n' Mary's, 39, 44
Buffet, Jimmy, 212
bugs, 53
Bull and Whistle, 158–59

Caloosa Cove, 48
Caloosa Indians, 3, 25
Cannon Patch, 18
Capitana, 18
Capote, Truman, 177
Captain Hook's Marina, 67
Captain Hornblower's, 159
Capt. Slate's Atlantis Dive
    Center, 11
Capt. Tony's, 154
Card Sound Bridge, 7
Card Sound Road, 8
Caribbean Club Bar, 22
Caroline Street, 152–54
Carysford, H.M.S., 16
Carysfort Reef, 13, 16
Carysfort Reef Lighthouse,
    77, 78
Casa Gato (Mercedes
    Hospital), 195–97
Castaway, 73
Castillito, 71
Charlotte's Story
    (Niedhauk), 44
Cheeca Lodge, 37, 38, 39,
    64
Chesapeake Motel, 36
Christ of the Deep Statue,
    16, 17
Cigar Factory, 137
cigars, 137
Coconut Grove, 73
Coffins Patch, 65
Community Swimming Pool
    (Key West), 165
Conch Houses, 190–93
Conch Key, 60
Conch Key Cottages, 72
Conch Reef, 18

Conch Republic, 140
Conchs, 6
Conch Train, 140–43
Content Keys, 67
Copa, 164
coral, 10–11
Coral Lagoon, 66, 73
Cottrell Reef, 223
Cow Key Marina, 113
Cracked Conch Cafe, 73
Craig Key, 50
Crane, Hart, 173
Crane Point Hammock, 69
Crocker Wall, 27
crocodiles, 28
Cuban Consul House, 194
Cudjoe Key, 77, 89, 105–8
Milton Curry Mansion, 153
Cypress House, 153

Davis Reef, 27
Delta Shoal, 67
Dildo Key Bank, 28
Discovery, 17–18
Divers' World, 11
diving, 66–67
    on Key Largo, 11–12
    on Key West, 222–23
Diving Site, 66
Dolphin Research Center,
    61
dolphins, 61–63
Dos Passos, John, 59
Drop Anchor, 33
Dry Tortugas, ix, 9–10, 75,
    133, 224, 226–27
Duck Key, 59, 60–61, 65
Durty Harry's, 158
Duval Street, 154, 158

Eastern Dry Rocks, 223
East Martello Museum and
    Art Gallery, 186–88
East Turtle Shoal, 67
East Washerwoman Shoal,
    67
Elbow, 16
El Infante, 18
El Patio Motel, 205
Elliott Key, ix
Eric's Floating Restaurant,
    33
Everglades, xi, 7
Eyebrow House, 190

Fanny's, 71
Fantasy Dan's, 111
Faro Blanco, 72
Fast Buck Freddie's, 161
Fat Albert, 108
Fausto's, 161
Fiesta Key, 50
Fisherman's Hospital, 71
Mel Fisher's Treasure
    Exhibit, 147–49
fishing:
    in Key West, 222–23
    in Marathon, 74–77, 80
Flagler, Henry, ix, 4, 54,
    59, 70, 124, 129
Florida Bay, ix, 28, 32
Florida East Coast
    Railroad, ix, 4–5
Florida Keys Angler, 75
Florida Keys Fishing
    Guides Association, 40
Florida Keys Wild Bird
    Rehab Center, 63
Fogerty House, 159

Forgotten Frontier, The
    (Parks), 127
Fort Jefferson, 224–28
Fort Taylor, 169, 184–86,
    187, 224
Fowey Rocks Light, 77
French Reef, 15

Galileo, 135–36
Garrison Bight Marina, 222
gingerbread houses, 193–97
Gingerbread Square
    Gallery, 170
glass-bottom boat, 17–18
Golden Orb spiders, 95
Golden Grouper, The, 72
Grassy Key, 5, 62, 97
Grassy Key Dairy Bar, 64
Graveyard (Key West),
    197–200
Great White Heron
    National Wildlife
    Refuge, 90
Grecian Rocks, 18
Green Parrot, 159
Green Turtle, 40
green turtles, 154
Grey, Zane, 77
guest houses, in Key West,
    206–208
Guild Hall, 163
Gulf Stream, ix, 16, 76
Gulf View, The, 72

Haitian Art Company, 169
Half-Shell Raw Bar, 154
Hariett's, 21
Harry Harris County Park,
    23–24

Harry's Place, 24
Hawk Channel, ix
Hawk's Cay Resort, 60–61
Hemingway, Ernest, 9, 130,
    143, 159, 173, 178–82,
    188, 197
Hemingway, Pauline, 178,
    180, 182
Hemingway Days, 177
Hemingway House, 178–82
Hens and Chickens Reef, 27
Herbie's, 73
herons, 29
Hersey, John, 173
Hideaway Cafe, The, 65
Hideout, The, 21
Higgs Memorial, 168
Hog's Breath Saloon, 220
Holiday Inn, 19
Holiday Isle, 27, 33, 34, 39
Hospitality House, 133, 190
Hospital Key, 225
hotels, 41–42, 65–67, 72–73,
    91–92, 110–111
  in Islamorada, 41–42
  on Key Largo, 19–21
  on Key West, 200–8
  in Marathon, 72–73
Houseboat Vacations of the
    Florida Keys, 15
Howard Johnson's, 19, 66
hurricanes, 35–36

Indian Key, 42–48
Inner Conch Reef, 27
Iris, 165
Islamorada, ix, 5, 39–40, 63,
    75
Islander, 42

Island Home, 26
Island Reef, 91
Italian Fisherman, 22–23

Jencks, Frederick Tingley,
    31
Jewfish Creek, 7
Jo-Jo's Diner, 105
Jules' Undersea Lodge, 12

Kelsey's, 72
Richard Kemp House, 153
William Kerr House, 194
Key Biscayne, 79
Key Colony Beach, 59, 66
Key deer, 92–93, 96–97
Key Largo, ix, 7–25, 35, 75,
    77, 92, 187
Key Largo, 9
Key Largo Dry Rocks, 16
Key Largo National Marine
    Sanctuary, 14
Key Largo Shoal Water
    Cruises, 32
Key Lois, 106–7
Key Vaca, 59, 67–80
Key West, ix, 4, 6, 9, 24, 35,
    45, 70, 77–78, 110,
    119–228
  bars on, 217–21
  beaches on, 167–69
  fishing and diving on,
    222–23
  galleries and antiques on,
    169–70
  guest houses on, 206–8
  history of, 125–33
  hotels on, 200–6
  land changes and, 123–25

oldest house on, 160–61
restaurants on, 210–17
salt ponds on, 167–69
shopping on, 136–38
streets of, 121–22
sunset viewing on, 143–44
writers on, 173–82
Key West Aloe, 137
Key West Aquarium,
    144–45
Key West Citizen, 170, 172
Key West Conch Shell, 164
Key West Hand Prints, 137
Key West Island Bookstore,
    177–78
Key West Pro Dive Shop,
    223
Key West Seaplane Service,
    113, 226
Knight's Key, 68, 70
Kokomo, 216

Lady Cyana, 27
Lakes, The, 223
Lake Surprise, 7
Land's End Village, 154
Largo Lodge, 20
Lash, Joseph, 173
Layton, 50
Lighthouse Military
    Museum, 79, 182–83
lighthouses, 77–78
Lignumvitae Key, 42–44
Lime Tree Bay Resort, 51
Literary Tour and Seminar,
    177
Little Palm Island, 102
Little Torch Key, 99, 100
Little White House, 145–46

Loggerhead Key, 107, 227
Long Key, 48, 52–55
Long Key State Recreation
    Area, 42, 52
Long Key Viaduct, 60
Looe Key, 77, 79, 89, 92, 100
Looe Key Reef Resort, 92,
    103
Lorelei, 40
John Lowe House, 191
lower keys, 89–115
Lower Matecumbe Key, 5,
    48, 51–52, 77, 79, 97
Lucky Street Gallery, 169
Lurie, Allison, 173

McGuane, Tom, 112, 173
Maine, 122, 124, 133, 183
Mallory, Stephen, 136
Mallory Square, 115,
    133–36, 140, 143, 190
manatees, 11, 28
Manchineel trees, 99
Mangrove Mama's, 91, 107
Manny and Isa's, 41
Man of War Key, 28
Marathon, 59, 66, 69–71,
    72–73, 74–80, 97
Marathon Guides
    Association, 76
Marathon Inn, 66
Marine Hospital, U.S., 145
Marine Patrol, 11
Marion, 149
Marker, 26, 39
Marquesas, 223
Marsh Sneaker, 28
Matecumbe Key, 24, 37–38
Merrill, James, 173

middle keys, history of,
    59–67
Peggy Mills Garden, 189
Missouri Key, 82
Molasses Reef, 14, 15, 16
Monte's Fish market, 105
mosquitoes, 3, 53
Mrs. Mac's Kitchen, 21
museums, 182–83, 186–88

National Key Deer Refuge,
    94
newspapers, 170–73
Niedhauk, Russel and
    Charlotte, 44
No Name Key, 97–98
No Name Pub, 98

Ocean Divers, 11
Ocean Reef Club, 8
Oceanside, 222
Oceanside Marina, 113
Ohio Key, 82
Old City Hall (Key West),
    139
Old Rhodes Key, ix
Old Town (Key West),
    190–93
ospreys, 89–90
Outer Conch Reef, 27
Outside Reef, 223

Papa Joe's, 41
George Patterson House,
    153
Richard Peacon House, 192
pelicans, 49
Pennecamp, John, 14

John Pennecamp Coral
    Reef State Park, 9–10,
    14–18
pepper trees, 95
Picture Show, 163
Pier House, 138
Pier House Market, 137
Pigeon House, 152
Pigeon Key, 81
Pilot House, 21
Pirate's Cove, 111
Plantation Key, 25–28, 38
Plantation Yacht Harbor
    Resort, 26
Poisonwood trees, 96–97
Ponce de León, Juan, 3, 142
Joseph Porter House, 159
punk trees, 96

Quay, 73
Quiescence, 11

Rabbit Key, 28
Rader, Dotson, 176
Rain Barrel, 27
Rainbow Bend Fishing
    Club, 64
Ramrod Key, 98, 103–5
Red Barn Theatre, 159
reddish egret, 52
Reef Divers, 105
Reef Raiders, 223
restaurants, 26, 33, 36–37,
    39, 64, 91, 107–8
    in Islamorada, 40–41
    on Key Largo, 21–23
    on Key West, 210–17
    in Marathon, 73–74

Rick's Cafe, 158–59
Riggs Wildlife Refuge, 168
Robbie's, 44
George Roberts House, 194
Rock Key, 223
Rockland Key, 112
Rock Reef, 20
Roseate Spoonbill, 29, 30–32
Rose Lane Antiquities, 165
Rose Tattoo (Williams), 175
Route 1, ix

Saddlebunch Keys, 88, 112
St. Paul's Church, 160
salt ponds, 167–69
San Carlos, 161–62
Sanchez, Mario, 187
Sandbar, 27
Sand Key, ix, 223
Sand Key Light, 77, 78, 79
San Jose y las Animas, 18
scuba diving, *see* diving
Sea Center Dive Shop, 105
Sea Dwellers, 11
Seafarer, 20
Seasports, 223
Seasports Dive Center, 154
Sea Store, 169
Seven-Mile Bridge, 68, 70,
    80–82, 98, 124
7-Mile Grille, 71
Shades, 137
sharks, 83
Shell Key, 42
Shell Man, 11
Shell Warehouse, 137
Shelter Key, 66
Sheraton, 19

shotgun shacks, 197
shrimping, 157
Side Door Lounge, 71
Sign of Sandford, 137
Sloppy Joe's, 159
Smathers Beach, 167
Snake Creek Bridge, 33
snakes, 101
Snook's Bayside Club, 21
Solares Hill, 172
Sombrero Beach, 68
Sombrero Light, 77
Sombrero Reef, 67, 79
Southern Cross Hotel, 159
southernmost point of
    continental U.S.,
    166–67
South Florida Fishing
    Tournament, 39
Spanish Harbor Keys, 85
sponges, 134–35, 138
Stars and Stripes, 214
Stevens, Wallace, 119
Stock Island, 113–15, 189,
    226
Stoneledge, 20
Straits of Florida, ix
Strand, 162–63
Sugarloaf Key, 85, 108–12,
    168
Sugarloaf Lodge, 92, 109
Summerland Key, 85, 89,
    96, 105
sunsets, 22, 68–69, 143–44
Sunshine Key, 82

Tarpon Basin, 20
Tavernier, 23–25, 44

Tavernier Towne, 24
Ten Fathom Ledge, 223
Tennessee Reef, 51
Theater of the Sea, 34, 39
To Have and Have Not
 (Hemingway), 130, 179,
 181–82
Torch Keys, 98, 103
Tortugas, *see* Dry Tortugas
treasure, sunken, 147–49
Treasure Divers, 27
trees, bad, 96–97
Trev-Mor Apartments,
 194–95
Truman Annex, 137, 145–47
Tugboat's, 21
Turtle Kraals, 154
turtles, green, 155–56

Underseas Inc., 105
upper keys, history of, 3–7
Upper Matecumbe Key,
 37–38

Valhalla Beach Motel, 65
Vera Cruz, 135–36
Vernon's Iron Skillet, 71

Jack Watson Nature Trail,
 95
Wellwood, 5
Western Dry Rock, 223
West Martello Tower,
 188–89
West Turtle Shoal, 67
Whale Harbor Restaurant
 and Marina, 39
White Banks Dry Rocks,
 15–16
White Street Pier, 168
Wilbur, Richard, 173
Williams, Tennessee, 173,
 175–77
Tennessee Williams House,
 175–77
Winchester, H.M.S., 5
Windley Key, 33–37, 39
Winner-Sombrero Docks,
 76
Wolf, 222
Wynken, Blynken and Nod
 Trailer Park, 19

Ziggie's, 39
Ziggie's Conch, 40

About the Author

JOY WILLIAMS is a novelist and short-story writer.

About the Artist

ROBERT CARAWAN is a native-born Key West Conch.
His etchings and serigraphs may be seen at the Gingerbread
Square Gallery on Duval Street.